README.1ST
SGML for Writers and Editors

The Charles F. Goldfarb Series on Open Information Management

"Open Information Management" (OIM) means managing information so that it is open to processing by any program, not just the program that created it. That extends even to application programs not conceived of at the time the information was created.

OIM is based on the principle of data independence: data should be stored in computers in non-proprietary, genuinely standardized representations. And that applies even when the data is the content of a document. Its representation should distinguish the innate information from the proprietary codes of document processing programs and the artifacts of particular presentation styles.

Business data bases—which rigorously separate the real data from the input forms and output report—achieved data independence decades ago. But documents, unlike business data, have historically been created in the context of a particular output presentation style. So for document data, independence was largely unachievable until recently.

That is doubly unfortunate. It is unfortunate because documents are a far more significant repository of humanity's information. And documents can contain significantly richer information structures than data bases.

It is also unfortunate because the need for OIM of documents is greater now than ever. The demands of "repurposing" require that information be deliverable in multiple formats (paper-based, online, multimedia, hypermedia). And information must now be delivered through multiple channels (traditional bookstores and libraries, online services, the Internet).

Fortunately, in the past ten years a technology has emerged that extends to documents the data base's capacity for data independence. And it does so without the data base's restrictions on structural freedom. That technology is the "Standard Generalized Markup Language" (SGML), an official International Standard (ISO 8879) that has been adopted by the world's largest producers of documents.

With SGML, organizations in government, aerospace, airlines, automotive, electronics, computers, and publishing (to name a few) have freed their documents from hostage relationships to processing software. SGML coexists with other data standards needed for OIM and acts as the framework that relates objects in the other formats to one another and to SGML documents.

As the enabling standard for OIM of documents, SGML necessarily plays a leading role in this series. We provide tutorials on SGML and other key standards and the techniques for applying them. Our books are not addressed solely to technical readers; we cover topics like the business justification for OIM and the business aspects of commerce in electronic information. We share the practical experience of organizations and individuals who have applied the techniques of OIM in environments ranging from immense industrial publishing projects to self-publishing on the World Wide Web.

Our authors are expert practitioners in their subject matter, not writers hired to cover a "hot" topic. They bring insight and understanding that can only come from real-world experience. Moreover, they practice what they preach about standardization. Their books share a common standards-based vocabulary. In this way, knowledge gained from one book in the series is directly applicable when reading another, or the standards themselves. This is just one of the ways in which we strive for the utmost technical accuracy and consistency with the OIM standards.

And we also strive for a sense of excitement and fun. After all, the challenge of OIM—preserving information from the ravages of technology while exploiting its benefits—is one of the great intellectual adventures of our age. I'm sure you'll find this series to be a knowledgable and reliable guide on that adventure.

About the Series Editor

Dr. Charles F. Goldfarb is the inventor of SGML and HyTime, and technical leader of the committees that developed them into International Standards. He is an information management consultant based in Saratoga, CA.

About the Series Logo

The rebus is an ancient literary tradition, dating from 16th century Picardy, and is especially appropriate to a series involving fine distinctions between things and the words that describe them. For the logo, Andrew Goldfarb, who also designed the series' "Intelligent Icons," incorporated a rebus of the series name within a stylized SGML comment declaration.

The Charles F. Goldfarb Series on Open Information Management

Turner, Douglass, and Turner

README.1ST: SGML for Writers and Editors

README.1ST
SGML for Writers and Editors

Ronald C. Turner
Timothy A. Douglass
Audrey J. Turner

For book and bookstore information

http://www.prenhall.com

Prentice Hall PTR
Upper Saddle River, New Jersey 07458

Library of Congress Cataloging in Publication Data

Editorial/production supervision: *Camille Trentacoste*
Cover design: *Andrew Goldfarb*
Manufacturing manager: *Alexis R. Heydt*
Acquisitions editor: *Mark L. Taub*
Editorial Assistant: *Dori Steinhauff*

The publisher offers discounts on this book when ordered in bulk quantities.
For more information, contact:

    Corporate Sales Department, Prentice Hall PTR
    One Lake Street, Upper Saddle River, NJ 07458
    Phone: 800-382-3419; FAX: 201- 236-7141
    E-mail: corpsales@prenhall.com

Printed in the United States of America

10 9 8 7 6 5 4 3 2 1

ISBN 0-13-432717-9

Prentice-Hall International (UK) Limited, *London*
Prentice-Hall of Australia Pty. Limited, *Sydney*
Prentice-Hall Canada Inc., *Toronto*
Prentice-Hall Hispanoamericana, S.A., *Mexico*
Prentice-Hall of India Private Limited, *New Delhi*
Prentice-Hall of Japan, Inc., *Tokyo*
Simon & Schuster Asia Pte. Ltd., *Singapor*
Editora Prentice-Hall do Brasil, Ltda., *Rio de Janeiro*

CONTENTS

6.   ELEMENT TYPE DECLARATION   73
Building the Markup Vocabulary

10. ENTITY MANAGEMENT   127
Managing Reusable Text

11. MARKED SECTIONS   143
Labeling for Special Purposes

12. READING A DTD   151
A Brief Walkthrough

FOREWORD

README.1ST: SGML for Writers and Editors is a first in more ways than just its title.

- It is the first book on SGML that was truly written for non-technical end users That is undoubtedly because its authors—Ron Turner, Tim Douglass, and Audrey Turner, of Soph-Ware Associates—were professional writers and educators before they became SGML experts.

- It is the first SGML textbook, in the sense that it was developed in a university setting. It was proven in classroom use at Eastern Washington University, home of the "Electronic Information Institute" World Wide Web site.

- It is a beginner's book—easy and fun to read—but without the mistakes common to such books. That is, it doesn't try to achieve simplicity by blurring vital distinctions or omitting key concepts. Instead, it simplifies advanced SGML applications like hypertext and the World Wide Web by explaining, step-by-step, how they evolve naturally from basic SGML facilities.

In achieving all this, the book is scrupulously faithful to the SGML International Standard. It uses the standardized professional vocabulary of SGML to teach the language's constructs. But it introduces and motivates the use of that vocabulary by relating it to the real work of writers and editors. The title says README.1ST. I wish I could have. You'll be glad you can.

Charles F. Goldfarb
Saratoga, CA
June, 1995

PREFACE

This book grew out of dismay on the one hand and enthusiasm on the other. Like many who work with documents that must move among various platforms and systems, we were dismayed at the effort that we needed to spend repeatedly just to move one from here to there to do this and that. For us, moving documents meant learning every sort of transfer trick we could devise: downloading and uploading, exporting and importing, converting with third-party tools, scanning, and writing pieces of ad hoc conversion code to make it all work.

Our enthusiasm came from the promise of SGML. If SGML were indeed a standard that applied itself in a *generalized* manner, then it would let us spend more of our lives writing, editing, and producing documents and less time moving them around and recycling them.

But we were also dismayed at how difficult it seemed to know *where to begin* with SGML. True, the standard is in place, the tools are on the market, there is an active and helpful community on the Internet, and the various methodologies are working for a multitude of writers. But we could find nothing like a "One-Stop SGML" that would give the novice everything necessary to achieve SGML productivity. This book and its ancillary software were the result: a true introduction to the standard, a readable introduction to the essentials of SGML, and sufficient desktop software to enable the reader to get productive with SGML.

These are austere times for writers. Budgets for dedicated technical writing groups are shrinking or disappearing. Writing is being forced "upstream," onto the desktops and benchtops of engineers, researchers, technicians and even secretaries. And this workplace cannot generally afford the luxury of week-long training sessions, on-site or at some hotel far away. Instead we must now engage in "just-in-time learning." *README.1ST* is a learning tool for this new breed of publishers. We have attempted to address each new topic by starting in familiar territory and moving intuitively into a more formal discussion of that topic. The presentation is therefore more verbose than you yourself would be in writing technical documentation. Also, you will find several instances of repeated discussion on the same topic. This sort of review, while perhaps out of place in a reference document, helps the reader of a textbook to "nail down" troublesome and unfamiliar concepts.

A persistent concern for writers unaccustomed to formal standards is that a standard like SGML will somehow deprive them of their creativity. Our first and probably most important task therefore is to convince you that SGML enables and supports a writer's creativity. It does so by allowing him or her to concentrate on creating text for a document without having to worry about how the document will appear.

How you decide to use *README.1ST* depends both on your job description and on your learning style. If you are a manager faced with the decision of whether to commit to the SGML standard, then you should read at least the first three chapters. If you are a writer who wishes only to get the idea of how standard markup fits within the scheme of electronic documents, you should study carefully the first five chapters. Chapters six through eight cover the essential syntax of an SGML document type definition (DTD).

"But do I really need to know about a DTD, what with all the SGML editing tools currently on the market?" While we devote a good part of Chapter twelve answering that question, we suggest that being able to read a DTD intelligently is like having available the "Reveal Codes" feature of a popular word processor—it means that you can always see what is *really* going on in your document. And while we do not target this book to designers of document types, we progressively design and build a DTD as the core of our discussion over several chapters. Watching a DTD develop in step-wise fashion into the definition of a rather robust hypertext document proves to be a satisfying and effective method for understanding both the what and the why of a DTD.

Today there is enormous interest in HyperText Markup Language (HTML), the markup scheme for documents on the World-Wide Web. We offer a close-up look at HTML that lets you understand HTML as a particular application of SGML. This will provide you with an insight into HTML that goes far beyond the beginner's concerns over which tags to put where.

At this point in a preface authors typically lament the travails of having gotten a project finally into print. Yes, we neglected several contracting opportunities in our company, our family lives suffered, house plants died from lack of attention, pets did not get petted as they ought, dust gathered where it ought not, and all of the other things happened that we find in the litanies of most prefaces. But one such common phenomenon did *not* happen to us: burnout. We are no less excited about SGML and its benefits than when we began this project. We hope that *README.1ST* succeeds in conveying that same excitement to you.

Acknowledgments

One tradition for a preface that we must not neglect is that of expressing thanks to those who have helped us along the way. The most important personage in the project has been Charles F. Goldfarb, who has patiently endured watching his child being mauled by pagans who, for purposes of this title, have frequently behaved more as practitioners and trainers than as theoreticians. While his name appears on the cover, and while his presence over our shoulders and in the series assures that what you read is *accurate*, we have aimed at creating a package that is also *readable* and *teachable*. If the book fails on those counts, we take all the blame.

Every vision requires an infrastructure to make it work. Mark Taub, editor at Prentice-Hall for the Charles F. Goldfarb series in the Professional Technical Reference Division, has assumed a unique professional profile that is well suited to the uniqueness of this series. To us he has functioned as coach, cheerleader, dispatcher, comforter, and referee. To the extent that the series is successful, it will be due largely to Mark's accurate sense of the publisher's role in the evolving electronic document workplace and to his own role in steering the corporate ship through the murky waters of an evolving technology.

This has been a textbook example of an SGML project. The manuscript, prepared as SGML text and then converted and transmitted electronically to the publisher, enjoyed all the benefits of electronic publishing that we describe in the book itself. But for this to happen required knowledge, patience, and courage on the part of the publisher's production staff. Prentice-Hall Production Editor Camille Trentacoste has abundantly exhibited all of these virtues, and without her invaluable assistance this project would not have been completed. Camille also deserves high praise for her work on the style for this book and the entire Charles F. Goldfarb series.

We also thank Eliot Kimber, whose pre-publication version of his book on HyTime guided us in doing Chapter fourteen. Daniel W. Connolly of HaL Systems, the designated watchman of the turbulent world of HTML, offered criticism and correction that was most welcome.

We are grateful to James Clark, whose programming resulted in the updated public domain parser SGMLS (included on the disk which accompanies the text). We enhanced that code further to produce the imbedded validating parser which supports our browser (also on the disk).

We want also to thank Microsoft Corporation and Novell (WordPerfect) for their cooperation in supplying pre-release copies of their SGML authoring tools. SoftQuad provided software and support for the editing environment of the book as an SGML document. And Frame Technologies likewise provided software for the final composition of the camera-ready text.

At several critical junctures we relied on computers at the Spokane Intercollegiate Research and Technology Institute (SIRTI). Charles Aude, manager of the Computer Laboratory at SIRTI, helped make everything work the first time.

For her behind the scenes work in providing us with a very helpful review of the manuscript and for the assistance she provided on testing the software that accompanies *README.1ST*, we would like to thank Beth Breidenbach.

The other indispensable contributors to the project are the patient souls who suffered through an earlier draft of this book in the premier go-around of the Electronic Document course at Eastern Washington University. They deserve much, and the least we can do is to immortalize them here: Charli Anderson, Rhonda Bowers, Heather Brown, Lou Chobot, Kathryn Conlin, Emilee Dhamakul, Lou Dunham, Cheryl Fronk, Mark Galioto, Katherine Gooding, Mahilani Gutina, John Herman, Mary Jordan, Celeste Kaylor, Georgina Olsen, Penny Robinson, Brian Schauer, Terry Shatto, Cathy Towne, and Connie Woodard. May their text (and yours) live forever!

And in the spirit of the interactive smart document, we thank in advance those of our readers who will share their comments with us to benefit readers of future editions of this book.

Ronald C. Turner
Timothy A. Douglass
Audrey J. Turner
Soph-Ware Associates
swa@comtch.iea.com

CHAPTER 1

WRITING WITH STANDARDS
Yesterday, Today and Tomorrow

SGML terms introduced:

application, document architecture, document type, text processing application

Overview

A brief "SGML Catechism" (based on actual questions posed by real writers and editors)

Q. Why is SGML a standard that we should take the time to learn?

A. Because it eases considerably our task of writing for digital publication.

Q. What is the nature of electronic document writing standards?

A. Rules that formalize (a) much of the standards-conforming activity we are already doing and (b) those aspects of our writing that are of concern to the global electronic community.

Q. How do these rules accomplish this?

A. By defining certain components of writing and editing activity in a manner that is totally unambiguous.

Q. Then is there any latitude for a writer's creativity within a standards-compliant writing environment?

A. SGML standards have no bearing on the semantic content of any document, only on its structure. And they may or may not even deal with details of page layout. So rather than stifling an author's creativity in any way, they enable the writer to expend all of his or her energy on *writing*.

Q. With the emergence of SGML tools and entire writing environments which claim to hide the "messy internals," why should a writer or editor even bother with the details of SGML?

A. As a professional, one should be naturally curious about what is going on "under the hood." But more practically, the minimal time spent in mastering some essential detail of SGML enables the writer or editor to grasp quickly and completely the "landscape" of *any* SGML-based project.

Q. Precisely how much essential detail of SGML should a serious writer or editor expect to master?

A. Slightly less than 25 percent (to be precise!). Of the 332 technical definitions in the SGML standard, about 75 have some impact on day-to-day authoring and editing. Throughout this book we discuss and apply the concepts conveyed by those 75 terms.

This chapter, on the one hand, is the most philosophical of the book. It dwells on the nature of standards—for communication in general and for writing in particular. It clarifies the semantics of the term "rule," as used in a writing standard. We survey prominent standards that have guided the writer's work. Then we explore how the exciting challenges of the electronic (digital) document call for a new kind of standard, a standard which can (1) enable the document's delivery in an undreamed of variety of media and venues and (2) enable the writer and editor to concentrate on writing and editing.

But like every other chapter in the book, this chapter presents some essential and practical SGML definitions and concepts. We look first at the text processing application, a topic which encompasses all of the familiar aspects of a writing project. "Text processing application" is a formal SGML term that will orient us well for further technical discussion throughout the book. SGML per se does not concern itself with issues of *how* a document gets processed, the *semantics of processing*—formatting, imaging, interchange, retrieval, for example. But there are entire standards emerging which do apply to semantics. This allows us to finish the chapter with a brief discussion of document architecture and to allude to standards of architecture.

1.1   Why Are Standards Necessary?

Why are standards necessary for writing? When we write, just as when we speak, we are communicating. For every message, written or spoken, electronic or print copy, prose or poetry, words or music, there are basic laws of communication in effect for both the encoder and the decoder. These parties may be speaker (or instrumentalist) and listener or writer and reader, but whatever the medium, each member of the pair must follow the same set of rules. Whenever any party in the communications chain violates this "contract," the message deteriorates to some degree, and the communication process suffers. So whether we speak of "rules" or "contract" or "basic laws," we understand there to be two dominant factors in effect for every successful communications event:

1. A collection of *explicit rules* which govern that particular brand of communication. These are quite possibly formulated and preserved by some external authority.

2. An agreement among all of the communicating parties to *adhere* to those rules.

With the advent of modern communications, we are certainly more aware of precisely defined rules, particularly for issues driven by technology: hardware and software requirements, broadcast frequencies, bandwidths, and rules of access. These are standards, and we need them in order to function. We define a standard then as a collection of rules.

But if we misinterpret the meaning of "rule" as used here with "standards," we are liable to misinterpret the spirit of the standards as well. Simply by frequency of use, we think of "rule" as implying "regulation," "prohibition," "mandate," and "legislation." And by extension that use of "rule" connotes "infraction," "penalty," and "submission or punishment."

The rules that comprise an international standard, on the other hand, are of the kind that we encounter in mathematics, computer science, linguistics, or any other discipline that requires formality and precision. We know that a computer can tackle only problems whose solutions are expressed with sets of precise, unambiguous instructions, known as algorithms. This is rule-ordered behavior. Likewise, the data which a computer processes must appear in a fashion that is totally understandable by its instructions (i.e., unambiguous data). "Rule" as we use it in this book therefore implies "formal," "precise," and "unambiguous." We have reached back to the Latin meaning of *regula* (from which "rule" derives): precise measurement.

1.2   Brief History and Survey of Standards

Standards in communication are nothing new. In fact, they have been with us since ancient times, though not nearly as well formalized as the rules for Associated Press newswriters, for example. In the fourth century an unknown guardian of standards for spoken Latin published an Appendix of Proofs (*Appendix Probi*) in which he (or she?) lists a considerable number of deviant pronunciations of Latin, each one contrasted with the "correct" (i.e., classical written Latin) form. Of course, spoken Latin, with all of its "deviant," "incorrect," and "non-standard" forms, eventually became what we hear today as French, Italian, Spanish, Portuguese, Catalan and Rumanian. That poor standards enforcer of the fourth century would be dismayed to visit modern Europe or Latin America!

Several European language communities throughout their histories have relied on national academies to codify standards for each language: spelling, pronunciation, word usage, and grammatical rules. The Académie Française and the Spanish Real Academia are two examples. For English word-level usage, there is no such official standards body, either in Britain or in the United States. Instead we rely on de facto standards (emerging spontaneously through popular usage), such as the *Oxford English Dictionary* or *Webster's* in the United States.

As for grammar (sentence-level usage), our de facto standards are textbooks and live usage itself. Although this would seem to allow English to run totally out of control, the actual linguistic "drift" of English is quite comparable to those languages for which official bodies make the rules. Thus de jure (legislated) standards and de facto (spontaneously emerging) ones seem to be equally effective... for word usage, pronunciation, and correctness in natural language.

But in modern written communication we rely on standards and conventions for much more than word usage and grammatical correctness. For example, when we deal in scientific or technical material of any kind, we must constantly *refer to* passages outside the sentence or paragraph we are writing. And we do this for various reasons. We must cite the origins of some scientific or technological finding whenever we refer to it. We must give complete credit to the owners of intellectual property, offering a full "audit trail" through its development. And we must frequently refer to other portions of our own text as well: footnotes, appendixes, bibliographies, figures, tables, and other material that is not strictly "in-line" to our text. The community that reads these citations has come to expect certain rules of navigation for accessing this material in a consistent fashion. This same community accepts and expects a consistent layout and format for presenting technical and scientific material. The standards that drive formal document writing thus serve the same purpose as any other communications standard: to make the flow of data more efficient and to assure that material is decoded (understood) precisely the way that it was encoded (written).

The freshman who struggles writing a research paper may not appreciate these benefits but may view the standards as so much pedagogical baggage. But a competent instructor will be quick to point out that a published standard achieves many benefits, even for a freshman research paper and even for the freshman! All of the specialized mechanics—structural organization, bibliography, tables, quotations, illustrations, citations—need only be referenced in the course syllabus by citing the name of the preferred style guide(s). In this way the professor does not have to consume weeks of class time restating rules in detail. The student, while writing the paper, does not need to reinvent formats for these details; they are in the style guide to be looked up as needed. And the reader has no problem navigating through the paper because everything appears in its expected place. These are the standards we adhere to when we follow some style guide, such as the *MLA Handbook of Style*, *University of Chicago Manual of Style*, or Strunk and White's *The Elements of Style*, to name a few.

The workplace also offers convincing evidence that standards make sense. The Associated Press publishes its own stylebook, which includes not only the AP standards for language usage but also the mechanics for filing stories properly on its wire services, as well as rules regarding libel. Here certainly, standards are a matter of career survival. And technical writers in any discipline should be aware of *Scientific and Technical Reports: Organization, Preparation, and Production*, a comprehensive ANSI standard (Z39.18-1987) covering every aspect of the technical document. This publication, in turn, is only 1 of over 50 titles in the *National Information Standards Series*.

A particular publisher may likewise establish standards, particularly in the area of page layout and design. This would entail such topics as fonts (and their various characteristics), margins, pagination, headers, footers, and sidebar material. A professional page designer lends a certain aesthetic "personality" to a book or series.

Finally, there are low-grade electronic transmission standards among publishers which simply *emerge*. Prior to the popularity of certain word processing or page layout software, a publisher would insist that an author submit textual copy as ASCII (character-only) files. But now a publisher might specify WordPerfect® or Microsoft Word® word processor files or that images be submitted in PostScript® format.

1.3   Objects of Standards

Standards are entrenched in the craft of modern-day writing. But what are we (through our various standards bodies) trying to standardize? And in particular, what sorts of standards are of greatest concern to the writer and editor? The language academies and authoritative dictionaries govern spelling and word usage, but these are word-level issues that are common to all types of writing. On the other hand, grammars and style manuals mainly treat usage at the sentence level, alerting us to incorrect forms and occasionally to specialized rules for various types of writing: journalistic, creative, and technical, for example.

The *Scientific and Technical Reports* standard, cited above, sets the stage for electronic documentation by specifying the *structure* of a document in two dimensions. In the section "Organization of Report," the standard details the *order* in which elements should occur in the document: Front Matter (cover, title page, abstract, contents, preface), Body Matter (summary, introduction, methods, results, conclusions), and Back Matter (appendixes, bibliography, glossary, index). And in "Preparation of Report" the standard discusses *subordination* only briefly. But the discussion of subordination in technical writing hints at the highly powerful attribute of *depth* in a document, something that will become paramount in the electronic document. That same section of the standard prescribes certain numbering systems or typographic progression schemes, plus indentation rules, in order to signal hierarchical relationships among segments. The intention is of course to clarify the meaning of a document through its structure; it streamlines the reader's access to information. In this sense structure helps to clarify a document. Thus the technical documentation standard, while it does not pretend to support electronic documents, seeks to enlarge our understanding of a document. The document therefore is not simply a sequence of concepts but a structured set of relationships among those concepts.

As publishers have watched the emerging popularity of word processing systems, it has become common to request manuscripts in machine-readable form. Besides receiving those manuscripts with a neat appearance and with a lower incidence of misspellings, a publisher hopes to eliminate costly total rekeying of text for typesetting. But with this industrywide trend there is a tandem aim for *compatibility*. It is not enough for a document simply to be machine-readable; it is important that it also be compatible with the publisher's typesetting "front end." So although we are still considering the printed page, it is significant that industry standards have helped set the stage for electronic documentation. The object of standardization here is *portability* among publishing systems.

With the emergence of electronic documentation, the author and publisher must now focus on every non-print, non-traditional medium possible and imaginable. The standards therefore must now broaden to encompass such optional media as interactive maintenance manuals, on-line hypertext (user-driven navigation) structure, multimedia, and electronic redistribution from regional centers. The object of standardization for the non-print arena therefore is *adaptability*—to known media and to those yet to be developed.

1.4   Impetus for an Electronic Standard

Automation

The central impetus to standards in writing has been the pervasiveness of automation—in every phase of the life cycle of the document: original authoring, drafts and revisions, typesetting, republication, electronic retrieval, and display for browsing and viewing. So just as technology in any industry spawns consistency and standards, so have modern publication and electronic delivery hastened the emergence of comprehensive standards.

There is a powerful negative impetus for standards as well. In spite of the efforts of computing and communications standards organizations, there are many aspects of hardware, software, and procedures that are inconsistent and incompatible. Sometimes this is intentional. Certain vendors may have hoped to trap a segment of a user community so as to assure prolonged future sales. . But whatever the reasons, and whatever the status of compatibility across computer platforms, we are not there yet. This difficulty of intersystem document sharing is not an abstract, academic topic, but an urgent economic need.

Here is the motivation for *Standard Generalized Markup Language*, as spelled out in its own Introduction:

> This International Standard specifies a language for document representation referred to as the "Standard Generalized Markup Language" (SGML). SGML can be used for publishing in its broadest definition, ranging from single medium conventional publishing to multi-media data base publishing. SGML can also be used in office document processing when the benefits of human readability and interchange with publishing systems are required.
>
> — ISO 8879, Clause 0

1.5   The Text Processing Application

The profession of creating and processing documents has reached a degree of maturity and complexity that simply demands standards. A serious professional writer in a modern electronic workplace cannot be a "one-man band," receiving rough outlines and producing camera-ready copy plus electronic media for whatever purpose. Instead, he or she may concentrate on writing and revision and not deal with page layout. If employed full-time in a single company, that writer will generate documents of a particular type. And the documents will treat subject matter of a particular vertical industry or type of organization. In other words, the profession has matured in its degree of specialization.

This specialization—or some would say fragmentation—has created some consistent patterns. The work has settled into some recognizable *tasks*: creating text, revising text, formatting text, doing page layout, preparing text for electronic storage and retrieval, and generating reports, for example. In addition, there are predictable *types* of text, depending on where it is to be used: office memos and reports, operations and maintenance manuals for devices of every description, articles and books for various publishers. There are therefore three *organizing criteria* for sorting these activities: (1) the arena in which the document moves (vertical industry or type of business activity), (2) the type of document (book, memo, installation guide), and (3) the process we apply to a document (create, revise, report from).

The SGML standard assists us in recognizing these criteria by formalizing the concept of **text processing application**. While the phrase seems rather commonplace, it is actually precise shorthand terminology for referring to entire classes of related document types and text processing activities. We note first that "text" here means any kind of human-readable material—character and non-character—that a document may contain: graphics, video, audio, spreadsheet, columnar reports, tables, as well as traditional text.

A particular text processing application centers around a particular writing community and is defined by the *types of documents* they produce and by the *ways that they process* those documents. For example, widely scattered technical writers within the financial services industry may produce an array of document types: software manuals for banking, policies and procedure manuals, market updates, investment offerings, newsletters, promotional literature, and year-end reports. Their various activities may be diverse: create, revise, format, prepare for on-line access, and make camera-ready copy. According to SGML, this particular grouping of *document types and processes* for the financial services industry might therefore constitute a text processing application.

Here is the formal definition of **text processing application** from the SGML standard (along with its associated definitions):

> **text processing application:** A related set of processes performed on documents of related types.
>
> — ISO 8879: §4.318

> **application:** Text processing application.
>
> — ISO 8879: §4.5

> **document type:** A class of documents having similar characteristics; for example, journal, article, technical manual, or memo.
> — ISO 8879: §4.102

The standard includes a NOTE to text processing application, offering three examples which help us summarize our discussion. The three applications (with their document types and processes) are

1. Publication of technical manuals for a software developer

    *   *document types:* installation, operation, maintenance manuals
    *   *processes:* creation, revision, formatting, page layout for a variety of output devices

2. Preparation of manuscripts by independent authors for members of an association of publishers

    *   *document types:* book, journal, article
    *   *process:* creation

3. Office correspondence

    *   *document types:* memos, mail logs, reports
    *   *processes:* creation, revision, simple formatting, storage and retrieval, memo log update, report generation

(Note that in this book, since we are treating only issues affecting writers and editors, we shall concentrate on creation and revision.)

When a grouping (such as the financial services one above) thus has an identity (and probably a name) as a separate text processing application, then the writers' task can be considerably eased. That is because it is now possible to standardize the various processes and document types according to the "family resemblances" within that application. Writers of software reference manuals, for example, should not have to reinvent a manual's structure for every new product within each company and writing group. And the overall process of creating such a manual would be highly similar from company to company.

The concept of a text processing application therefore serves as an electronic gathering place for a community of writers who create similar documents and who perform similar tasks. The community can then quite naturally coalesce under a single standard, as has happened in the case of *Electronic Manuscript Preparation and Markup*, the first SGML industrywide text processing application. (The standard is commonly called the "AAP Standard" because the SGML application is based on the Association of American Publishers' *Standard for Electronic Manuscript Preparation and Markup*. This has now been adopted as international standard ISO/IEC 12083.)

Why an SGML-based application as a standard? Because it offers attractive benefits to a wide variety of producers and consumers. The Association of American Publishers in their ANSI/NISO

Z39.59-1988, the original standard for the AAP application, is emphatic about the standard's benefits to the industry:

> to establish a standard means of identifying and tagging parts of an electronic manuscript so that computers can differentiate between these parts, and,
>
> to provide a logical way to represent special characters, symbols, and tabular material, using only the ASCII [plain text] character set.
>
> By following these procedures, any manuscript can be processed on any computer. Just as important, publishers will be able to file a manuscript on a computer as a searchable database.
>
> — ANSI/NISO Z39.59-1988, Foreword p. ix

Why standards? And why SGML as an electronic document standard of choice? We have emphasized some major benefits to writers and editors:

- *Confidence* that the conforming document's structure will be totally understandable, even by a computer.

- *Freedom* to concentrate primarily on writing and editing.

- *Increased productivity.* One now creates a single document that will (1) "play" on a variety of media, (2) appear in a variety of formats, and (3) enjoy a much prolonged life cycle.

A further motivating factor for electronic standards has to do with our sophisticated demands on the document and, in particular, on how it moves about and gets processed. No longer content with the traditional page, we insist that a document be *smart* or *lively*. When we say that, we usually are thinking about *how a text application gets processed*, that is, the *semantics* of a text processing application. We will look at some characteristics of "smartness" or "liveliness" in a moment (neither of which are formal definitions, by the way). The job of defining semantics is one of the chief tasks of a **document architecture**. Since that is the case, we need (1) to define formally what a **document architecture** is, and then (2) to describe what might make for a document to be "smart" or "lively."

In general, the architecture of a document refers to issues that are not of direct concern to SGML. Specifically, **document architecture** is a set of rules that apply to **text processing applications**. Those rules typically go beyond issues of internal document structure and reach instead to details of processing. So a conforming document may indeed *specify* some sort of processing in a formal way; this is entirely proper. For example, the author may insert very specialized "hooks" for hypertext navigation processing or for retrieval processing. Hypertext and retrieval are text processing applications, and they rely heavily on conforming documents, to be sure. But it is not up to SGML or to the author to specify how those processes will eventually work.

On the other hand, various user communities are *very* interested in *how* processes work: how the document will be formatted, what will be the nature of its transmission and delivery, and precisely how the document works in a retrieval system, for example. Out of these processing concerns come formal rules, and those rules are what we refer to as a document architecture.

To summarize the distinction, SGML concentrates primarily on the various internal structural issues of a document: the various building blocks (e.g., front matter, body, end matter), their internal sequencing, and the hierarchical relationships (structuring) among these elements. But architecture goes beyond the internals of the document. It deals with the document's purpose, its audience, its possible media, and the variety of ways that the document will be played, performed, displayed, accessed, transmitted, or read. A document architecture therefore is a set of rules that tell how this should happen. And since there is such a variety of processing options, it is possible for a single application to be part of several architectures. Finally, it is important to note that architectures themselves are becoming standardized. We shall look at some of these later on.

1.6   Smart Document Architecture

In general a "smart" system of any kind is more open, more accessible, more interactive, and in general more responsive to the user. A "dumb" system is the opposite: more closed, less accessible, less interactive, and less responsive to the user. We can apply the same criteria to buildings, to electronic hardware, to software, or to objects we have never thought of as either "smart" or "dumb." We consider a house, for example, to be "smart" if it is designed with sufficient electronics to enable it to respond to people's needs in some flexible manner: programmable security, scheduled entertainment, highly automatic and responsive environmental controls, and automatic maintenance scheduling. We call a computer "terminal dumb" if it has sufficient electronics only to receive and send a single character at a time from the computer and to receive keystrokes from the user. But a "smart" terminal typically can store large amounts of data and manipulate that data in more interesting and efficient ways, possibly without the help of the main computer.

But a smart *document*? What can make a document smart? Here we are not referring to the contents of the document, but to how it gets processed. The traditional written document, of whatever genre, is something that we read linearly, from beginning to end or from top to bottom. We may occasionally choose to read in reverse order, not a bad way to proofread your writing. Or, we may use an index or table of contents to go directly to the segment of the document that concerns us. But even with this direct-access method of entering the document, we generally read each segment beginning to end, top to bottom.

Non-linear access gives us a hint of how a document can be more "open," more responsive to the user. This is what we expect of a reference manual, but what if every kind of technical document—user manual, installation guide, parts catalog, maintenance and operation manual—were more open to the user? And what if every kind of written corpus—journalistic prose, legal document, dictionary, poetry anthology, novel, short story—were likewise more responsive? And what if we included non-print media: painting, sculpture, video, and audio records? Redefining "document" in this way suggests that we must redefine how we produce, transmit, deliver, and receive such media. This is not futuristic brainstorming. Our computing systems, communications networking, publishing methodologies, and fundamental assumptions about intellectual property demand that we supply formal and standard definitions for documents and their related activity. This is precisely the concern of document architecture. And an architecture that transcends our notions of the traditional print document is what we call *smart document architecture*.

What are some aspects of the smart document? We suggested a few above: non-linear, highly interactive, direct-access. Following is an expanded list of characteristics:

- Portable across different hardware architectures

- Multimedia-aware or -compliant

- Accessible through various modes (totally open-ended)

- Offering a wide variety of "deliverables"

- Applicable in multiple venues of delivery

- Conforming to all applicable standards

- Accessible to physically challenged users

- Responsive to intellectual property issues (automatic charge-back for access to copyright materials)

- Offering the reader semi-interactive access to author(s)

- Achieving seamless "authoring gateways" (write once, deliver anywhere, in any manner—total reusability of the document)

The most essential point for the author is that for a standard document architecture to work properly, the underlying document(s) must likewise conform. Conforming to SGML therefore makes possible all of the promise of the electronic document.

Summary

Why standards? And why SGML in particular? Because it offers a reasonable hope for benefits that we have sought since before writing began. And now the key player is not some industry giant or some pervasive technological breakthrough but instead is the *writer*.

CHAPTER 2

SGML AS A NEW PARADIGM
Structure before Style

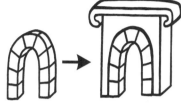

SGML terms introduced or reinforced:

application, descriptive markup, document, document type, element, markup, mark up, process, tag.

Overview

When we change the way we *do* something, we are likely not creating a revolution. But when a considerable segment of a worldwide community begins to think differently about its primary object of attention, then it is reasonable to assume that there is what historians call a "paradigm shift." The community of authors and editors of electronic documents are beginning to think in new ways about the document and about how they do their work. We would suggest therefore that this suggests a paradigm shift, one which demands something from the writer and which promises much in return.

This chapter explores certain key notions that SGML introduces to the digital workplace. We suggest that SGML lightens the writer's load considerably and frees up the document as well. We introduce the basic notions of SGML that enable a new level of simplicity for document creation. We contrast the important notions of *deducing structure from a document's appearance* (what a human does) versus *rendering a document's appearance* based on markup of structure (what a document process does). This helps us to reorient our thinking in ways that help us take advantage of the power offered by SGML. Finally, we look at an example of descriptive markup using two common element types: lists and list items.

2.1 Paradigms and Paradigm Shift

The term "paradigm shift" denotes a radical development in the way people think. In this chapter we are considering some fundamental aspects of preparing a document, and we are discussing how SGML alters that task. SGML changes the writer's task in ways that may seem at first burdensome. But as we shall see, SGML actually makes the author's and editor's agenda much less complicated. At the same time, it gives new power and flexibility to the document itself. Because we need to think differently therefore about writing and editing and about the document itself, we maintain that SGML entails a *paradigm shift* in our thinking, a practical shift for the better.

Let us first be clear on the significance of paradigm (pronounced "para-dime"). Broadly speaking, a paradigm is a thought pattern, a widely accepted method of observing, considering, and discussing some portion of our reality. The paradigm for a body of knowledge—scientific, technological, historical, or whatever—implies much more than simply the facts pertaining to that knowledge. Beyond facts, it is also the collection of commonly held assumptions that give structure and meaning to those facts. It binds together the community of theorists and practitioners of that knowledge with shared beliefs, specialized terminology, and probably a corpus of shared literature. And a paradigm usually implies some far-reaching side effects.

The most notable paradigm in astronomy that eventually underwent a drastic shift was the concept of a geocentric (i.e., earth-centered) universe. This was a centuries-old assumption shared by most of European civilization. And one of the significant side effects of that paradigm was that it afforded a sense of particular importance to the earth and to all its inhabitants. But that paradigm finally expired as knowledgeable people began to think and believe otherwise. Realizing that the earth revolved around the sun forever changed civilization as "we" knew it. And it also impacted an entire culture's sense of comfort and security.

Futurists in the 1960's used (and abused!) the phrase "paradigm shift" in describing this or that revolution in technology, world view, transportation, communication, diet, dress, education, politics and whatever seemed highly interesting and undergoing change at the time. Because of overuse, therefore, the phrase now quite often connotes simply "different" or "novel."

But there is a true paradigm shift awaiting writers and editors who aspire to become SGML-literate. It is certainly not nearly as cosmic as the sixteenth-century shift to the paradigm of a heliocentric universe. It has to do with (1) what writers consider to be the *outcome of their work* and (2) how writers view the *domain* of their work. In other words, we are considering both the nature of the document that writers produce and the nature of their activity in producing that document. And although we establish a clear difference between traditional and SGML authoring and markup, we shall look at how closely SGML markup echoes the markup rules of traditional style guides.

2.2   The Document

Printed Page versus Information to Be Processed

For nearly all technical writers, the metaphor of the printed page has traditionally defined their work. Writers speak of stages of a document using terms like "draft copy" as opposed to "cam copy" or "repro"—terms which are tied to the page metaphor. To revise is to "mark up" and traditionally involves red-lining and blue-lining. (We will see shortly how SGML has capitalized on the terms mark up and markup and given them powerful and useful meaning for the electronic document.) Prior to word processing and desktop publishing, we typed our manuscript according to in-house or publishers' style guides. The purpose for standards at that time was to enable as easy translation as possible from (1) typewritten draft to (2) editorial markup and revision to (3) typeset pages.

With the advent of desktop publishing, writers themselves could create "finished" (i.e., print-quality) pages, complete with fonts, page design, graphics, and everything placed (i.e., "pasted up") properly. But more than ever before, writing and editing activity in desktop publishing focuses on the *appearance of the printed page.*

As the professional typesetting industry well knows, the advent of desktop publishing surely was revolutionary (catastrophic for many small typesetting firms). The revolution consisted of the writers' preparing print-ready copy without expensive typesetting labor and equipment. In fact, the status of editorial workflow currently is such that the writer now frequently delivers diskettes to a service bureau which can create photographic film directly for the printer. Or the document on disk may possibly be input directly to the publisher's electronic typesetting machinery. In other words, electronic publication has revolutionized the workflow between authoring, editing, and final printing.

A revolution, to be sure. But is this change in publishing technologies a paradigm shift? Not really…at least not solely because of desktop publishing. While there are dramatic cost savings and while the time required for manuscript preparation and book production has collapsed (theoretically, at least!) to electronic speed, people in the desktop publishing community still think and work among the issues of appearance of the printed page: attractiveness, visual consistency, fonts, placement of graphics, and other considerations of page layout. And so, with such a revolutionary improvement over the old typewriter-to-typesetter methodologies, why should we even hope for anything more (or for something different) for creating and delivering documents?

The answer to that question quite simply is that to offer the serious writer an enhanced ability as a compositor does not really enhance his or her productivity as a writer. Even with highly available electronic assistance, the writer must continue to think both *as a writer and as a compositor.* Again, the printed page is still the guiding metaphor in thinking about the document. But even though the current desktop page formatting technologies are superb for creating a document, they are generally very stingy with the variety of options they provide us for delivering that document. For example, a mid-size, state-of-the art page layout product—Adobe PageMaker® for example— is meant primarily to print pages. A package such as this does offer certain export options so that a document can be imported by another page layout program or by a commercial typesetting system. So in a limited sense, such products do indeed allow us to move a document. But even this is almost never easy, either because of software or hardware incompatibilities or because of undocumented anomalies among the various systems.

A document is thus typically locked in to a particular computer, operating system, network, or page layout program. This is not really the fault of the computer manufacturer or the software providers. The central mission of each company is, after all, to enhance and promote its own products. It has not traditionally made good business sense for a company to spend inordinate effort to create documents primarily so that they can move elsewhere.

But during recent years that has changed. And computer users have forced a change upon providers not only for documents but also for accounting information, database systems, and nearly every application that exists for the computer. Those demands translate into phrases such as *open systems architecture* and *enterprisewide computing*, and *workgroup authoring*. Not surprisingly, it has required some tough thinking and some rather heavy-handed standards formulation and enforcement to move the industry toward such an era of openness. And we are not there yet.

For document processing, the issue of "unlocking" the document is particularly acute since nearly all computer hardware doing nearly all flavors of computing do some document processing to a greater or lesser degree. To expect hardware manufacturers and software providers all suddenly to change their products into a single, seamless entity would be totally unreasonable. But the document creator and document user communities nonetheless demand that the document be unlocked. This has been particularly true for writers and users in governmental agencies, in which the proliferation of documents is rampant and continuing unabated (no matter how governments may attempt to legislate against it!). And unlocking the document is also critical for major segments of industry, in which easy interchange of documents is vital to conducting business. So it is no surprise that there is a worldwide consensus that demands openness in documentation.

What are the characteristics of the "open document"? From a purely economic standpoint, such a document does not necessarily consume paper; while it may on occasion appear as hard copy, it can be rendered electronically at will. It certainly is not bound to particular printing or viewing devices but is portable across a variety of hardware and software platforms and among a variety of *topologies* (arrangements of computers, workstations, networks, servers, and clients). The document's entire community of users no matter how spread out geographically—must be able to share the document. And the community may elect to "reuse" the document—as a database, for example. These are a few aspects of an expanded notion of document. In the next chapter ("Features and Benefits of SGML") we shall view these in greater detail as the payoffs that come with our standards. For now we concentrate on how they have expanded our definition of the document.

The dream of documents that are totally open—rendered in ways unknown to the author and only later defined, shareable across all computing architectures, portable among an entire community, reusable in ways also as yet undefined—would have remained no more than an impossible dream without some radical redefinition of some part of the writing process. Either we must standardize all of the necessary hardware and software used by the entire authoring and writing community or we must strictly enforce a single universal authoring and processing standard over that entire community. But neither of these agendas appears even remotely possible.

So what is the magic that SGML offers for achieving such noble objectives (portability, shareability, etc.)? Basically, SGML expands first our notion of the document itself. The formal

SGML definition of document is as follows: "A collection of information that is processed as a unit..." (§4.96). The subtle but profound implication here is that the document as a "collection of information" is separate from whatever it is when it gets *processed*. It is a first and then relationship: First there is a document and then something processes the document.

This distinction between "document" and "process" is so fundamental and so persistent in SGML that we must understand clearly each term and the distinction between the two worlds that these terms represent. "Process" for an SGML document is anything that anyone wishes to do with the document: view, print, typeset, interrogate, search, navigate via hypertext links, play back (if there is video or audio content), project, transmit, broadcast, translate (to Braille), or whatever this generation or succeeding generations of users care to do with the document. In a word, "process" is so open-ended that no one even knows all of its meaning for any given document. The significant point for an SGML author or editor is that it is up to the *processor* to make all of this activity happen—to render the appearance of the printed page, to specify the colors and placement of text in video output, and so on.

The *document*, on the other hand is a collection of information. But note that SGML deals primarily with internal elements, components of the document's structure; it has practically nothing to do with "information" or "semantics" in the popular sense of those terms. For now, we should recognize that the structural hierarchy "book," "chapter," and "paragraph" are elements of the document type defined as "book." (We shall revisit the terms "structural element" and "document type" in great detail in later chapters.) Ideally, the document does not include processing-specific information: colors, centering, backlighting, type styles. Instead it uses SGML to describe its own internal structure in a highly precise and unambiguous manner. Using that structural information alone, the processing software or hardware decides how to render the text or graphics or video or audio. The SGML document therefore remains unaware of what will finally become of it when it is processed.

But documents do not simply self-generate in a vacuum. They are created and edited by real people who naturally visualize the final processed forms of the document all along. So SGML does not force us suddenly to stop thinking of the document's rendition. As we shall see later, traditional page layout is a powerful means for visualizing and specifying structure, which is our central task in SGML anyway. And SGML typically does insist that we keep the document itself general and that our markup be generalized, not bound to any particular processing scheme.

2.3   Writers and Editors

Makers of Pages or Describers of Structures

Having established the clear distinction between the SGML document and the processing of the document, we turn next to what that redefinition of "document" implies for the agenda of the writer and editor. In a word, it means that they (1) write their material, (2) specify the structure of (the relationships among) all of the elements of their document, *and then stop.* In other words, if the properly marked-up document is the "deliverable" for SGML, then the writer's job is done when he or she has (1) written all of the content required and (2) properly marked up the document (with *tags*) so as to describe the internal structure of the document in a totally precise and unambiguous fashion. That activity of tagging is called descriptive markup in SGML. Again, that markup describes the structure of the elements within the document and not how the document is to be processed.

> With generalized markup [of which SGML is an example], the markup process *stops at the first step*: the user locates each significant element of the document and marks it with the mnemonic name (generic identifier) that he feels best characterizes it.
>
> — ISO 8879 A.2 (italics added)

2.4   Traditional Markup versus SGML Markup

We assume that the reader is well acquainted with traditional editorial markup. We need only to emphasize that this markup typically commingles two aspects of a document: content issues, which typically require correction (spelling, punctuation, word usage, deletions, insertions, for example) and layout and design issues (centering, indenting, italicizing, bulleting, item numbering, and folios). Even in an electronic document workplace, the copy editing will continue to enforce internal correctness: spelling, punctuation, word usage, and clarity of content. But the elaborate and intricate detail traditionally supplied by design editors is no longer part of the author's task in an electronic environment. (See the sample layout specification figure 2-1.) By declaring all of that effort to be "processing," we have thus released the author from the task of being also a compositor.

We have emphasized that "document" bears a new meaning in SGML: a collection of information (the author's own content information plus information about the document), all of which is precisely defined, unambiguous, and "unaware" of its own eventual processing. In addition, by restricting the domain of the document we have relaxed the requirements for authoring and editing and consequently have redefined and simplified the writer's and editor's agendas. Again, after applying proper descriptive markup to a document, the writer can simply stop.

We turn now first to the format of the SGML document with its text and descriptive markup. In the remaining discussion, we discover yet other "relaxations" of the author's effort. As an example of how SGML descriptive markup differs from traditional markup, we look finally at how a typical SGML application treats a list and list items, two common types of elements among the structures of practically every type of document.

Type specs for <u>COMN-PILER USER'S GUIDE</u> 3rd ed
See attached grid   Trim = 8½" x 11"
<u>Type area</u>: 42 pi x 59 pi [Note: Text width area was 43 pi in <u>2nd ed</u>;
                          should be 42 pi in 3rd ed]

<u>Margins</u>: gutter = 6pi
          outside = 3 pi
          top = 4 pi
          bottom = 3½ pi

> <u>Type</u>: Note : In all specs that follow, typefaces
> are identified only as "serif" & "sans serif." Please
> match the typefaces in <u>2nd ed</u> as closely as possible

<u>Chapter number and title</u>: Pls. match <u>2nd ed</u> as closely as possible. The following
          specs may be incomplete:
          Ch. number: 52 pt.? sans serif f. l., followed by 8pt. # to
          2 pt. rule (x 42 pi.); then 36 pts. b/b to first line
          of ch. title.
          ch. title: Sans serif roman 28 pt. type, f. l., u/lc
<u>A-heads (section heads)</u>: 12 pt. sans-serif boldface caps, f. l., followed by
      4 pt. # to 1 pt. rule (x 42 pi); 24 pts. # b/b to first line of text
<u>Text</u>: 9.5 or 10/12 serif type [pls. see 2nd ed: can't tell whether typesize is
    9.5 or 10 pt; leading <u>is</u> 12 pt.], f. l. /ragged right on 42 pi measure. No
    end-of-line word breaks. <u>NOTE</u>: Question <u>numbers</u> (used in options
    lists) are boldface; questions themselves, roman. Turnovers hang on
    first word of text. Pls. match horizontal spacing, indentations,
    alignments in list formats as in 2nd ed.
    Add 6 pts. # between complete sub-sections (18 pts. b/b), both in main
    text and in Appendices.
<u>Running heads</u>: Folio – 10 pt. serif type boldface, <u>flush outside</u>; em-space
    to chapter number (CHAPTER X): 7 pt. bf caps, followed by centered
    bullet; then chapter title: 7 pt. roman caps
<u>Paging instructions</u>: Paging may run short as necessary to <u>avoid</u>: (1) breaking
    up subsections of less than 5 lines; (2) separating figures from the text
    to which they belong (no need to balance bottoms of spreads).
<u>Figure titles</u>: 9 pt. sans-serif boldface type, u/lc, centered on text
    width. (Set en-dashes in figure and table numbers.)
<u>Tables</u> table title: bf. text type, centered over body of table; 18 pts
    b/b to column heads.
    column heads: rom. text type, followed by 4 pt. # to 1 pt rule to
    width of table.
    table body: rom. text type; SEE sample tables in 2nd ed—pp. 19,
    15, 56, 79
<u>Throughout</u>: set en-dashes as marked.
<u>Figures</u>: Leave 1 line # (24 pts b/b) above figure heading; appr. ½ line #
    (18 pts #) from base of figure <u>heading</u> to top of figure; appr. 1–2½ l #
    below figure to next text unit.

Figure 2-1 Sample typesetting specification

2.5   The Format of the SGML Document

Plain Unformatted Text

The best guarantee for a document's portability from one computer to almost any other computer on the planet is for that document to contain nothing but ASCII ("plain text") characters. The entire markup philosophy of SGML, since all markup is itself in plain-text format, really does allow us therefore to focus our attention on writing and on describing the document's structure. This is indeed a significant reduction of effort on the author's part, compared to the additional labor of preparing camera-ready page copy.

At first, this reduction sounds as though we have surrendered all of our advanced document technology and expertise to the cause of portability and open systems. If what we retain is only unformatted text, then this would seem to be the lowest of low common denominators. But this reduction is only partly true, for the following reason: SGML, while itself is simple unformatted text, carries along all of the information it needs for the document to be totally reconstructed by any conforming SGML document processing system. Since our aim is to allow the document to move to another platform (another brand of hardware, a totally different viewing and printing facility, or some totally different medium) we no longer concern ourselves primarily with page layout and appearance of the document. Instead we allow SGML to bear the information required for some process to reconstruct and redisplay the document on the target device (which may be totally unknown to the creator of the document).

In Chapter 1 we read explicit language in the standard SGML application for the Association of American Publishers(AAP), specifying that any computer must be able to process any manuscript. That standard was explicit in demanding a plain-text means of conveying the document. The aim of the AAP standard, to somehow convey even non-ASCII symbols within the document, is stated as follows:

> to provide a logical way to represent special characters, symbols, and tabular material, using only the ASCII [plain text] character set. By following these procedures, any manuscript can be processed on any computer.
> — ANZI/NISO Z39.59-1988, Foreword p. ix

The document that we share in this utopian open environment certainly bears little resemblance to the highly polished, camera-ready page image that we strive for with PageMaker or Illustrator. Instead we "reduce" the document to precisely what the AAP standard says: "plain text."

Understanding this division of labor between the author's and editor's activity, on one hand, and processing activity (proper appearance on the screen, behavior of the database, typesetting details), on the other, is basic to our understanding SGML. An authoring and editing system (procedures, hardware and document-producing software) generates a conforming SGML document... period. Some process downline may perhaps also create a camera-ready version, one that is just like what we are accustomed to with PageMaker, but not necessarily. The work of receiving the SGML document, interpreting the critical information that the SGML apparatus bears about the document, and then displaying, printing, retrieving, or playing the document is left to the processing system. Naturally this means that the particular workstation or printer or typesetting machinery or data retrieval device or video player has some significant knowledge of SGML. That processing system handles everything that pertains to receiving an SGML document, interpreting the text and its markup codes, and then processing the document in some way.

The magic that (1) reduces effort so dramatically on the author's part and (2) enables such dramatic portability on the document's part is descriptive markup.

2.6   Example of SGML Markup

List and List Items

In order to capture the meaning of document structure in the SGML sense, let us study one part of one *application* of SGML: the structure definition for lists and list items in a manual, as we shall define them in Chapters 5 through 9. (See figure 2-2, Elements of a Manual.) You will see at once that we approach the manual from the outside in. The "outermost" element is the manual itself, and as we move "inward," we encounter three additional types of elements: Title, Author, Section. (This is not a complete or formal SGML definition of our document type, but it will help us later to understand the complete definition.) Each time we move inside an element we encounter another set of sub-elements, until finally we cannot move inward any further. Without becoming any more technical at this point, let us remember only that the "freight" that SGML carries for the document is the information about relationships among all of the various elements in a document.

Two issues typically occur to an author at this point. First, a writer will recoil at the notion of such a rigid scheme of relationships for a document. "With that tight a definition for my document's structure, how can I hope to be original and creative?" (That is precisely the response we would expect from a conscientious professional!) One answer to this objection is that with or without SGML we are already conforming to technical standards more than we realize. In presenting research or writing user manuals, we follow style manuals: APA, MLA, Chicago, Turabian, AP. We deliver in-house documents according to style books (or at least guidelines) that our company provides. For purely technical documentation, we no doubt follow something akin to the ANSI standard *Scientific and Technical Reports—Organization, Preparation, and Production*. And even artistic works are highly constrained by technical definitions: harmonic progressions in rock music, screenplays for commercial television, and the metrical and rhyming conventions for a sonnet.

The second reaction to SGML by most authors is that this sort of definition of structure is not really all that revolutionary. Everyone knows that a book is made up of a title plus chapters, and so on. And this is true. The structural elements of a book or article or serial are present, no matter who or what defines them. The difference between that and the way SGML defines structure lies in the markup apparatus. Within a chapter, for example, when we encounter a short line of boldface type with some extra vertical space above and below the line, we infer that this is a heading for a new

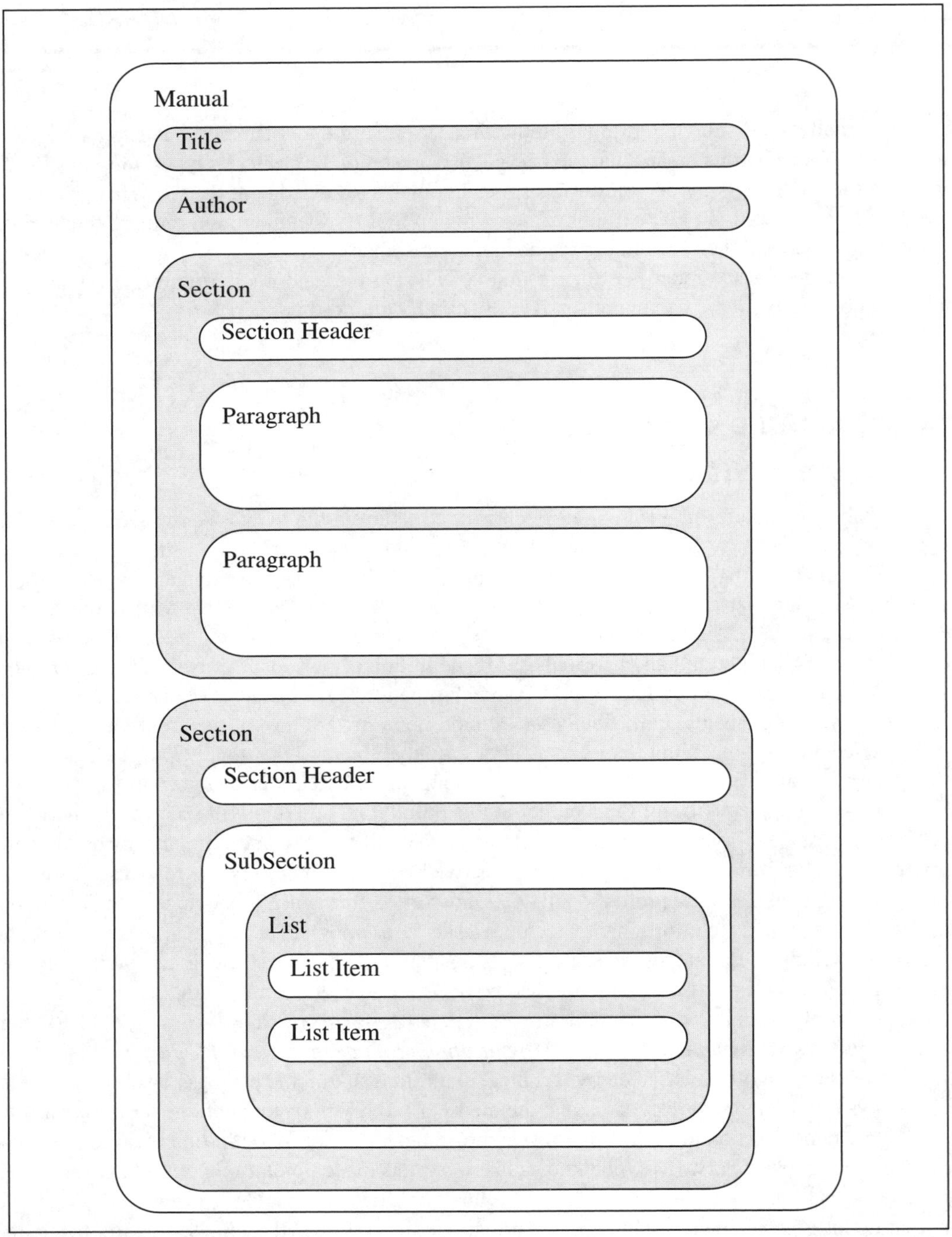

Figure 2-2 Elements of a Manual

section of the chapter—a "secondary heading," we might call it. In an SGML tagged manuscript, we would typically find no such boldface type, simply an `<h2>` tag (within the AAP application). The typesetter or viewing workstation would read that structure tag and probably create boldface type from that.

In the familiar setting of a printed list of items, we would encounter something like the following:

1.List item #1

    Second line of item #1

2.List item #2

3.List item #3

We are conditioned to scan a printed page and take our structural cues indirectly from the visual layout of the page. Here, we recognize the element "list" by there being certain predictable indentations, numbering, and horizontal alignment. *We view the appearance* and *deduce structure from it.*

As an example of this contrast between SGML and printed rendition, study Figures 2-3, Sample Tagged Manuscript, and Figure 2-4 Sample Typeset Document. Figure 2-3 is an SGML document. Figure 2-4 is one possible rendition of that SGML document. Note here in particular how we tag a secondary header with the `<h2>` tag. And note how it handles lists, using two varieties of list tags: `<l1>` and `<l2>`. (Ignore the format for tagging for the moment.) Compare these two tagged lists with how the typeset version renders each of the lists in Figure 2-4. This contrast between the tagged document and the typeset rendition tells us that the SGML markup is explicit about describing structure among elements, while disregarding totally any consideration of visual appearance. While we as readers (and authors, traditionally) rely upon physical page layout to imply structure and relationships among elements, SGML can express that structure solely by means of tagging. In other words, we as readers deduce the structure of a document from its appearance. In the SGML world, on the other hand, the document's typesetting or viewing device reconstructs the appearance of a document totally on the basis of the structure expressed in SGML. This means that SGML plus an appropriate display process—with its structure-first, appearance-later sequence—redefines the concept of "document" so that a computer can receive and process it in whatever way is appropriate. That inversion (appearance as primary for humans, structure as primary for the computer) is partly why we claim that SGML methodology represents a new paradigm for authoring and delivering a document.

One further irony awaits us. The mechanisms hinted at in SGML tagging (`<h1>`, `<h2>`, `<l1>`, `<l2>`) are very reminiscent of the terminology used by page designers and manuscript editors for years. So while SGML and descriptive markup may be a radical departure in some ways, the nomenclature and notation are by no means revolutionary. So once again, "revolutionary" is not synonymous with "new paradigm"!

```
<memo><h1>Internships: General Guidelines</h1>
<h2>Problem</h2>
<p>Having completed our first year's experience with undergraduate and graduate interns from the region's universities
and colleges, we have identified some persistent problem areas. The common thread of the various issues is that there is a
wide difference between our definition of <quote>internship</quote> as an entry-level work opportunity and <quote>
internship</quote> as a formal academic program within the universities.</p>
<h2>Items for Department Discussions</h2>
<l1>Here are some questions which we will need to discuss in our various department meetings and then resolve in the
formal personnel policy meeting next month:
<ListItem>How are we to view internship positions? Are they really a contribution to regional training or are they simply
a means of cheap labor?</ListItem>
<ListItem>Should they be paid positions or not? Or should some be paid and some not?</ListItem>
<ListItem>What should be our procedure for defining and then filling an internship position?</ListItem>
<ListItem>Should interns participate in formal training programs? If not, how can we formalize the training
process?</ListItem>
<ListItem>Who should manage and evaluate interns, the Human Resources Department or designated managers within
the departments?</ListItem></l1>
<h2>Interim Procedure</h2>
<l2>Although we do not yet have a permanent policy, please follow these steps in dealing with internships:
<ListItem>Submit a <quote>Request for Internship Position</quote> memo to the Human Resources
Department.</ListItem>
<ListItem>After HR approval send a posting of the position to each of the area colleges and universities, using the
contacts and addresses available in the HR Office.</ListItem>
<ListItem>If the student is doing the internship for academic credit, make certain that you, the intern, the university,
and our HR Office agree on the statement of work: learning objectives, activities, and method of evaluation.
</ListItem></l2></memo>
```

Figure 2-3 Sample Tagged Manuscript

Internships: General Guidelines

Problem

Having completed our first year's experience with undergraduate and graduate interns from the region's universities and colleges, we have identified some persistent problem areas. The common thread of the various issues is that there is a wide difference between our definition of "internship" as an entry-level work opportunity and "internship" as a formal academic program within the universities.

Items for Department Discussions

Here are some questions which we will need to discuss in our various department meetings and then resolve in the formal personnel policy meeting next month:

- How are we to view internship positions? Are they really a contribution to regional training or are they simply a means of cheap labor?
- Should they be paid positions or not? Or should some be paid and some not?
- What should be our procedure for defining and then filling an internship position?
- Should interns participate in formal training programs? If not, how can we formalize the training process?
- Who should manage and evaluate interns, the Human Resources Department or designated managers within the departments?

Interim Procedure

Although we do not yet have a permanent policy, please follow these steps in dealing with internships:

1. Submit a "Request for Internship Position" memo to the Human Resources Department.
2. After HR approval send a posting of the position to each of the area colleges and universities, using the contacts and addresses available in the HR Office.
3. If the student is doing the internship for academic credit, make certain that you, the intern, the university, and our HR Office agree on the statement of work: learning objectives, activities, and method of evaluation.

Figure 2-4 Sample Typeset Document

CHAPTER 3

FEATURES AND BENEFITS OF SGML

SGML terms introduced or reinforced:

conforming SGML document, document architecture, document type, document type definition, markup, reference concrete syntax, tag

Overview

This chapter presents several of the notable features of the SGML environment and emphasizes various benefits—for the writer and for the document itself. Following is a list of such *features*, followed by their *benefits*.

1. The document exists simply as **plain text**.

   The text requires no difficult conversions; it is easily **portable.**

2. Writing and markup are the **total** task of the author.

   The author is **free to write** and need not concern him- or herself with details of page appearance.

3. Processing-specific data **need not be part of the document.**

   The author's job is **easier, and the document is portable** and **open-ended.**

4. The SGML environment offers a **precise terminology and formulation** of rules.

   The writer and editor can **know precisely** what the boss, client, or customer wants.

5. There are industry-specific **standardized applications**.

   The writing group can enjoy **wider community** support, generalizable training, **uniformity**, higher quality of their own work, and **far less local reinvention.**

---

6. Standardized **architectures** have emerged which encompass the semantics of processing.

   To the extent that the writer and editor must be concerned with processing details, that task is **eased**, and they can be assured of more uniform processing.

7. SGML can assure **open-ended processing.**

   We can expect that a document will be **reusable** (targeted even for media as-yet not implemented)

8. The markup we apply is **multipurpose**.

   The tagging can serve for hypertext **links** and data **retrieval** as well as for **page composition**.

9. The underlying **notation for defining** SGML and a particular document type is highly similar to that used for computer languages.

   Our markup can describe concisely and uniformly the **hierarchical** relationship among the elements of document.

10. SGML **Reference Concrete Syntax** underlies most applications.

    The writer and editor can expect to **understand structure** even among different document types.

3.1   Standards

Nice-to-Have versus Need-to-Have

In Chapter 1 we surveyed an entire history of standards in human communication. For most of that history, standards have served to *enhance* the communication process. Writing standards have dramatically eased the writers' task, helping them to concentrate on content and relieving them of the pain of reinventing local conventions of style, organization, and page layout. This in turn enhances the document's readability and extends portability of documents to the widest readership possible. Writers adhere to certain usages and style conventions in order to facilitate the flow of the document and by all means never to obscure meaning. Page designers and publishers follow their layout rules in order to assure that all of the physical appearance of the document will assist the reader in recognizing logical segments, emphasized passages, bibliographic references, and the relationship among figures, tables, and the text which they support. And even in the case of the publisher's requiring machine-readable manuscript, that is only an enhancement to production. For all of these aspects of documentation, standards are highly desirable, and sometimes necessary. But however necessary they may be, they are in addition to the document and *enhance* the document.

With SGML, however, the standard *defines* the document. We now speak of a standard that is not only desirable but whose rules define precisely how the author does part of his or her work.

Chapter 1 listed several features of the smart or lively document that we would like to see: portability, multimedia awareness, interactivity, open-ended processing options, and retrievability, to name a few. But just wishing will not make this happen. For every one of those diverse features, the document needs to fit perfectly with the "host" application: search and retrieval software, viewing device, multimedia navigation engine. We achieve that guaranteed fit only through *precision*. And SGML offers both the writers of documents and the processors of documents the precision that is necessary to make it all happen. In that sense, therefore, the drive to make this list a reality has motivated SGML. We *need* the precision of SGML to make our documents *live* and *move*.

3.2   Features and Benefits of the Lively Document

It would certainly not be highly motivating to a writer for his or her boss or client simply to expect absolute compliance with a highly demanding standard unless there were also some highly enticing rewards for doing so. Nor would a writing group be eager to buy into a new standard if indeed everything about the new environment would be unfamiliar. We looked briefly above at some items on the dream list for the document of the future, noting that the cost for achieving those results is a new level of precision in how we do writing. Our task now is to dwell first on the *features* of a conforming SGML document, the SGML rules that apply to the writing process, and the writer's activity within an SGML environment. After surveying those features, we will examine the *benefits* of SGML.

Nearly every feature of SGML applications and of the SGML workplace derives from the following related fundamental principles:

1.   The markup for a an SGML application is *explicit* and *unambiguous*.

2.   SGML clearly distinguishes between the *document* and the *processing of the document*.

3.   The author and editor of a conforming SGML document deal primarily (and perhaps exclusively) with writing and markup, not with *processing* the document.

Processing the document is of highest concern in electronic documentation. Without the ability for us to retrieve, view, read, navigate, or listen to such a document, it would remain forever as some useless, disembodied abstraction. Processing the document is like a sound system's rendering a high-quality recording or to a projector's showing an award-winning film. In either case, the processing system must accurately render the medium. And while the writer of an electronic document naturally is thinking rendition and delivery all along, his or her primary task is to conceptualize about the document—its contents, its writing style, and the structural relationships among all of its parts. The writer normally does *not* concern him- or herself with the document's existence beyond its becoming a conforming document.

This may sound as if the standards makers have sold us a bill of goods. Hearing the promise of portability, we might expect to see in SGML a miraculous superstandard, one that demands at least everything found in existing standards plus many mechanisms used in popular word processors and page layout systems. On the contrary, SGML achieves portability and other benefits by redistributing the various tasks of creating documents, not by heaping further restrictions on the workplace. The result is that for the final deliverable presentation of the document (as hard copy, on-line hypertext, or whatever), it demands *very little* from the author, but it expects *everything* from the typesetting system or the on-line delivery software. The corollary to this is precisely what spells out a benefit to the author: The author concentrates on the document—its contents, its style, and the structural relationships among its parts.

We emphasize this for two reasons:

1. It is rather shocking—surprising, at least—for the writer to be out of the document production and delivery business. It is in fact so radical for some writers that it may inhibit them from hearing what the SGML standard itself is really saying.

2. We will frequently advise (or admonish!) you by dismissing some issue with the phrase "That's implementation," or "That's a processing issue," meaning "Don't worry about that right now."

3.2.1 Portability

We quoted language from the SGML standard itself which cites the need for documents to "be processable by a wide range of text processing and word processing systems" and for means "to facilitate interchange between dissimilar system" (§0.2 "Objectives"). SGML has responded to that need by guaranteeing a document that is totally portable. And in the process it has also presented the writer with several attractive benefits. As we stressed above, it has accomplished this by directing the writer toward concepts, leaving production and delivery detail to implementation.

But what really *is* the "deliverable" for which the SGML-conforming writer is responsible? That deliverable is so simple that it appears to be trivial. Specifically, the SGML document is (1) a pure character text file into which (2) the author has inserted markup tags, generally of the form <{tag}>. For example, a paragraph may appear as follows:

```
<p>Here is a very short paragraph.
```

The most striking aspect of SGML is what we do *not* find. There are no hidden, non-text control codes, such as those we find in every word processing file. There may be extremely few formatting cues in the document. In the tagged paragraph above, the author simply tagged the start of paragraph, without even an indent. Again, the SGML file is always pure character text, something that is readable and modifiable by any text editor or word processor in existence. And it contains markup tags which are in turn pure text; "<p>" is simply a string of three characters from an ordinary keyboard. It is true that there now exist many SGML markup tools, some quite sophisticated, that assist the author in the markup process. And it is true that the underlying rules for markup require serious orientation. (That is the purpose of this book!) But whatever platform and software the author uses, the final document will always be a text file with markup tags.

The ability for an SGML document to be read by any text editor is a significant aspect of SGML's portability, relieving the author of most concerns about cross-platform compatibility. But that is a very low-level type of portability. There are other aspects which are of even greater benefit to the author.

3.2.2   In-House Typesetting

Although the emphasis of this book and of the SGML standard in general is on the electronic document, we constantly refer to hard copy as a delivery medium of choice for documents. Again, whether the document eventually is to be on-line or printed as hard copy or both is of no concern to the author. But should the manuscript be destined for typesetting, then SGML is a dramatic time-saver to the author and to the publisher's production staff. In the old days, designers (of pages, covers, and dust jackets) wrote highly detailed specifications for how the final "camera copy" of a page should look: fonts and faces, headings, lists, the various margins, and the placement of all figures and tables. If the author did not produce that camera copy, then a production editor did. In any case, the role of the typesetter was to make it right. With more advanced personal word processing and page layout software, an author can more easily produce camera copy, but it is still tedious and costly.

By requiring the entire typesetting phase of publication to be an SGML process, the publisher now can rely on the typesetting software to handle all of the details of receiving a document from the author and producing camera-ready copy. Again, the SGML methodology has redistributed the publication tasks. The author conforms to the SGML standard but does not worry about page layout. The publisher invests in machinery that interprets the SGML document and produces a page that conforms to the publisher's company specification. This sort of portability spells dramatic savings in time and money. One early example of this streamlined process was the case of the SGML international standard itself (a lengthy publication). After Charles Goldfarb, the inventor of SGML, had entered his corrections in the final draft, he boarded a plane for Geneva. A few hours later in Switzerland, he was handed a package of printed copies of the published standard.

3.2.3   Word Processing

SGML is benefiting word processing activity, albeit in a very indirect way. Since the advent of word processing, the only reliable method of document transfer was via text files—plain text, with no control characters or formatting information. The good news was that the text was indeed portable under this transfer scheme. The bad news was that nothing else was portable; most formatting information was lost, or worse, badly mangled. There have been several transfer formats in use over the years, but there has never been anything universal enough to satisfy the whole community.

The most helpful transfer schemes have come from the providers themselves, who will often include import (and perhaps export) utilities from (and to) competitors' word processing formats. Finally, there have always been third-party conversion software products. But even these have not provided an absolute guarantee of portability.

SGML is not simply another word processing format. Since SGML is not concerned (within itself) with formatting details, it is not yet practical to consider portability between word processors and SGML in terms of simple *conversions*. But there are products and procedures for moving documents in this way. Some of them are quite expensive; you will see why as you learn more about SGML. But in time, we may speak less guardedly about automatically *converting* a word processing document to or from SGML. When it becomes routine and requires as little skill as importing a text file into Microsoft Word or WordPerfect, then we will say the "c-word" with greater assurance. And when that happens, the word processing community may finally have an exchange format that is nearly universal.

3.2.4   System platforms

The term "platform" allows us to refer in a general manner to the hardware and software that is supporting our work. So we say, for example, that we run our word processor on a PC platform; this implies a single-user, IBM-compatible microcomputer, probably with MS-DOS® or Microsoft Windows® as the operating system. Of course, the range of possible platforms for doing documentation is enormous and constantly evolving. For most main-line word processing and page description languages, the user community can expect eventually to see a version of their favorite package that runs on their platform. When it happens that way, well and good. But a work group may find itself with powerful hardware and no compatible document processing software, at least no software that accomplishes the specialized tasks of the group. Or even more frequently, the provider of a particular document processing system may become inactive, leaving its community with obsolete and perhaps unconvertible document files. Another likely cross-platform scenario is that the same company, department, or even the same work group may have highly incompatible hardware and operating systems and yet must accomplish useful work as a team.

Any one of these scenarios is an excellent motivation for SGML. An SGML document file, by definition, is simply a character text file, the most portable kind of document file possible. SGML therefore is a possible large-scale remedy to cross-platform incompatibility, an issue that has plagued writers from the dawn of computing. The big requirement for this solution is of course that there must exist an adequate set of SGML tools on every platform required. At first it would seem that we have only traded bottlenecks: requiring a given word processor to run on all platforms versus requiring that there be SGML tools for all platforms. That is true to an extent, but there are many reasons for optimism with SGML. In fact, SGML answers some cross-platform questions that have not even been asked because we have always thought in terms of traditional word processing and file formats. Users typically develop strong preferences for the tools they use, which tends to lock them into that tool (word processor), its file format, and platform. This leads them to view their data (documents) strictly in relation to word processing, since the file format problem prevents their easily using it in any other way. With SGML all tools on all platforms use a common file format, so the users are free to choose the tool they like best. In addition, we have seen that SGML documents can be used in many ways besides conventional word processing. We are now free to visualize our documents as *data* that can be manipulated in many different ways with many different tools. Because of this there is potentially a much wider market for SGML tools than there is for conventional word processors.

3.2.5   Device Types

What kind of hardware does SGML run on? The answer quite simply is "anything it needs to." The types of activities that surround an SGML document are literally endless, because the standard is abstract enough to support terminals, players, media, keyboards, monitors, projectors, synthesizers, animation systems, and varieties of hardware that have not even been invented. The benefits of SGML to the writer of documents are twofold: (1) a solid assurance, guaranteed by the standard that the document will enjoy a life cycle far beyond that of traditional word processed or page layout documents; (2) absolutely no need to concern him- or herself with the final display or transmission environments of the document.

3.3   Precision of the Specification

If there is one trait above all others that characterizes the digital writing environment, it is that the rules are precise and unambiguous. Precise terminology and precise rules may at first seem to be a burdensome inhibition to a writer. But the significance of precision for SGML is that in preparing a conforming document the writer knows beforehand precisely what the boss, client, or customer wants. When the writer knows that the product is to be of a certain document type, then a large number of structural details are perfectly clear, requiring no further clarification or explanation. That is because the document type is described according to formal rules in a document type definition (or DTD). The DTD is of major interest to the writer because it is the SGML apparatus for enabling the markup which the writer will apply to the document. The markup for a book, say, will be different in some respects from that for a technical manual. These differences between document types are spelled out in precise detail by the set of rules which comprise each separate DTD. And the rules, in turn, follow their own internal scheme for how they are written. In subsequent chapters we will become fluent in reading and sometimes modifying these rules. But for now, we should only be aware that writing "against" a particular DTD that is either an international standard or at least agreed upon by both writer and client is a comforting guarantee that the product will be acceptable the first time.

But we hasten to remind ourselves that SGML, for all its precision regarding structure, has virtually nothing to say about the semantics or internal content of any written work. So a document may be totally conforming and therefore "correct" in the SGML sense while at the same time be ungrammatical, full of misspellings, and loaded with inaccurate information. Such a document is certainly far from acceptable to the client! Nor does SGML speak to issues of writing style and creativity of the content. We emphasize, therefore, that SGML detracts nothing from the need for writing skills and creativity. In fact, by relieving the writer from the purely mechanical issues of a document's structure—those issues covered by the SGML rules, as stated in the DTD for the document—SGML allows the writer to dedicate more effort and attention to the important professional issues of accuracy of content, a convincing writing style, and personal creativity. Not only does the boss, client, or customer get a document that conforms to the "contractual" specification for a particular document type, but the product should be more polished internally as well.

3.4   A Wider Community

When the writer is conforming to a standard document type definition, which in turn is written according to SGML rules, we can then be sure that there is an extensive community of writers and editors who share common ideas about document structure. This is little more than saying that a standard is a standard. But the implications for there being a wider community are significant and practical. Most of all it means that there will be a minimum of local reinvention of structural definitions. It is one thing for writers to be creative—as writers. But it is quite unproductive for writers and editors to expend great effort in reinventing and enforcing structures at the local or work-group level. To do so means to stop productive writing in order to create and maintain original internal style manuals and to enforce those original standards with constant internal training.

3.5   Familiar architectures

We have already discussed document architecture as having to do with the semantics of processing—how a document gets processed—including fine details of its representation. When an entire architecture becomes standardized, then we are able to speak in a "shorthand" manner about large clusters of such details, without needing to explain or reinvent the details. Such is the case for Standard Page Description Language and Document Style Semantics and Specification Language both of which are international standards, known as "SPDL" and "DSSSL" respectively.

3.6   Open-Ended Document Processing

SGML enables the writer to stop far short of specifying a document's rendition or representation. As we have noted, this reduces the demands on the writer. But it has important benefits for the document as well. When a document that marked up in some standardized manner, following precise rules—as is the case for a conforming SGML document with a standard DTD—the document is highly *open-ended*. That is, one particular software system might process the document as browsable hypertext. Another may present the same document as a retrievable unit of data and then print a user-specified columnar report, reorganizing and summarizing data contained in tables within the document. The dramatic benefit of an open-ended document is therefore is that the document becomes *reusable*. We can represent the document in ways that even its writer may never have thought of. And on a more cosmic scale, this reusability may conceivably extend centuries into the future and toward technologies that do not yet exist.

3.7   Flexibility of Markup

In later chapters we will work closely with tagging as a means primarily of identifying the structural elements of a document. (This markup of course is the most easily recognizable characteristic of an SGML document.) But the rules for defining the markup for a particular document type—book, maintenance manual, or poetry anthology—may anticipate the various uses that we envision for the document. For example, if we intend for the user to browse the manual with hypertext links, then the markup should serve as a tool for producing hypertext. With proper markup we will identify what text items should be represented as "hot" (i.e., pointing to other text for the user to click on, navigate to, and then return). And the same applies for a large poetry collection that we wish not only to view and to print selectively on demand but also to produce as a retrieval system for scholarly research. Proper tagging will assure that all of the necessary apparatus for a database is present when the retrieval processing software operates on the collection: authors' names, dates, places, metrical schemes, glossaries to difficult vocabulary. All of this is to say that markup, because it is rule-driven, is highly flexible, serving whatever needs the document may have.

3.8   Standard Notation for Defining Document Types

For many readers the notion of a DTD notation's being a desirable feature with benefits sounds doubtful, to say the least! Admittedly, your initial confrontation with a "raw" DTD for an industry-standard document can be a bit daunting. Realizing that, the authors of this book in fact promise to make you fluent enough in reading a DTD—any DTD—that you will no longer feel as though you are in totally unfamiliar surroundings. But before we arrive at the mechanics of a DTD, we need to stress some very important characteristics of the notation.

First, we should be clear on the distinction between the layers of SGML apparatus that support your conforming document. At the bottommost level are the rules that use "raw" SGML to create a standard syntax. This is the set of writing rules which an SGML programmer uses to create the DTD. (Note that we are discussing rules for a developer to write a DTD and not rules for you to use in writing a document.) This standard syntax is called the reference concrete syntax. The big benefit of the reference concrete syntax is that any SGML programmer within the entire community can create document-type definitions for an infinite variety of types and still use the same syntactic notation. This is one level of benefits for SGML notation. Even serious users of SGML do not typically dwell much on the details of the reference concrete syntax; it is simply there to be used.

The second level, the one of greater interest to the writer, is the formal description of a document type (the DTD). At this level, a programmer uses the concrete syntax to express rules that (1) describe the elements of our document type and that (2) specify the markup we are to use when we write. Using a standard (reference) concrete syntax to create a DTD means that anyone who can read one DTD will probably be able to read any other DTD.

But there is another benefit in using SGML that is of great importance to the document itself. The notation enables us to describe a hierarchical (or "tree") structure quite easily. And since every document is treelike, this notation becomes a highly adequate tool for its description. We hesitate to say at this point that the SGML notation for a DTD is "intuitively obvious." But we do maintain that it is a highly appropriate tool for the job of describing a document's structure accurately and unambiguously.

3.9   Markup for Structure Only

It is true that there is a learning curve for becoming competent in creating conforming SGML documents. But we argue that the most difficult portion of SGML to master is not the *mechanics* of the standard but rather the *orientation* with which you as a writer should view your document. That is the reason for the lengthy discussion of paradigms in Chapter 2. If you have mastered this concept well, then you will not encounter great difficulty with the mechanics of SGML markup, because as we have said repeatedly, the structural elements of a document have been with us forever. Another item of comfort for you is that there is a healthy variety of commercial products now appearing to assist you in the markup task. The greatest benefit to you of course is that your job of maintaining a document through all of its revision history is trivial compared with that same task in the environment of desktop publishing, in which every revision of the text usually means yet another revision of the page.

Summary

Some of the benefits of SGML seem to be almost cosmic in nature, like the promise of an infinite life span of a digital document. And some, like the standardization we enjoy because of a concrete reference syntax, may seem somewhat removed from the everyday work of writing and editing. But the vast majority of the features and benefits of SGML have immediate bearing and payoff for writers. Much like modern computing systems, the digital writing workplace has redistributed its various tasks and subtasks. The writer no longer needs also to be a page layout specialist (unless he or she happens also to be one). In a collaborative writing group—even one which is geographically spread over several continents—the various writers need not concern themselves with the portability of their text across different hardware and operating systems. Thanks to emerging document architectures, writers can share large clusters of detail about how their documents are to be processed. And the most persistent issues of revising documents—unquestionably the biggest headache for writers and editors—are dramatically eased with SGML. So while the features of SGML are striking enough, the benefits to writers and editors are compelling.

CHAPTER 4

DOCUMENT ANALYSIS
Recognizing a Document's Structure

SGML terms introduced or reinforced:

descriptive markup, document type definition, element, element structure, element type, tag

Overview

In this chapter we reiterate the significance of a document's structure being hierarchical: Elements are related to one another by a tree-like relationship that is peculiar to the particular document type. We move toward a formal definition of SGML structure by first *describing* these relationships with words, the most significant words being "order" (among the elements) and "subelements" (subordination and nesting or containment of elements within other elements). We then summarize the discussion with a table that pictures these ordering and subordination relationships.

4.1   What Is Document Structure?

"Structure" is a writing term that can have a number of interpretations. And although it is not by itself an SGML standard term, it bears a meaning that is closely related to other SGML concepts. Generally, a document's *structure* refers to the role of individual elements in relation to the whole of the document. More precisely, these two terms—element and structure—do represent a formal SGML concept, one which we need to understand fully. In Chapter 3 we alluded to SGML's viewing a document as always being treelike, having a "hierarchical" structure. When we use the SGML phrase element structure therefore, we always imply that the elements in the document are arranged in treelike fashion. In this chapter we will therefore speak of *elements* as members of a document's *structure*, a structure that is a tree or *hierarchy*[1]. That is, while of the three terms— element, structure, and hierarchy--only element is a formal SGML term, we use "element" and "structure" together within the context of the single SGML definition of element structure:

> The organization of a document into hierarchies of elements, with each hierarchy conforming to a different document type definition.
> — ISO 8879: §4.113

As a member of a hierarchy therefore, an element may likely include subelements; a manual (topmost, or "document," element) may include sections (subelements) each of which includes chapters (subelements) which include paragraphs (subelements).

The identity of an element is based on what it is trying to communicate. We do not refer here to the semantic meaning or information content, of course, but to information of a structural nature, something that enables the reader to sense the overall structure of the document and to know precisely where he or she is at any point within that document's structure. A structural element has a single, unambiguous purpose. It is never used to identify something else, even if two elements are similar in purpose. They must have exactly the same function to be considered the same type of structural element. For example, consider the title of a document. The title is a structural element that has a specific meaning relative to the rest of the document. It is a brief "identifier" for this particular document. If there are chapters in the document a chapter title does not have the same *meaning* as the overall title, so we say that these two types of titles are distinct structural element types. A paragraph is another structural element, one that has a more general meaning. It is simply a block of text that relates to a single common theme. Any text with a more specific purpose should not be identified as a paragraph.

All writing involves structure in one form or another, from the highly structured rows and columns of an automotive parts list to the free-form text of a modern novel. The particular elements may change, but there is always a structure defined for each document type.

4.2   The Purpose of Structure

Document structure serves to enhance the communication of the written words. The different structural elements act to emphasize certain points and to establish order. Structure provides organization that enables the reader to locate and identify particular items of information that might otherwise be lost in the mass of text. Traditionally, with paper documents, structure is indicated by visual clues such as type size and style, indentation, numbering, and borders. For example, the indentations in an outline communicate a hierarchy of ideas, with the most general being least indented and the more detailed indented further. Bold type might indicate titles and numbers and letters might identify the sections.

---

1. In terms of formal data structures we would say that the document is a graph that is represented by a tree with connections among the leaves (through hyperlinks). This model handles documents of any structural complexity.

A table of contents in a manual is a simple map of the basic structure of the manual and is an excellent example of an element that conveys structural meaning. The table of contents allows readers to see quickly how the different parts of the manual relate to each other and also enables readers to go directly to the portions in which they are interested. The table of contents is organized around the structure of the manual. Another structure, the index, is quite different in purpose even though at first glance it might appear similar. An index locates individual pieces of information, ignoring their position in the overall structure of the manual. In brief, the index is a structural element that allows the reader to "short circuit" the overall structure of the manual to get directly at the particular information it contains. On the other hand the table of contents enables the reader to move directly to the structural element that contains the information he or she desires.

Document structure forces organization by grouping common elements under a single structural element. We saw this in our discussion of elements and nested subelements above.

When the structural elements of a document are identified explicitly (by the use of SGML,) the document becomes accessible in a variety of ways that are impossible with a normal paper document. A document that is tagged for structure can become a hypertext document or a piece of a database, and it can be searched in a variety of ways that would be impossible otherwise. The key word for document structure therefore is *access*. Good structuring, whether it be visual or whether it be with SGML, makes the information in the document more accessible. By improving the reader's ability to extract information from the document, we increase the value of the document.

4.3   Indicating Structure Visually

In traditional document formatting, structural elements have been indicated by the visual attributes we associate with them. This serves the purpose of drawing the reader's eye to the different elements in some sort of organized fashion. Figure 4-1 presents a list of items, each item consisting of a paragraph of text, which shows how this works.

```
            THIS IS THE LIST HEADER
               This is item one.
               This is item two.
               This is item three.
```

Figure 4-1 Sample list

Notice how the large type, use of all capital letters, and center formatting tends to draw attention first to the title, or header of the list. At each element the bullet at the left margin separates and highlights. In addition a blank line between each item in the list helps keep them separated. Using these structural clues, we only need to glance at the page to determine that we are looking at some sort of group of three items with a heading. Because the structure visibly groups the items together, we know that by simply reading the heading we will have a general idea of what the rest of the list is about. Visual representation of structure relies on the reader to interpret the formatting and to translate that format into structure. Because of this, different readers may, in cases with more complex formatting, come up with different interpretations. This is one of the weaknesses of visual structuring.

In Figure 4-1 it is the visual elements which tell us what is most important and what is less important. But what happens when the visual clues are not there? U.S. Government publications, in response to the Paperwork Reduction Act, have widely adopted a style in which the visual elements of structure (especially white space) are severely reduced. One immediately noticeable change is that subitems are no longer indented. Instead they all appear in simple paragraph form with only their section and subsection numbers as a clue to their interrelated structures. The structure still exists, but it is very hard to see it because the visual clues have been removed. It is virtually impossible to skim through this sort of document because you cannot identify major points without close reading. Figure 4-2 demonstrates not only that such a visually neutral document is difficult to read but that it might also actually mislead even a careful reader. Note that the printed character "i" is used for both lowercase "i" and "small Roman numeral I": 2.i "Employees shall not be permitted to drink…"; and 3.h.i: "Facilities shall be accessibly located…"

When relying on visual elements to identify structure, yet another problem can arise: how to interpret the structure when the meanings of the formats used are ambiguous. In a short printed document this may not be too much of a problem, since the reader will probably be able to figure out the difference, but if the document is long or is to be processed electronically, then this ambiguity will create problems.

Ambiguity, either through using one visual style to indicate more than one structural element type or by inappropriate selection of style, is always a problem with visual structuring. For example, if a subsection is titled using a more emphatic type style than that for the main section title, it can leave the reader unsure as to whether this starts a new section or whether it is some other type of structure altogether. Equally confusing is the use of different types of formatting to indicate the same element types, for example indicating section headers by using italics in some places and boldface in others. This leaves the reader unsure as to whether he or she perceives the structure the way it was intended, thus reducing the effectiveness of the communication.

The widespread use of PCs and desktop publishing has forced writers to become layout editors as well, often without any clear idea of how page design and layout affects the communication of the written word. Gradually, through trial and error, most users become capable of producing good quality page layout, if for no other reason than because they are used to seeing it. Proper (or at least adequate) visual structuring comes fairly easily to most writers, even though they may never really understand the theory behind it. But sooner or later the limitations inherent in visual indications of structure began to surface and detract from the message, even in documents prepared by expert layout artists. Clearly a better solution is called for.

WAC 296-306-320 Field Sanitation--Requirements.

Agricultural employers shall provide the following for employees engaged in hand-labor operations in the field, without cost to the employee:

(1) Orientation: Orientation shall be given verbally to all employees in a manner readily understandable by each employee and shall include:

(a) Potable water: The location(s) of potable water supplies;

(b) Nonpotable water: Identification of nonpotable water at the worksite and prohibition of the use of nonpotable water with an explanation of the possible consequences of using nonpotable water;

(c) Handwashing facilities: The location(s) of handwashing facilities with an explanation of when and how they should be used and the consequences of nonuse; and

(d) Toilet facilities: The location(s) of toilet facilities with an explanation of the necessity to use them and to keep them sanitary as well as the possible consequences of nonuse.

(2) Potable drinking water.

(a) The water shall be provided and shall be placed in locations readily accessible to all employees.

(b) Potable water containers shall be refilled daily or more often as necessary.

(c) Potable water dispensers shall be designed, constructed, and serviced so the sanitary conditions are maintained. They shall be capable of being closed and shall be equipped with a tap.

(d) Open containers such as barrels, pails, or tanks for drinking water from which water must be dipped or poured, whether or not they are fitted with a cover, are prohibited.

(e) Marking: Any container used to distribute drinking water shall be clearly marked, in English and with appropriate international symbol as to the nature of its contents.

(f) Use: Any container used to distribute drinking water shall not be used for any other purpose.

(g) The water shall be suitably cool and in sufficient amounts, taking into account the air temperature, humidity, and the nature of the work performed to meet employees' needs.

Note: Suitably cool water should be sixty degrees Fahrenheit or less. During hot weather, workers may require up to three gallons of water per day.

(h) The use of common drinking cups or dippers is prohibited. Water shall be dispensed in single-use drinking cups, personal containers, or by water fountains. Single-use drinking cups mean a container or any type or size whether disposable or not, and may include personal containers so long as the option to use a personal container is exercised by the employee, not the employer.

(i) Employees shall not be permitted to drink from irrigation ditches, creeks or rivers. Potable water shall meet the standards for drinking purposes by the state or local authority having jurisdiction or water that meets quality standards prescribed by the local health department in accordance with the United States Environmental Protection Agency's National Interim Primary Drinking Water Regulations, published in 40 CFR Part 141.

(3) Handwashing facilities.

(a) One handwashing facility, providing a tap with an adequate supply of water, soap, single-use hand towels and either a basin or other suitable container for washing shall be provided for each twenty employees of fraction thereof.

Note: Nonpotable water shall not be used for washing any portion of the person, except as specifically permitted by the health authorities having jurisdiction.

(b) Running water: Each facility shall be provided with running water.

(c) Soap: Each facility shall be provided with a dispenser containing handsoap or a similar cleansing agent.

(d) Towels: Each facility shall be provided with individual single-use hand towels.

(e) Cleanliness: Facilities shall be maintained in a clean and sanitary condition in accordance with appropriate public health sanitation practices.

(f) Waste: Waste receptacles shall be provided. Disposable of wastes from the facilities shall not create a hazard or cause an unsanitary condition.

(g) Reasonable use: Employees shall be allowed reasonable opportunities during the work period to use the facilities.

(h) Location:

(i) Facilities shall be accessible located in close proximity to toilet facilities within one-quarter mile of each employee's place of work in the field.

(ii) Where it is not feasible to locate facilities as required by (h)(i) of this subsection, the facilities shall be located at the point of closest vehicle access.

Figure 4-2 Government document example

(4) Toilet facilities.

(a) One toilet facility shall be provided for each twenty employees or fraction thereof.

(b) Each employer shall ensure, at the beginning of each day, that the toilets are inspected. If any toilet facility fails to meet the requirements of this section, immediate corrective action shall be taken. Inspections shall be documented and the record shall be maintained at the work site for at least seventy-two hours.

(c) Toilet facilities shall be adequately ventilated; appropriately screened, and have self-closing doors that can be closed and latched from the inside and shall be constructed to ensure privacy.

(d) Cleanliness: Facilities shall be maintained in a clean, sanitary, and functional condition and in accordance with the appropriate public health sanitation practices.

(e) Toilets shall be provided with toilet paper.

(f) Waste: Disposal of wastes from the facilities shall not create a hazard or cause an unsanitary condition.

(g) Reasonable use: Employees shall be allowed reasonable opportunities during the work period to use the facilities.

(h) Location:

(i) Facilities shall be accessible located in close proximity to hand washing facilities and within one-quarter mile of each employee's place of work in the field.

(ii) Where it is not feasible to locate facilities as required by (h)(i) of this subsection, the facilities shall be located at the point of closest vehicular access. [Statutory Authority: Chapter 49.17 RCW. 89-ll-035 (Order 89-03),

Figure 4-2 Government document example (Continued)

4.4   Using SGML to Indicate Structure

SGML provides a way of marking document structure that is entirely unambiguous and does not rely on any reader interpretation. This system centers around the tag which is a code used to mark a particular structural element in the document. The key is that a tag identifies only the structure, not the appearance. This allows the creation and use of as many types of tags as are necessary to identify fully all the structural elements in a document. Obviously, in order to tag the structure of a document, it is first necessary to understand that structure and be able to identify the parts. To gain an understanding of how this works we can consider a typical document. We will first discuss the structure of a document, using language that is familiar to all writers and editors. Then we will summarize that discussion in Table 4-1. The table will function both as "training wheels" and "springboard" into formal SGML notation.

4.4.1   Document Structure

A Discussion

During this "guided tour," consult Figure 4-3which shows a page from the *Users Manual for Video Display Terminal SaferVu-777*, a technical manual which embodies much of the same structure we are discussing here.

At the very top level we need to agree that the document itself (here, a manual), in its entirety, is a structural element. It is necessary to have some starting point that all the other structural elements tie to. Certain things are immediately obvious about the "manual" element: (1) It can appear only once in the document; (2) it must be able to contain other elements; (3) if "manual" is not defined, it is implied; that is, we agree that the element "manual" exists simply because the document exists. If we intend for this element (manual) to be usable in other contexts, we need to define

CHAPTER 2: INSTALLATION

General

This chapter contains unpacking, installation, and initial turn-on procedures for the SaferVu-777 large-screen workstation.

Unpacking

The SaferVu-777 is shipped complete in one shipping container. Refer to the following steps and figure 2-1 to unpack the SaferVu-777.

1. Place SaferVu-777 shipping carton on level surface.

   NOTE
   Make sure that the carton has the correct side up according to locator arrows on the carton.

2. Open the top of the carton and carefully remove the contents as shown in figure 2-1.

3. Make sure that the following items are contained in the carton:

   a. Keyboard module

   b. Workstation module

   c. AC line cord

4. After unpacking and inspecting for shipping damage, continue with the normal installation procedures.

   NOTE
   Retain all packing and shipping materials.

Terminal Installation

The location of the SaferVu-777 in a working environment should conform to the environmental specifications outlined in Chapter 1. However, the reliability of the SaferVu-777 requires the operator to adhere to the following guidelines:

1. Locate the SaferVu-777 such that there is free air flow through top and bottom air vents.

2. Do not place working material on or near the SaferVu-777 air vents.

3. Do not locate the SaferVu-777 where the screen is exposed to sunlight or intense lighting.

Figure 4-3 Video display terminal manual page

what its purpose is. Only a structural element that is clearly defined can be applied to any document without ambiguity. The definition assures us that the element means the same thing in any document where it is used. We can define the element manual as indicating a particular collection of writing or information dealing with a single general topic.

The next element that becomes evident in our typical document is the title. Once again there are certain properties about the element "title": (1) it can occur only inside a document element;

(2) It can occur only once in the document; (3) no other elements can appear inside it; (4) the entire element may be omitted from the document if the document has no title. The definition for the element "title" is "a general or descriptive heading for the document."

Following the "title" element, we find the name of the author. This is an important structural element because it allows for some sort of identification of documents by their authors. This element, unlike the title, may be repeated if there are multiple authors for the document. Like the title however, it can appear only inside the document. No other elements may appear inside it, and it may be omitted if desired. A brief definition of the "author" element is "the name of the person, or the name of one of the persons, who wrote the document."

At this point we get down to sections, nearer the actual "meat" of the document. This part of the document contains the actual information to be communicated. There are several properties to observe about the "section" *element type*: (1) There may be any number of sections contained in the manual element, while in a simple manual there may only need to be one; (2) the section element can only appear inside a manual element; (3) a section element can contain a number of other types of structural elements, specifically a section header, some number of subsections, and various types of textual material. A section is defined as "a distinct part or major subdivision of the manual, containing information that is internally related."

A section may contain a section header. This is a descriptive title for the particular section. The properties for a section header are very similar to those for the manual title. The main difference is that the section header is contained inside the section element, it must only be used inside a section, never anywhere else, and may appear only once in a particular section.

A section may also contain subsections. Subsections are very similar to section elements, but at the next lower level. The main difference is that a subsection is an optional element and may be omitted entirely if it is not needed. The properties for the subsection element type are as follows: (1) There may be any number of subsections in a particular section; (2) the subsection element may appear only inside a section element; (3) a subsection may contain a subsection header if desired, although it is optional, like the section header. A subsection must contain at least some occurrence of textual material. A section is defined as "a distinct subdivision of a section, containing closely related information of a greater level of detail than that of the section containing it."

There are two types of textual material elements that may appear in our document. The first is a simple paragraph. This element has the properties that it (1) may be repeated as many times as desired and that (2) no other elements may appear inside it. The definition of a paragraph is the one that you would expect: "A block of written material pertaining to a single topic sentence." The second textual material element is a list. The list element type is more complicated than a paragraph because it is a tree-type structure. A list element itself has the following properties: (1) It may be repeated; (2) it may contain other elements, specifically a list header and list items; (3) it must contain at least one list item. We define a list as "an ordered series of related items." The list header, defined as a descriptive title identifying the list and its contents, is optional, may appear only once in the list, and may not contain any other elements.

The "list item" element is defined as a single point or item in a list. This should imply to us that it can be repeated as many times as needed. We can also conclude that a list item can appear only inside a list. As a final property, in order to provide additional flexibility in our documents, we will allow the list item to contain either paragraphs or another list element. This makes for what is called a recursive structure, one which may include another instance of itself. For example, a list contains a list item, which may contain another list including list items of its own. This can continue for as many levels as are desired. It is the fact that a list item may contain a list element that creates this recursive behavior.

Because paragraphs and lists are peer elements, that is, they can appear at the same structural level in the document and are elements that may appear in more than one place in the document, we will use a little bit of "shorthand" to simplify our description of them. To accomplish this we will create an entity called "text matter," which is simply a container to hold both paragraph and list elements. The text matter entity is only used in defining the element types, not in actually identifying the parts of the document.

4.4.2   Docment Structure
Summary by Table

In Table 4-1, Table of Element Types (at the end of this chapter), we find all of the elements we discussed here laid out in tabular form. One very important thing about the table needs to be understood however. The element type column identifies each class of structural pieces of the document. In that column the *vertical order* indicates the order in which these elements may appear in the document and the *level of indentation* indicates inclusion of elements. In other words, because "title" is indented and occurs below "manual," we know that title is included *inside* the manual element. Because "author" follows "title" in the table, we know that they must appear *in that order* in the manual, but because they are at the same level of indentation they are equal under the manual element.

The set of *element types* described in this chapter is not intended to be all-inclusive. There are obviously many additional structural elements that appear in real documents: copyright notices, figures, tables, bibliographic references, glossary items, and appendices, for example. The list of possible structural elements is huge and in many cases is very specific to the type of document being analyzed.

When dealing with an existing document—one that was written without a formal structural definition—it is often difficult to define its structure. And based on our discussion thus far, we can see why. Without the formalism we are applying in our description of elements, a writer can very easily introduce ambiguous and inconsistent structure. This is the heart of the problem of what is known as the "legacy conversion" task—converting non- or pre-SGML documents to conforming SGML documents.

Understanding document structure is the first step toward being able to tag (i.e., do **descriptive markup** in) our document and to write with structure in mind. A clear understanding of how to recognize and codify the structure of a document is the first step toward creating conforming SGML documents.

Table 4-1 is an intuitive and informal document structure definition. The document type in this case is "manual," While it is not a rigorous **document type definition**, it serves to describe the structure we will use in the next chapter for writing a conforming document. There are still a number of ambiguities found in this table. One example is that it does not explicitly tell where we may and may not insert text for the content data. Furthermore, the usage column contains both forward and backward references, that is "appears inside this" and "may contain this." While the rules are in plain English and relatively easy to follow, they are far too wordy and cumbersome to be practical in a high-production writing group. And of course they are completely useless in a computer environment. Other problems become apparent with further close study. Obviously, if we intend to produce a completely unambiguous definition of the structure of our document (and one that enhances the productivity of our work group), we will need to go further than this. That conclusion, of course, leads us directly to using true SGML notation to create a **document type definition**.

Table 4-1: Table of Element Types

Element Type	Definition/Meaning	Usage
Manual	A piece of writing or information dealing with a single general topic.	1) May only appear once. 2) May contain other elements. 3) Is implied by the existence of the document.
Title	A general or descriptive heading for the document	1) May appear only once 2) May only appear inside the manual element. 3) No other elements may appear inside it. 4) May be omitted
Author	Name of (one of) the person(s) who wrote this document.	1) May appear multiple times, once for each author. 2) May only appear inside the manual element. 3) No other elements may appear inside it. 4) May be omitted.

Table 4-1: Table of Element Types (Continued)

Element Type	Definition/Meaning	Usage
Section	A distinct part of a document which contains information that is somehow internally related	1) May be repeated inside the manual element. 2) May only appear inside the manual element. 3) May contain other elements. 4) At least one section must appear in a manual.
Section-Header	A descriptive title identifying this section.	1) May only appear once inside a section. 2) May only appear inside a section element. 3) No other elements may appear inside it. 4) May be omitted.
Text-Matter	see below	1) May only appear once inside a section. 2) Must occur at least once.
Sub-Section	Like a section, only entirely contained inside a section, both physically and by topic.	1) May be repeated inside the section. 2) May only appear inside a section element. 3) May contain other elements. 4) Is an optional element in a section.
Sub-Sec-Head	A descriptive title identifying this sub-section	1) May only appear once inside a sub-section. 2) May only appear inside a sub-section 3) No other elements may appear inside it. 4) May be omitted.
Text-Matter	see below	1) May be repeated inside the sub-section. 2) Must occur at least once.
Elements of Text Matter		
Text-Matter	A "container" for elements only, the paragraph and list elements included in this entity hold the information content of the document.	

Table 4-1: Table of Element Types (Continued)

Element Type	Definition/Meaning	Usage
Paragraph	A block of text relating to a single topic.	1) May be repeated. 2) No other elements may appear inside it.
List	An ordered series of related items.	1) May be repeated. 2) May contain other elements. 3) Must contain at least one list item.
List-Header	A descriptive title identifying the list and its contents.	1) May only appear once inside the list element. 2) May only appear inside a list element. 3) No other elements may appear inside it. 4) May be omitted.
List-Item	A single point or entry in a list.	1) May be repeated inside the list element. 2) May only appear inside a list element. 3) May contain other elements.
Text-Matter	see above	1) May be repeated inside the list item element.

CHAPTER 5

DOCUMENT TYPE DEFINITION
Writing for Structure

SGML terms introduced or reinforced:

attributes, conforming SGML document, descriptive markup, document instance, document type definition (DTD), element structure, element type, generic identifier (GI), markup, (markup) minimization feature, reference concrete syntax, SGML application, tag, text processing application, validating SGML parser

Overview

Simply to recognize that standards are necessary and that standards exist does not of itself create documents that are standards-compliant. The writer of course must create those documents. In technical writing, the professional has typically had style books, in-house format and layout standards, and even national standards to follow. But now that we have altered the notion of what conforming to standards means, we must offer some guidance for the writer who aims toward this new flavor of standard. In particular, we must identify precisely how the standard for electronic document architecture representation both resembles and differs from traditional standards for technical writing (ANSI Z39.18, for example). We address some questions of great practical importance for the writer:

1. What is there among traditional standards that hints strongly of SGML and so can help us more easily to understand SGML as an enabler of writing standards?

2. If the object of conforming to an SGML application standard is not to generate a stunning page layout, then what is the deliverable that the writer now seeks to produce?

3. What are the basic rules of tagging, as specified by SGML?

4.   If the writer no longer refers to visible, literal templates in a style book, then what precisely drives him or her? In other words, what is the nature of the markup that determines what the conforming author does?

5.   How does the writer know what to do—and not to do—at each juncture of the document?

6.   Does the writer who aspires to write conforming SGML documents have to understand SGML as a language… really?

In this chapter we will dwell at some length on ANSI Z39.18-1987 as a typical writing standard for technical writers. This is a published standards document that requires compliance in quite traditional term but also hints strongly at the emerging technology of electronic architecture. Then, after a brief introduction to the mechanics of tagging, we will develop a document as an instance of our own "Writers And Editors (WAE) Document Type" based on Table 4-1.

5.1   Traditional Writing Manuals

One of the most revealing aspects of a writing manual's perspective for our purposes is the number of pages and paragraphs dedicated to *structure*. One such manual (taken at random from the authors' office shelf) allocated all of two pages to a section entitled "Structure of the Document." Unfortunately that is the good news! The bad news is that the passage simply urges the writer to structure his or her writing and then cites at length from the American writer Sinclair Lewis's *Babbitt*. Babbitt delivers his real estate speech to the luncheon meeting after some very haphazard outlining. A poor job of structuring, says the writing handbook, and we would probably agree. But like most other traditional manuals, this one does little more than to admonish us to outline our document carefully.

5.2   Abstract of ANSI Z39.18-1987

The full name of this standard is *Scientific and Technical Reports—Organization, Preparation, and Production*. (The current edition was approved in 1987, a revision of the 1974 edition.) The abstract of the document hints strongly at the degree of ambivalence in standards compliance only a few years ago. Notice how the second sentence is almost apologetic in tone:

> It [the standard] is designed to impose only that degree of standardization
> that will help the author(s) or editor(s) disseminate the results of scientific
> research…

But the abstract later hints strongly at the emerging requirements of electronic document mechanisms:

> The standard provides for the inclusion of data elements critical to librar-
> ies, abstracting services, and other information processing organizations…

But note carefully that the document indeed prescribes *organization*:

> For organization of a report, it suggests techniques for ordering and speci-
> fying preferred and optional elements.

Finally, note that the rest of the abstract reverts to purely physical and content-related aspects of the technical document:

> For report preparation, it sets forth some parameters for formatting; for
> using symbols, terminology, illustrative materials, and footnotes; and for
> keyboarding a manuscript. For report production, it covers such matters as
> graphic design and typography and the steps involved in markup, reproduc-
> tion, and binding.

As we have said, traditional writing guides and style manuals, even one so highly standard-ized as the ANSI *Reports*, dwell almost exclusively on appearance of the page—what the SGML world calls "presentation" or "rendering"—rather than on structure.

5.3   ANSI Z39.18-1987 and Document Organization

Section Three of the standard, "Organization of Report," is of greatest interest to us, since this material comes closest to dealing with structure as we have defined it. But even here the stan-dard constantly intermingles considerations of page layout, wording, and writing style with issues of structure. In §3.2.1, "Title Page/Report Documentation Page," the standard lists the required ele-ments and specifies their behavior in page layout figures.

The notable exception to the ANSI standard's preoccupation with page layout is §3.1, "Order of Elements." Here, at least at the topmost layer, the standard focuses on the important structural elements of a document: front matter, body, and back matter as the three top-level components. As we have noted, the designer of an SGML application (using SGML rules to create a text process-ing application for an entire industry, for instance) will tend to be as general as possible on such matters as how the text is finally processed. In other words, while a text processing application may be industry-specific (as for financial services, as we cited in an earlier chapter), the SGML applica-tion itself will contain concise rules about descriptive markup (use of tags, which express element structure) and not dwell on appearance and presentation. The ANSI 1987 standard, in rather signif-icant contrast, lists the precise order and title preferred for each subsection of the three main divi-sions. True, it does refer to "heading" and "subheadings," but not in the *generalized* fashion of an SGML application.

The significant implication of SGML-flavored structure, as you have gathered from the previ-ous chapters, is that it lends an additional *dimension* to the document. The elements of a document do not simply follow one another in a totally linear fashion. In addition to their linear order, they are also related to one another in a hierarchy. The document is thus a two-dimensional structure: the sequence of the document's elements plus the system of subordination among those elements.[1]

The structured document as a two-dimensional construct is highly similar to the notion of an indented bill of materials used in manufacturing, inventory, and parts ordering systems. A machine or device comprises discrete parts, perhaps many thousands of numbered parts, as in the case of an automobile or airplane. But a single-dimensioned, non-structured (i.e., flat) list of all those parts would be of little help in maintaining the vehicle. The maintenance and operations people need documentation that describes the *interrelationships* among all of the parts. The indented bill of materials offers precisely that sort of hierarchical description. In the case of the airplane, the starboard wing may be one part on a list, but the indented bill of materials entry for that part will "explode" to many deeper layers, exposing entire structural, hydraulic, and electrical subsystems, each of which will also have its own "indented" lists of parts. The notion of *hierarchy* is thus closely related to that of *indentation*.

ANSI Z39.18 comes close to structural considerations, as we have defined them, in §4.1.1, "Subordination." The first paragraph of this section should sound familiar. But there is something here is that is slightly foreign to our discussion:

> Subordination of ideas is indicated by the use of headings and subheadings that divide the report into manageable segments, call attention to main topics, and signal changes in topics. In a well-organized report, no more than three levels of headings are necessary. Primary headings identify major sections of the report, and each major chapter equivalent should begin on a new page.
>
> — (p. 21)

In this discussion, the standard assumes the three levels of headings to be simply *visual identifiers* of the final printed report. We, on the other hand, shall insist that headings and all of the other structural elements of an SGML application are the *essence* of the document. In the old days, headings were part of page layout; now they are key elements of the document's very definition.

The remainder of §4.1.1 reveals our former fixation on the visual, rather than structural, implications of subordination apparatus:

> Many scientific and technical reports use a decimal numbering system to show subordinate relationships and to simplify extensive cross-referencing. The system becomes cumbersome, however, if more than three levels of subordination are needed.
>
> An alternative format for subordination uses typographic progression for subordination. Headings, and subheadings are indicated by boldface type

---

1. Actually there are additional "dimensions" as well, such as those formed by cross-references among the elements, such as a reference from a paragraph to a figure.

with initial capital letters for principal words. Primary headings are set in larger type than secondary and tertiary headings. Primary and secondary headings are flush with the left margin, and tertiary headings are run in with indented text. ANSI publications use a combination of the two formats for ease of cross-referencing.

— (p. 21)

This constant commingling of visual layout with structural relationships was quite natural, as long as there was no need to separate the two realms. But with SGML we consciously relegate everything visual—all of the issues that pertain to the details of page layout—to "presentation" or "rendition" of the document. Presentation issues are important, to be sure. But within the paradigm of electronic document architecture, they are of concern to the purveyors and suppliers of document viewers and browsers, printers and projectors, typesetters, and CD-ROM mastering specialists. The writer concentrates on structure…period. In so doing he or she is able to produce a document that delivers all that we discussed in the earlier chapters of this book.

5.4   The Deliverable in Electronic Authoring

If the author's task for the electronic document is not the layout of the final page or screen or viewer, then what is the end product or "deliverable" for which he or she is responsible? The answer is quite simple: a conforming SGML document, one whose text and markup accurately reflect the document type's structure definition and otherwise conforms to the International Standard.

In Table 4-1 of the previous chapter we invented a small set of element types in order to give us a hint of what might be an adequate set of structures for a piece of text. We derived them by observing documents that were already typeset and which therefore gave us strong visual hints as to the presence and nature of each structural element: title, author, section, paragraph, list.

We turn now to some purely mechanical issues of tagging. By now we are surely convinced that tagging is only the visible apparatus of the author's markup. But before we launch into discussions of formal markup in Chapters 6 through 8, let us dwell on the generic rules for markup itself.

5.5   Mechanics of Markup

In Chapter 4, we used the term "element" in describing the structural building blocks of a document. Elements,[1] we noted, are related to one another in a hierarchical or treelike sense. "Manual," "Section," and "Subsection" are three such units of our example, such that a paragraph is part of a sub-section, which is part of a section, which in turn is part of a manual. The writer must know those structural relationships for the document in order to begin the task of marking up the document. We concluded Chapter 4 with a rather verbose description of the structure of our document ("Manual"), summarized in Table 4-1, Table of Element Types. Understanding those structural relationships beforehand means that the writer can produce text that fits the structure for that document (paragraph within subsection, subsection within section, section within chapter).

But having understood the structure of a particular type of document, the issue now is much more practical: How do we do mark up our text in a way that identifies that structure explicitly and without ambiguity? In other words, how do we prepare text in such a way that even a computer can infer all of the conforming structure that we built into our document? The answer is that we add what SGML defines formally as **descriptive markup**. We explicitly tell the computer everything it needs to know about the structure of our text: "Here is a document whose type is 'Manual.' Inside 'Manual' is a 'Section'—possibly several sections. Inside 'Section' there are 'Paragraphs.'" Furthermore we delimit each of these structural units of text: "Here is where the 'Manual' begins and here is where it ends. Here is where a 'Section' begins and here is where it ends, and so on." These delimiters are called **tags**. You may have seen SGML text before, and if so you probably recognize the familiar "angle brackets" that SGML uses for tags (e.g., <manual>, </manual>, <paragraph>, </paragraph>).

These markup tags which indicate the start and end of an element are in fact explicitly mentioned in the formal definition of an SGML element:

> **element:** A component of the hierarchical structure defined by a document type definition; it is identified in a document instance by descriptive markup, usually a start-tag and end-tag.
> — ISO 8879: §4.110

In other words, the computer (and the human reader of an SGML document) recognize a document's elements by the start-and end-tags which the author inserts into the document. This means that the tags carry all of the "freight" of expressing that structure. (Remember that the computer cannot rely on the appearance of the document to infer structure, even though the human reader can.) We suspect therefore that markup entails both precision and conformity to rules in order to select and place tags properly.

5.5.1 SGML Syntax for Tags

An important general rule is that tagging, like writing itself, follows syntactic conventions. You probably already know that an SGML document's tags consist of angle brackets: "<" and ">".

---

1. Note the difference between "element" and "element type." Element type refers to a class, while element refers to a particular instance (occurrence) of that class. For example, we may talk about the characteristics of the paragraph *element type*, which apply to all paragraphs, such as saying that they begin with a tab. We may also refer to a particular paragraph *element*, such as the one you are reading right now, saying it appears in a footnote.

That convention is set by the SGML reference concrete syntax. This is a set of standard syntax rules that allow the writer simply to assume that certain rules, including these rules for start- and end-tagging, will be universally understood.

The syntax of tags is simple. A tag opens with "<" and closes with ">". The other special symbol—special because the reference concrete syntax defines it to be so—is the forward slash "/". This appears as the second symbol of an end-tag. So we might find that for a particular document type a start-tag for the element "Paragraph" would be defined as "`<paragraph>`" and the end-tag would be "`</paragraph>`". Note that it is SGML syntax that prescribes how to delimit a start- and end-tag. But it is up to the document type definition (DTD) for Manual, Book, or whatever, to prescribe the element type names (generic identifiers, or GIs) that may occur in the tag: "p", "para", or "paragraph", for example. In addition to the GI for the element, the start-tag may contain other information about the element in the form of attributes, which will be discussed in Chapter 8.

5.5.2   Tags Enclose an Element

The *usage* of tags is likewise simple for the writer. First, just as the formal SGML definition says, the tags for an element enclose the element. So a section would begin with "`<sect>`" and end with "`</sect>`". The word "usually" in the formal definition implies that there may be exceptions. We will discuss one such exception shortly.

The location of an element's start- and end-tags on the page is relatively unimportant, as long as they appear before and after the content data of the element. This is because the appearance of the marked-up document is of no concern to the computer that reads the document. You may choose to reserve separate lines for certain tags, where possible, just so they stand out more prominently to the human reader. In the case of "`<sect>`" and "`</sect>`" the tags could each appear on their own separate lines, above and below the text of the section:

```
<sect>
.
.
Write your section's worth of text here, including sub-sections, paragraphs,
and whatever.
.
.
</sect>
```

Or you may embed the tags so that they physically enclose the text with no intervening line breaks:

```
<sect>Write your section's worth of text here, including sub-sections,
paragraphs, and whatever.</sect>
```

To the computer interpreting your marked-up text, there is absolutely no difference between the two examples above.

5.5.3 Elements Can Be Nested

In the example above we noted that "your section's worth of text" could include subelements: subsections, paragraphs, and more. So, using our easier-to-read (for humans) formatting option, let us expand on our example:

```
<manual>
    <title>WhizzyCalc Installation guide</title>
    <section>
        <section-header>Getting WhizzyCalc Onto Your Hard Disk</section-header>
        <paragraph>Type "B:" (your drive name), then type "INSTALL."</paragraph>
    </section>
    <section>
        <section-header>Registering WhizzyCalc</section-header>
        <paragraph>Mail the registration card to WhizzyCorp.</paragraph>
    </section>
</manual>
```

We are interested just now in the way we apply markup to the text to show nesting or subordination of subelements: A manual contains (or embeds) a title and sections, and sections contain paragraphs. Look again at the example above and note how each start-tag is balanced off by its own corresponding end-tag. We might redraw these relationships as follows, this time without any other text at all:

```
<manual>
    <title></title>
    <section>
        <section-header></section-header>
        <paragraph></paragraph>
    </section>
    <section>
        <section-header></section-header>
        <paragraph></paragraph>
    </section>
</manual>
```

It is worthwhile to observe that while we speak of subordination and embedding, it is not necessary to use indentation to indicate those relationships. In fact, it is not good practice to insert tabs or indent characters into the marked-up document at all. A validating SGML parser (recognition and interpretation program), when it parses (analyzes) text, does not even "see" such page formatting. The parser examines each character of the document and decides whether it is part of the markup (such as tags) or data (the information content).[1] In doing so, it will ignore white space that isn't part of the data.

---

1. Note the distinction between "text," which is the entire marked-up document, and "data" by which we mean the information content of the document, that is, what you write. These terms are used with these meanings in this book, so when we refer to "text" it means "information content and markup" and when we use the term "data" it means "information content only."

So to illustrate our rule of nesting in a slightly more formal manner, let us invent three elements whose start-tags in descending order are `<manual>`, `<section>`, and `<paragraph>`. This simplest of all examples (which includes no data at all!) shows the way those elements (including their tags) must be nested:

```
RIGHT:<manual>…<section>…<paragraph>…</paragraph>…</section>…</manual>
```

The rule of nested elements, on the other hand, dictates that we must NOT do something like the following:

```
WRONG:<manual>…<section>…<paragraph>…</section>…</paragraph>…</manual>
```

This of course is second nature to a writer, since the wrong example above involves starting a new section in the middle of a paragraph and then continuing on with the same paragraph as though nothing had happened!

5.5.4   Easing the Writer's Task
Markup Minimization

Now for possible exceptions. The formal SGML definition above tells us that a start-tag and end-tag usually identify an element. For the writer/editor that means that we *usually* mark up each element with both a start-tag and an end-tag. There is never any harm in doing that in any SGML document. That sort of invariable, exhaustive approach (sometimes referred to as "rigorous" or "full" markup) is the sort of strategy you would expect to use for a brainless robot. But you might have guessed from the examples above that even a computer could guess that a paragraph should end when a new subsection begins or that a subsection ends when a new section begins. And we have a sense that there should be some way to tell the computer that such obvious things should happen automatically. The benefit of such an automatic rule would be that we as authors would not have to insert every single end-tag. In the description (DTD) for every real-life document type, there are rules which state precisely where you are free to omit end-tags (described in Chapter 6). This feature of SGML is called markup minimization, something that is formally described for a particular document within that document's DTD. (This, by the way, is one important reason why it is a very good idea for you to be able to read a DTD on your own, as we will discuss in our DTD walkthrough in Chapter 12.) So part of the benefits of SGML for the writer/editor is that the rules for a document type include shortcuts like this which lessen the mechanical burden of tagging.

5.5.5   Further Help
Validating SGML Parsers

An SGML tool which greatly assists the author is the validating SGML parser. Validation means that as you edit a document, the computer scans your marked-up text to find any improperly nested elements, any illegal tags, or any other such errors in the text. Note that SGML validators never look at the semantics or check the spelling, grammar or syntax of your document. The SGML validator only makes sure that you have applied the rules for that document type (the rules in the DTD) properly in your markup of the text. A validating parser can either be highly streamlined and smart, hiding most detail from the author, or it may be quite minimal. In either case, it is most effective when *you* know the material you are now learning in this book.

5.6   The Ever-Present DTD

The persistent interplay between (1) a document's type, as defined in its DTD, and (2) your marked-up text, called a **document instance**, is what sets your activity apart from traditional writing and editing. The existence and control exerted by the DTD are your guarantee that the document will be portable. But in addition it simplifies your text processing task. Now you need only to produce a document in character (ASCII) text that is marked up properly.

That plain-text version of your document, as we said before, is your deliverable. This means that any text editor, no matter how little intelligence it may have, is theoretically suitable for authoring and editing an SGML document. Furthermore the DTD itself offers minimization rules (markup shortcuts) to reduce your markup effort. So while your deliverable as an author is only the marked-up text (which you must actively produce), the other component of the deliverable is the DTD (which you should be able to read but probably will not need to design or even modify). The summary paragraph on "Rigorous Markup" in Annex A (A.3) of the SGML Standard recapitulates this dynamic well:

> The document type definition enables SGML to minimize the user's text entry effort without reliance on a "smart" editing program or word processor. This maximizes the portability of the document because it can be understood and revised by humans using any of the millions of existing "dumb" keyboards. Nonetheless, the type definition and the marked up document together still constitute the rigorously described document that machine processing requires.
> — ISO 8879: Appendix A.3 (final paragraph)

In the world of markup, as we have defined it, the author is finished when the document is written and the *tags* are properly selected and placed. The writer inserts *tags* to signal the start and end of elements. But since processing the document depends on a proper interpretation of its markup, we would expect that the concise definition of the elements of the document must also accompany the document itself. And so that description must accompany the document *everywhere*, whether physically attached to the document or simply referred to from the document. In the real world of SGML documents, remember that there are no visual clues to structure that we can infer from the page layout of the document. As we saw, in fact, there is really no page layout in a tagged document at all. The text of a tagged document is just that... text: no special faces (bold, italic, underline), no reserved positions on the page, and no special spacing and margin settings. Similarly, the software that processes the text cannot infer anything about structure; it needs the precision of the **document type definition**. The entire "freight" for expressing structure is in the definition of the elements, including the **generic identifiers**, which are the element type names that are used in the **tags**. This is why the *definition of the element types always goes with the document.* So once again, the SGML author's deliverable is the dual component of (1) the marked-up document together with (2) the formal definition of the document type used by the author in preparing the document.

5.7 Document Type Definition

Basics

One important observation about tags in an SGML writing environment is that the **descriptive markup** we actually see in the writer's deliverable product—acronyms or abbreviations surrounded by angle brackets—are only the visible indicators of the structure. The subtle but important point for the writer is that in descriptive markup (what the writer does) he or she uses tags to express the elements of *structure* in the document. This means that we must be fully conscious of the structural meaning behind each tag. How much of SGML mechanics does the writer *need* to master in order to conform to a particular SGML application? We suggest the following:

1. The **set of element types** that make up a particular application. For each element type that will need explicit markup in our text, there will be a name or **generic identifier**. Its purpose is to identify elements of that type. That name (the "generic identifier," or "GI") appears in the tag which we use during markup to signal the start and end of an element, so the writer should master the set of GIs, including the meaning and structural relationship of each element type identified by that name. (Other information besides GIs may occur within tags, as we will see later.)

2. The **order** in which the various elements of the document may occur. As we noted above, this requires that we know the relationships of subordination (indentation) among those elements.

3. The **properties** of each element type: whether it is optional or obligatory, whether there can be multiple instances of the element type within the document, and further information about the element that the tag may identify.

Our work in this and future chapters will focus on understanding these items of information about a particular document. That information is borne by the document type definition in a manner that is highly uniform from type to type. So as a result of your work in this small book, you will be able to analyze any document type's element structure to determine proper markup for that type.

Having expanded the concept of SGML tagging, it is worth noting that a word processed document cannot simply be *converted* to SGML in the way that one would convert a document from MS Word to WordPerfect or from Wordstar® to MS Word. The conversion process must somehow deal intelligently with the definition of the element types, just as the typesetter or software developer for the SGML browser/viewer must design with the document's structure in mind. In other words, any person or computer which processes an SGML document must also process the definition of its element structure. The products now available for such conversions do in fact contain embedded "intelligence" for using a document's DTD while converting the document.

5.8   Document Type Definition

Working Discussion

In Section 5.4 we stated that the author's deliverables include markup that reflects the structure of the document. Now that we have a grasp of what comprises a formal description of the elements underlying the markup, we can begin a working discussion of a document type definition.

A document type definition (we'll use DTD from now on throughout the book), briefly defined, is a set of rules which (1) governs the author's activity while he or she designs and produces the document and which (2) informs processing and presentation software of any kind (for typesetting, viewing, and retrieval, for example) precisely what to expect so that each process can present the document in some final form. The final form may be an elegantly designed, camera-ready page layout of the document (in a typesetting system), a screen representation (with title, headers, list elements, and paragraphs all appearing in some easy-to-recognize format on the screen of a browser/viewer), or a "hit" from a user's query on a CD-ROM database. The DTD accomplishes all of this by specifying everything that the author and the implementor need to know about the tags.

5.8.1   Allowable Element Types
Their Names and Their Meaning

Our collection of element type names from Chapter 4 is limited, but so is every such list. Every element type that an author might use in a conforming SGML document must be accounted for (i.e., defined) in the DTD. The author naturally must know the proper name of each element type as well as its meaning (e.g., `ti` for "title", `p` for "paragraph", `lh` for "list head"). In many cases the DTD will be accompanied by documentation providing this information. Other times it may be included in the actual DTD as comments. But occasionally the author will need to be able to read the DTD directly to extract the needed information on his or her own.

5.8.2   Tagging Communicates Structure

In our WAE (Writers And Editors) Table of Element Types (Table 4-1), we specified that a `manual` begins with a `title`, that there is a `section-header` within a `section`, and that there can be any number of `paragraphs` within the `section`. But note that it would be absurd for us to insert a `section-header` in the middle of a `paragraph` or a `title` in the middle of an `author` block. In other words, there are rules about which structural elements can occur at which points in the document. Naturally our intuition, based on our experience with various document types, gives us most of the information we need when we write a document, with or without SGML.

The comforting aspect of electronic document architecture is that the DTD itself is able to tell us at each juncture of our task precisely permissible what element is allowable. This is because the DTD is unambiguous in its definition of the allowable relationships among structural elements. Not only is this of immense help to the writer, but it also continues to guide the document into its presentation or rendition. When we hand off the document to a computer, typesetting device, browser/viewer, retrieval system, or who knows what, we cannot assume even the least degree of intelligence, intuition, or background experience, because we are essentially dealing with a robot. In more formal terms, we say that our human activity is highly context-sensitive (the context being our experience and intuition), while the structural definition of the electronic document must be totally context-free (bearing all of the necessary structural information within itself). The electronic document thus achieves this context freedom by incorporating the DTD within itself.

Communicating the structural knowledge that your document must bear is the mission of the DTD. The "language" that the DTD uses in communicating that knowledge is in fact much like a computer language, hence, the "L" in Standard Generalized Markup Language (SGML). Fortunately for the author, the grammar and syntax of a DTD are normally hidden. The author need only be aware of those aspects of the DTD that define the element types and their associated markup.

5.8.3   Additional Properties of Element Types

There are additional properties of the document's element types of which the author must be aware. First, he or she must know whether the element is optional or obligatory. For example, a particular DTD may include the element type "subtitle" among the list of available element types for the document. The author may choose to omit a subtitle in a particular document *only if the DTD specifies that the element "subtitle" may be omitted.* Similarly, an author working in a security-sensitive area may not know the precise level of security clearance for a particular document. Yet the DTD for all documents in that area specifies many elements that must not only be tagged but in addition must be provided with the proper security level, restriction(s), release level, codeword(s), and additional security information. The author must do this *because the DTD specifies that this additional security information is obligatory.* In other words, the author must know not only the name and meaning of the element type but also any other properties associated with it. Finally, an author who is publishing the findings for a large research project needs to ascribe proper credit to each member of the research team. Each team member of course expects to see his or her name as a co-author of the published paper. The author will of course enter their names as authors, *but only if the DTD allows for multiple authors of a document.*

The main point of this chapter is that an author of an SGML-compliant document must be aware of the ever-present DTD for that type of document. We have referred to our intuitive DTD of Chapter 4 Table 4-1, (which is at this point not really a DTD, but just a table of element types) to illustrate the aspects of the DTD we must understand in order to do productive work. The good news for writers and editors is that they do *not* need to be fluent readers of the entire DTD. In the next few chapters we will examine DTDs from both ends of the spectrum: (1) our own uncomplicated WAE document type definition, with little structural complexity, and (2) a full-blown industry standard DTD that supports a rich variety of publications. And we shall offer keys to allow any writer or editor to find essential structural information, even within a complex DTD.

Let us look again at our intuitive structural definition from Table 4-1. Although the table does a rather adequate job of portraying the elements of "manual," it is far from being a formal DTD because it contains no formal rules that apply SGML to markup. But since we are about to experiment with a real-life document and need to do descriptive markup, we need a repertoire of generic identifiers or GIs to put in the tags we will use. So we take a theoretic shortcut and simply use the table's element type names as GIs. What they lack in SGML rigor, they achieve in faithfulness to the structure of the document. (After we have applied these long GIs to an exercise in writing a manual, we will rework the table, creating a formal SGML application with formal GIs.)[1]

The remainder of the chapter is a discussion example of how a DTD drives the work of an author. First, we hereby adopt Table 4-1 as representing a standard DTD for our universe of writing activity and give it the name WAE (for "**W**riters **A**nd **E**ditors"). It is therefore now an example of

---

1. Note that the SGML standard uses "element type name" and "GI (generic identifiers)" synonymously, but in this book we usually reserve the former term for the full name of the element type, not restricted by SGML syntax.

an SGML application. Now let us apply WAE to the task of creating an actual conforming document, in this case a policy manual regarding sick leave.

5.9   Creating a Structured Document
A Case Study

5.9.1   Description of the Document

Bolton and Sons Manufacturing is still a small company (68 employees in all). It has found that with their mix of contract, salaried, and hourly-pay employees, they must clarify how their policies of sick leave apply to the three different classes of workers. Management has already found itself in difficult circumstances trying to enforce their policy, due to the lack of a clearly written manual. Also, state industrial health and safety regulations now impose certain guidelines on the employer, and Bolton wants these to be clarified to each employee. The writer for the project has received some notes for the document from the personnel director, and fortunately the notes at least resemble an outline. The writer needs to determine first whether WAE will be sufficient for the document she is about to produce: a brief stand-alone company statement regarding sick leave. The document, later to be printed as a small brochure, will have various numbered sections, perhaps an occasional subsection, and three instances of listed items. After comparing these requirements with Table 4-1 for WAE, it does in fact seem to be a good match.

The rough-draft notes look like this:

BOLTON Sick-Leave Policy
by Cynthia Ann Weiler, Personnel Director
(tech writer: include your name as a co-author)

Why a revised policy is necessary: splitting management between contract and salaried now creates three groups—sick leave now too complicated without a formal policy.

Policy itself adopted by management and by the Machinists' Union. Basically the same for all three groups, but some differences in the number of days, depending on the category of the employee and the number of years worked for Bolton. Grounds for sick leave: sickness or injury requires physician's care and/or bed rest. A single parent may also claim same days leave for care of child who is homebound while sick or injured and requiring constant care.

Contract employees (professional and administrative working under a written contract for a stated annual rate of pay, with a given duration of time). Less than five years' employment: 25 days; greater than five years: 35 days; leave accrued through five contract years; company-provided long-term disability insurance for longer leaves.

Salaried employees (hired without contract but with a stated biweekly rate of pay). Less than five years: 15 days; greater than five years: 30 days; accrual to next anniversary of hire date only; disability insurance company-subsidized at 50%.

Hourly ("bargaining unit") employees. Current contract with Machinists' Union specifies 12 days for up to three years' employment, 15 days for up to five years, and 18 days for ten or more; accrual for current year of union contract in force; disability insurance optional with no company subsidy.

Our first impulse as writers is likely to be to clean up the English of the draft notes. There are numerous incomplete sentences, and there is blatant misuse of the colon. Second, we would probably want to unwind these dense, fact-filled paragraphs into some sort of more readable layout. Then we could no doubt *produce an attractive, informative booklet* for human resources. Our task in the structured document environment, however, is to *generate a document which conforms to a DTD*. With that in mind, let us postpone all sentence-level grammar considerations and concentrate first on the document as a whole, in the light of the WAE DTD.

5.9.2   Structure of the Document

First, we need to reference the DTD from inside the document by means of a DOCTYPE declaration. Then we will look to the DTD to define and structure the document. We find that it must first bear a title. "BOLTON Sick-Leave Policy" is obviously the element we need, so we tag that as `<title>BOLTON Sick-Leave Policy</title>`. Once again, note that the title's eventual visual presentation in the document has no bearing on the document's conforming to the WAE DTD; the *tag tells all*.

The DTD also demands an author and in fact allows for multiple authors. So depending on company policy, your name (as writer) may appear with Cynthia Weiler's as multiply tagged authors.

Cynthia's first paragraph hints strongly at the notion of an overview or introduction to the entire document, although she has not used the word "Introduction" or "Overview" in the draft. If we choose to view the paragraph in that way, we might wish to rewrite and expand the draft such that this paragraph will become an entire section, with its own header and possibly with several paragraphs.

The second paragraph contains information that is common to all the employees, so this too may be a separate section. The grounds for claiming sick leave sound like a list, albeit a list of only two items. If we choose to make those into a list, then each one would be tagged ultimately as a List-Item in WAE.

The final three paragraphs of the draft have a definite kinship; they each describe comparable policies for a class of employees at Bolton. So with our DTD in mind, we would probably be inclined to group these three draft paragraphs into a single section with an appropriate section header. Then, after a brief overview of the section, we might start a separate subsection for each class of employee. Within each class (i.e., under each subsection) we could structure the terms for sick leave as a list.

Having thus mapped out the structure of the document with the guidance of our WAE DTD, we are now ready actually to begin rewriting the document. Please note that we have deliberately described this process with highly non-directive language: "This may be," "hints strongly," "we might wish to," "if we choose to," "we may be inclined to," and the like. This is meant to be a strong reminder that *the DTD does not force us into a single method of structuring our document*. And it certainly does not dictate anything about the semantic content of the company's policy book on leave policy. It only assures us that, however we select from among structuring options, the document will be WAE-compliant. Even if we chose the most minimal approach possible and simply drafted the Leave document as a manual with a single section of five paragraphs, and even if we left the language in rough-draft form, the document would still be WAE-compliant. So the writer's options are practically infinite, even within the constraints of the DTD.

5.9.3   Marked-Up Document

As we emphasized above, there is no single correct way to mark up this document. There is only a single DTD to which the document must conform. With that in mind, study now the following marked-up text. Note that we have set the tags in boldface only for readability's sake.

```
<!DOCTYPE manual SYSTEM "c:\pub\dtds\wae.dtd">
<manual><title>BOLTON AND SONS Sick Leave Policy</title>
<author>Cynthia Ann Weiler, Personnel Director</author>
<author>Renn J. T. Loring, Staff Writer</author>
<section><section-header>OVERVIEW</section-header>
<paragraph>A revision of the sick leave policy is necessary and will apply to
Bolton and Sons Manufacturing.</paragraph>
<paragraph>The sick leave policy was adopted by management and by the
Machinist's Union. It will be the same for all three groups except for some
differences in the category of the employee, in the number of days, and in the
number of years worked at Bolton Manufacturing.</paragraph>
<paragraph>Sick leave is defined as;</paragraph>
<list><list-item>A sickness or injury to the employee which requires bedrest
and/or Physician care.</list-item>
<list-item>A single parent may take "same days leave" for the care of a child
that is sick or injured and or requires constant care.</list-item></list>
</section>
<section><section-header>CONTRACT EMPLOYEES</section-header>
<paragraph>Contract employees are professional and administrative personnel
working under a written contract for a stated annual rate of pay with a given
duration of time. Sick leave policy for contract employees include the
following:</paragraph>
<list><list-item>Less than 5 years of employment-25 days of sick
leave</list-item>
<list-item>Greater than 5 years of employment-35 days of sick leave</list-item>
```

```
<list-item>Leave accrued through 5 contract years</list-item>
<list-item>Company provided long-term disability insurance for longer
leave</list-item></list></section>
<section><section-header>SALARIED EMPLOYEES</section-header>
<paragraph>Salaried employees are hired without a contract but with a stated
biweekly rate of pay. Sick leave policy for salaried employees include the
following:</paragraph>
<list><list-item>Less than 5 years of employment-15 days of sick leave
</list-item>
<list-item>Greater than 5 years of employment-30 days of sick leave</list-item>
<list-item>Leave accrued to next anniversary of hire date only</list-item>
<list-item>Company provided disability insurance subsidized at 50%</list-item>
</list></section>
<section><section-header>HOURLY ("Bargaining Unit") EMPLOYEES</section-header>
<paragraph>Hourly employees are currently contracted with the Machinist's
Union. Sick leave policy for hourly employees include the
following:</paragraph>
<list><list-item>Up to 5 years of employment-15 days of sick leave</list-item>
<list-item>For 10 or more years of employment-18 days of sick leave</list-item>
<list-item>Leave accrued for current year of union contract in force
</list-item>
<list-item>Disability insurance optional with no company subsidy</list-item>
</list></section>
<paragraph>Current employee contract negotiations will result in an expanded
definition of "salaried employees." An updated employee contract will go in
effect July 1,1996.</paragraph></section></manual>
```

5.9.4   Document as Printed

Figure 5-1 is a *possible* rendition of the above document. Note that the production specialist or the typesetting system has made certain decisions about how to represent such items as the following:

1. A document title (<title>): very large and bold

2. A paragraph: double-spacing between paragraphs, indentation of about seven spaces

3. Section header: large and bold

4. List items: double-spacing between items, ordered with alpha identifiers

5. Authors: italics

Summary

We suggested in earlier chapters that the writer using SGML, while aware of printed or on-screen *appearance*, is primarily interested in *document structure*. Since the primary deliverable is in fact the marked-up document, we may use the document's DTD directly in the authoring process. The DTD therefore, as a structuring mechanism, becomes a powerful tool for the author.

BOLTON AND SONS
SICK LEAVE POLICY

Cynthia Ann Weiler, Personnel Director
Renn J. T. Loring, Staff Writer

I.   OVERVIEW

A revision of the sick leave policy is necessary and will apply to Bolton and Sons Manufacturing.

The sick leave policy was adopted by management and by the Machinist's Union. It will be the same for all three groups except for some differences in the category of the employee, in the number of days, and in the number of years worked at Bolton Manufacturing.

Sick leave is defined as:

a)   A sickness or injury to the employee which requires bedrest and/or Physician care.

b)   A single parent may take "same days leave" for the care of a child that is sick or injured and or requires constant care.

II.   CONTRACT EMPLOYEES

Contract employees are professional and administrative personnel working under a written contract for a stated annual rate of pay with a given duration of time. Sick leave policy for contract employees include the following:

a)   Less than 5 years of employment-25 days of sick leave

b)   Greater than 5 years of employment-35 days of sick leave

c)   Leave accrued through 5 contract years

d)   Company provided long-term disability insurance for longer leave

III.   SALARIED EMPLOYEES

Salaried employees are hired without a contract but with a stated biweekly rate of pay. Sick leave policy for salaried employees includes the following:

Figure 5-1 Bolton and Sons sick leave policy

a)   Less than 5 years of employment-15 days of sick leave

b)   Greater than 5 years of employment-30 days of sick leave

c)   Leave accrued to next anniversary of hire date only

d)   Company provided disability insurance subsidized at 50%

IV.   HOURLY ("Bargaining Unit") EMPLOYEES

Hourly employees are currently contracted with the Machinist's Union. Sick leave policy for hourly employees includes the following:

a)   Up to 5 years of employment-15 days of sick leave

b)   For 10 or more years of employment-18 days of sick leave

c)   Leave accrued for current year of union contract in force

d)   Disability insurance optional with no company subsidy

Current employee contract negotiations will result in an expanded definition of "salaried employees." An updated employee contract will go in effect July 1, 1996

Figure 5-1 Bolton and Sons sick leave policy (Continued)

CHAPTER 6

ELEMENT TYPE DECLARATION
Building the Markup Vocabulary

SGML terms introduced or reviewed:

comment, comment declaration, content model, descriptive markup, document instance, document type declaration, document type definition (DTD), element, element type, element type declaration, end-tag, mark up, markup, occurrence indicator, start-tag, tag

Overview

Once we recognize the need for some sort of marking or tagging scheme to identify the structural components that make up a document, we see the necessity of a clear definition of that marking scheme. The intuitive approach that we have followed so far has its weaknesses, most notably (1) ambiguous relationships and(2) a reliance on the understanding of the writer. The formality of SGML provides the tools for creating a rigorous marking scheme that can be tailored to fit any document.

In this chapter we explore the problems with an intuitive marking scheme, and then work from that intuitive scheme (Table 4-1, Table of Element Types) toward a full SGML Document Type Definition (DTD). We will introduce the basic syntax for a DTD and discuss the use of it. At the conclusion of the chapter we will then present the formal WAE DTD created from Table 4-1. In the process we will develop a more complete definition of how various structural components behave so that we will have a better understanding of the ability of SGML to apply to any type of structure.

6.1 Weaknesses of an Intuitive Tagging Scheme

In Chapter 4 (Table 4-1) we introduced the WAE (Writers And Editors) structure definition, which was a common-sense or intuitive approach to describing document structure. This simple

---

definition was quite useful for identifying and even marking the structure of many different types of documents. But the simplicity of that intuitive approach introduces some problems when it comes to using it for marking a live document. First, the GIs in the tags are lengthy, a result of trying to make them self-explanatory. Verbose tags are space-consuming and clumsy, adding to the work of tagging if we have to type them. The second problem we find in the WAE structure definition is that it has several areas of ambiguity. Some of the information we need for understanding the tagging method is either implied or explained outside the table. Worst of all, some of the element types and their usage appear to be inconsistent or missing altogether. For instance, the order in which the elements may appear is not clearly defined anywhere; we know intuitively that a document's title cannot follow a section, but the chart does not tell us that explicitly.

Whether all the information about an element type is present and well organized in our structure definition is not simply a matter of theory or aesthetics. Because a tag is merely a descriptor of an element, we cannot begin to tag a document accurately unless we understand everything about the element type definitions for the document. So while our verbose and intuitive approach has helped us to understand the mechanics of tagging, there is a very real need to tighten up our definition of the element types: less verbose, no ambiguities, no aspect left to intuition, and every case explicitly spelled out. Note that we are not about to throw out the *structure* of WAE; we only want to revise and formalize the *definition of the structure* to eliminate any ambiguity.

6.2   Formal Tagging Convention for WAE

In order to remedy these shortcomings and ease the process of actually creating tagged documents, we are going to rewrite the WAE structure definition from its table-based form into a shorthand notation. The particular notation that we will use is SGML, which is used to define all the parts of a document type definition (DTD). This will enable us to describe the element types and all of their related usage and behavior clearly, consistently and unambiguously. The end result of this activity will be a formal specification of WAE structure definition as an *SGML DTD*.

The first task is to agree on a set of working abbreviations, called generic identifiers or GIs, for the element types. These will provide names for use in the tags we insert to start and stop or enclose the various structural components of our document. With this we are not addressing any aspect of our WAE table other than simply the repertoire of GIs for the element types. True, an element type's name—whether intuitive or as a formally defined name—may imply some *container* or *environment* relationship, as in `Section` and `SubSection`. But we will spell out those relationships explicitly in a formal and concise manner later on.

The process of abbreviating the tags to produce a more compact specification is quite straightforward. There are several systems commonly used to develop abbreviated names. The one we are going to use calls for us to reduce each GI to the smallest number of characters that will adequately identify the particular element type. We will also attempt to make the more commonly used names shorter than the less frequently used ones. This is a scheme that is particularly useful when you may need to hand-tag documents. Note that SGML does not dictate how we "spell" the GIs in our set, only how we build the definition of the set of element types. Following the strategy of frequent-gets-short, we arrive at the following set of generic identifiers presented in Table 6-1.

Table 6-1: Element type names to GIs

Element Type	Generic Identifier (GI)
Manual	`manual`
Title	`ti`
Author	`au`
Section	`sec`
Section-Header	`shd`
Sub-Section	`ssec`
Sub-Sec-Head	`sshd`
Paragraph	`p`
List	`l`
List-Header	`lhd`
List-Item	`lit`

Now that we have a complete set of usable GIs for marking a document, we need to establish a clear and consistent marking technique that will allow us to indicate the start and end of each tagged structural component. The SGML standard dictates that we write a **start-tag** by enclosing the tag itself in angle brackets: *<tag>*. The **end-tag** is similar except that it uses a slash after the opening bracket: *</tag>*. Using this convention we would tag the title of a WAE document this way:

```
<ti>This is the Document Title</ti>
```

Again, note that we have not recast much of the WAE Table 4-1 into formal SGML notation as yet; we have only formalized the set of GIs. We have yet to deal with the other critical data in column one of the table—the structural relationships implied by indentation.

6.3 Formal Description of the Element Type's Usage

In Table 4-1 the third column contains a description of the "usage" of the element type. This is a highly verbose part of the table, and it contains much essential information about each element type. Converting this into a formal definition means that we need to break out every piece of that information and decode exactly what it means. What precisely do we learn from the written out usage definition in column 3? If we scan that column, we will find that there are really three basic items of information about each element type:

1. Type of occurrence: only once, one or more, or may be skipped

2. What other elements this element type may contain

3. The environment in which this element type may occur

If we consider carefully the information in item 3—where this element type may occur—we discover that it is the logical complement of the information in item 2. For example, if a document contains a section, it follows logically that a section may appear inside a document; a section is a subcomponent of a document, and a document forms the environment of a section. So one way to eliminate redundant information (i.e., tighten up) in our new format for specifying an element type's usage would be to describe only the *contents* of each element type. That is, we could agree that for each element type we would only look "inside and downward," viewing only its subcomponents and ignoring the "outside and upward" view of its environment. Doing this will lead us to define *each element type as a self-contained structure*, without regard to higher-order structures of which it may be a part. This makes each individual element type completely context free, in much the same way as we discussed making an entire document context-free by the use of SGML.

To transcribe the "usage" of an element type (and therefore the usage of its GI) into more formal terms will then mean to account for only two of the characteristics of that element type: (1) occurrence and (2) contents. In practical terms, we must always know if and when an element of this type can occur and if it does, what its subelements might be. Without knowing that, we are unable to tag a document.

6.3.1 Occurrence of an Element

The following list summarizes the basic parts of an element type's usage that have to do with occurrence. That is, they tell us when and how frequently an element of the given type must or may appear. In slightly more precise terms, there are two variables: (1) whether the element is required or not and (2) whether the element can be repeated or not. When we consider all the combinations of these two variables we have four cases to consider:

1. An element type that must occur once and only once at this level. (A required element that occurs one time, is required, and not repeatable.) There is no such element type in the WAE structure as we know it.

2. An element type that must occur at least once and may be repeated any number of times after that. (A required element that occurs one or more times, required, and repeatable.) `Section` is such an element type in WAE.

3. An element type that may be skipped, but which if it appears, may only occur once. (An optional element that occurs zero or one time, is not required, and non-repeatable.) `Title` is an example of this in WAE.

4. An element type that may be skipped but may be repeated any number of times when it does appear. (An optional element that occurs zero or more times, is not required, and may be repeatable.) `List` is such an element type in WAE.

To summarize, we describe the *occurrence* characteristic of an element type by referring to (1) whether it is optional or obligatory, and (2) whether it can be repeated. Later we will look at the SGML shorthand for describing this characteristic.

6.3.2   Contents of an Element

In our WAE Table 4-1, we explicitly state whether an element of a given type may or may not contain other elements. A `manual` "may contain other elements," but for an `Author`, "no other elements may appear inside it." So column 3 is explicit about whether or not an element is a container of subelements. As for *which* subelements the element may contain, we must look at the first column of the table. And we must look carefully, because the table expresses the relationship between element and subelement *purely on the basis of indentation*. So for `Section` we read in column 3 that it "may contain other elements," and we deduce from column 1 that those subelements are `Section-header` and `SubSection`, and the elements contained in the text matter entity, `Paragraph` and `List`. (For now, we will not count `SubSec-Head` and the nested elements under `List` as subelements of `Section` because they actually occur inside one of the other subelements.)

Our WAE Table 4-1 describes the important characteristic of an element's *contents* in two ways: (1) general language in column 3, and (2) explicit indentation of subordinate elements (subelements) in column 1. Again, we shall look later at the concise SGML way of describing this container/subelement relationship.

6.4 Formal Description of Order of Appearance

In Table 4-1 the order of appearance of items was strongly implied by (1) the indentation among the element types in column 1, (2) the vertical order in which the element types appeared, and (3) our background common knowledge of order among the element types. After all, we simply *know* that Section must normally follow Author. But the visual representation in the table leaves a lot of room for errors in interpretation, which must be avoided in a formal definition so that the document can remain context independent. The main area where the table approach fails is for indicating instances in which elements *may appear in any order*, rather than in the order they are listed in the table. The example of this in WAE structure is Paragraph and List, two element types which can appear in any order, as we know from the examples we have studied as well as from our own intuition. We cannot easily determine that from the table, however. Once again, we sense the need for concise expression, this time to describe all the permissible orders of occurrence among the element types in our set (the GIs in our markup repertoire). And again, SGML has exactly what we need. But first we must further amplify precisely what it is that we are trying to define.

When we begin to formalize a method for describing the order of appearance, we must be clear what the starting point or point of reference is: We are always describing the order that *subordinate elements* appear inside the *current element*. The current element is what delimits the context for us. For instance, Title and Author must appear inside the Manual element, *in that order*. When we analyze the structure definition, we will discover that for any list of element types there are only three sequence scenarios that we need to consider:

1. Elements of the listed types must appear in the order they are specified.

2. Elements of the listed types may appear in any order.

3. One and only one element of the listed types may appear.

As we noted above, the current format of Table 4-1 does not describe the order of occurrence among elements as explicitly as this. And we will find that we need that degree of precision in order to know how to tag a document properly.

It should be apparent that the *order* and the *usage* characteristics combine to produce the entire description of the set of element types for a particular document type. The order of appearance says that certain items must appear in some prescribed order, but that if a particular one of the items is optional, then that element may be skipped. All of this is what a comprehensive description of an element type should convey. And our table *plus our intuition about documents in general* would carry us a long way toward a clear definition. But since our tagged document is being (or may be) sent to a computer, in which there is absolutely no intuition or common sense about anything, we must express our description in a totally unambiguous manner. That is precisely the motivation for SGML. So we turn now to SGML for the notational tools we need for doing it right!

6.5   Recasting WAE as a Formal DTD

At first glance the shorthand notation for listing the element types and for defining their properties of *occurrence* and *order* in a DTD is somewhat daunting, but we are about to decompose it into pieces that we can readily understand. The basic form of an element type declaration[1] in a DTD follows this scheme:

```
<!ELEMENT name   tag minimization        contents>
```

Each component of the line above, even the spaces between the words, has some special meaning of its own, meanings that are already familiar to us. In order to discuss each component clearly, let us rewrite this scheme or "template" in table format (Table 6-2).

6.5.1   Opening Delimiter to Name Parameter

Item 1 is the literal "spelling" of the start of an element type declaration. It uses the same left angle bracket that we use with a tag when we mark up a document. But remember that this declaration defines a *type* of element, the structure which is identified by the tag. The word ELEMENT is a special word or "keyword" in SGML. As part of a declaration it bears the prefix "!" (exclamation point).

Item 2 is a delimiter, one or more spaces in this case, to separate the keyword ELEMENT from the name, which follows.

Item 3 is the element type name. This is the generic identifier for the elements, which will then be usable in a tag. As we will see, the "abbreviated GIs" from the table above will go into this slot: doc, ti, au, sec, etc.

Item 4 is another delimiter (one or more spaces).

6.5.2   Omitted Tag Minimization Parameter

Item 5 is the tag minimization section. The codes in this slot tell whomever or whatever references our document type definition whether the start- and end-tags may be omitted when tagging this element. We have only hinted at this possibility so far, but it is a significant feature of SGML. It allows us, for example, to omit certain end-tags in our markup when there is no chance of ambiguity. Note that omitting an end-tag has nothing to do with the *occurrence* characteristic of the element. We shall see shortly how SGML handles that part of the description. The minimization slot contains two characters. The first refers solely to the start-tag (<p>, for example). The second refers only to the end-tag (</p>, in this case). If the tag *must* appear, the character is a "-"

---

1. Note that the standard (ISO 8879) actually calls this an "element declaration" rather than an "element type declaration." This is an error that is expected to be corrected in the next edition of the standard.

Table 6-2: Element type declaration parts

1	2	3	4	5	6	7	8	9
Opening delimiter & declaration name	separator	parameter	separator	parameter	separator	parameter	separator	closing delimiter
<!ELEMENT	one or more spaces	*name*	one or more spaces	*tag mini-mization*	one or more spaces	*contents*	zero or more spaces	>

(hyphen); if the tag *may be omitted* the character is an "**O**". This is the letter O, for "omissible," not zero. It is important to use the right character because, to a computer, zero and the letter "O" are quite different. For `Title`, which must have a start-tag, but whose end- tag may be omitted, the first six parts of its declaration would appear as follows (remember, the space delimiter fields are significant!):

```
<!ELEMENT ti   - O  contents >
```

The significance of being able to omit certain tags is primarily that it reduces the total effort involved in tagging a document. But is important to understand that we can only omit a tag if the context implies its existence unambiguously. For the title element in our WAE DTD we know that we can omit the end-tag because no other elements may appear inside a title element. Because of this, encountering any start-tag for another element tells us (or the computer reading the document) that the title element has been ended. If other elements may appear inside the current element, as with the section element, neither the start-tag nor the end-tag could be omitted, because there would be no way of knowing if we had reached the end of the section element. (Most SGML authoring tools automatically insert both start- and end-tags on all elements, regardless of allowable minimization)

Item 6 is another delimiter (one or more spaces).

6.5.3   Content Model Parameter

Sequence

Item 7 is the *contents* slot, in which we describe the elements that this element type may contain. Both *sequence* and *occurrence* information for the subelement types is encoded here. This information is known as the **content model** for an **element type**. In its simplest form the contents field will simply contain a list of the valid element types or data that can appear in an element of the current type, each item separated by a comma"," and the entire list enclosed in parentheses. A written term paper might consist of a title, a body, and a conclusion. In SGML terms, we would write its **content model** as follows:

```
(title, body, conclusion)
```

As we might expect, every symbol is important. In the content model the spaces are not significant, but the commas are *very* important. They are *connectors* that tell us that these three subelements—title, body, and conclusion—occur in precisely the order listed. So the full SGML element type declaration for the `TermPaper` element type would read as follows:

```
<!ELEMENT TermPaper - O  (title, body, conclusion) >
```

The content model in this format would indicate (because of the comma connectors) that each one of these elements *must* appear in the "TermPaper" element in the exact order specified. Note that the comma has the special meaning "followed by." We read the declaration as follows:

"The element TermPaper, which must be marked with a start-tag and may optionally be marked by an end-tag, must have a title, followed by a body, followed by a conclusion."

If an element type's structure allows subordinate elements to appear in any order, the content model uses an ampersand (&) instead of a comma to connect them, as in this declaration of the body element type:

```
<!ELEMENT body O O  (paragraph & list) >
```

The ampersand has the special meaning here of allowing variation in the order of the two items it joins. So we read this content model as "either a paragraph followed by a list or a list followed by a paragraph." Both elements *must* appear, but the order is up to the author.

The final sequence option, where one and only one of the elements is allowed, is indicated by connecting each item in the content model with a vertical bar (|):

```
<!ELEMENT body O O  (paragraph | list) >
```

Once again, a single symbol bears some special meaning. Now the content model reads: "Either a paragraph or a list, but not both." Since only one element can appear, the order is not significant.

By means of the comma, the ampersand, and the vertical bar we can express every possibility of *order* or *sequence* among the subelements in a content model.

6.5.4   Content Model Parameter
Occurrence

We have thus far been discussing how the content model describes *sequence* among subelements. The content model also specifies *occurrence* behavior for an element: required or optional, once only or repeated (see Section 6.3.1). SGML accomplishes this by adding notation to the *sequence* specifications we discussed above.

We have already seen the first type of occurrence—once and only once—used in the content model example above (Section 6.5.3). Just the subelement type name without any further embellishment says "once and only once."

The remaining three *occurrence indicators* each have a special symbol. A plus sign (+) indicates a repeating element type that *must* occur one or more times.

```
<!ELEMENT body - -  (paragraph+) >
```

This occurrence indicator requires at least one paragraph but allows for more to occur in a body element. The plus sign is the formal notation for the text "May be repeated" that we found in column 3 of Table 4-1.

To indicate an optional element type (may be omitted) for which only one element can occur if it occurs at all, we use a question mark (?).

```
<!ELEMENT TermPaper O O  (ti?, au?, sec+) >
```

We read this content model as follows: "A `TermPaper` element may contain an optional `ti` (title) element, followed by an optional `au` (author) element, followed by at least one `sec` (section) element." Again, note that (1) comma means "followed by," (2) "+" means "required and repeatable" or "one or more" and (3) "?" means "optional and non-repeatable" or "zero or one time."

The final occurrence indicator is for an optional element type that may occur multiple times. This is indicated with an asterisk (*).

```
<!ELEMENT paper      O  O  (ti?, au*, sec+) >
```

All that is changed from the previous example is that now we may have any number of `au` (author) elements or none at all (zero or more).

In the content models of all of our examples, note the parentheses. For independent subelement types, just the required outermost parentheses are sufficient. For example, `title`, `body`, and `conclusion` are all on the same structural level (also known as "peer" elements) in our definition of a student term paper, so the only structural relationship among the elements that we are concerned with is that they occur in sequence. But SGML also allows the use of parentheses to group certain items with different occurrence characteristics separately from the other items in the list.

In the following definition `ssec` contains the subelement types `sshd` (subsection header), `p` (paragraph), and `l` (list). This is exactly what we found in Table 4-1. But there is an either/or relationship between `p` and `l` that does not apply to `sshd`. We already know that the vertical bar "|" expresses "either-or," but we need the parentheses to show that this connector applies only to these elements. The parentheses also have the effect of enabling an occurrence indicator to apply to the entire "model group" of items inside. In the example below, the plus sign applies to the parenthesized inner model group of `p` and `l`.

```
<!ELEMENT ssec - -  (sshd?, (p|l)+) >
```

The plus sign means "either a paragraph or a list element must occur in this position and that after that paragraph or list element occurs, either one may occur again, repeatedly."

We would paraphrase this declaration as follows: The subsection element must be marked with both a start-tag and an end-tag; a subsection consists of an optional single subheading, followed by either a paragraph or a list, both of which may be repeated and intermixed as many times as the writer desires.

Why didn't we simply do it this way:

```
(sshd?, (p+|l+))
```

If we consider exactly what this says, the answer becomes apparent. The `(p+|l+)` would be read as "one or more paragraphs" *or* "one or more lists." We can see right away that this does not properly express what we want, which is to allow any number of paragraphs and lists mixed in any order with the minimum requirement of one paragraph *or* one list.

To review the mechanics of grouping, we read this definition from the inside out, so we consider the `(p|l)` as a single item which is either a paragraph or a list. This item must appear at least once but may appear multiple times. We read the final definition of `ssec` as follows: "a subsection (ssec GI) will consist of an optional subsection header (sshd GI) followed by at least one paragraph (p) or one list (l), after which any number of p or l elements may occur in any order."

Using parentheses to group members of an expression is precisely what we do when we mix multiplication and addition in arithmetic and need to group our numbers properly: (6 x 3) + 4 as opposed to 6 x (3 + 4), two expressions which give totally different results. Similarly, the various element types in a DTD *must* be grouped properly in order to correctly express the structure of a document. And, like using parenthesis in arithmetic, the phrases are read from the inside out, considering first what is inside the innermost parenthesis, then evaluating the next level and so on.

Item 8 in the element definition template is an optional delimiter (zero or more spaces).

Item 9 is simply a closing angle bracket ">" that indicates the end of the declaration.

There is one final construct used in the DTD version of our WAE structure definition. Table 4-1 version does not explicitly tell us where text, that is, any written material (information content), can go. SGML provides the keyword #PCDATA to indicate that text appears at this point. The #PCDATA keyword appears in the content model like an element type name, but it simply means that you can put text of some sort at this point in the structure.

6.6 Comments in the DTD

We stress throughout this book the importance of the DTD as something *to be read by the writer.* So while the DTD of course maintains only a *background presence* in the writing process, it is imperative that it be as lucid as possible for human readers. SGML itself, because of its own rigorous consistency, helps to maintain this readability across all DTDs. But when we design or modify a DTD—which we are in fact doing as we build and modify our WAE DTD—we can do much to enhance readability by inserting *comments.* Every real-world DTD contains comments, so SGML users everywhere expect to find them at strategic locations within the DTD.

A comment is an explanation or remark intended for human readers. It is technically a *declaration*, declared in the same way that we declare an element type or an entity. The syntax of a comment is extremely simple, as we can see from the table format in Table 6-3. A typical comment would look something like this:

```
<!-- Writers And Editors (WAE) DTD -->
```

Anything that appears between the opening "--" and the closing "--" delimiters will be totally ignored by the SGML parser. That text is purely for consumption by a human reader. Note also that the comment delimiter offers a means to "deactivate" a portion of a DTD, for whatever reason: an obsolete or alternative declaration or some currently unused portion of the DTD.

Note particularly that complex industry-standard DTDs will frequently contain large commented blocks of the DTD plus instructions (all as part of the "comment") to "uncomment" this or that block in order to activate some SGML markup declaration(s).

Table 6-3: Comment Declaration Parts

1	2	3	4	5
Opening Delimiter	Comment Delimiter	Comment	Comment Delimiter	Closing Delimiter
< !	-- (two dashes)	Anything you please, including declaration(s) you wish to "deactivate"	-- (two dashes)	>

6.7   Document Type Declaration

We need finally to declare to the system the *type* of document we have designed and where its definition (the DTD) can be found. The type of document is indicated by the top-level element type in the document, which is called the document element. The element name for the document element is also the name of the document type. The document type declaration (which has the declaration name DOCTYPE) includes the name of the document type, which is used to connect your text (the document instance) with the document element type declaration in the DTD. If we assume that the actual path and name of the file containing the text of our DTD is "C:\pub\dtds\wae.dtd", we could declare the document type in our document instance like this:

```
<!DOCTYPE manual SYSTEM "C:\pub\dtds\wae.dtd" >
   <manual><ti>The Worlds Greatest Manual</ti>...
   [and all the rest of the actual marked-up text of our document instance.]
```

This notation (using SYSTEM) tells the SGML parser that the operating system can use the text "C:\pub\dtds\wae.dtd" to find the DTD. Moreover it tells the parser that the GI of the document element is "manual."

6.8   Structure Definition

Here now is the entire WAE structure definition using standard DTD notation:

```
<!--              Writers And Editors (WAE) DTD                   -->

<!--        Element Type Declarations                             -->
<!--        ELEMENT    MINIMIZATION    CONTENT                     -->
<!--        =======    ============    =======                     -->
<!ELEMENT   manual     O O             (ti?, au*, sec+) >
<!ELEMENT   ti         - O             (#PCDATA) >
<!ELEMENT   au         - O             (#PCDATA) >
<!ELEMENT   sec        - -             (shd?, ((p|l)+ | ssec)+ ) >
<!ELEMENT   shd        - O             (#PCDATA) >
<!ELEMENT   ssec       - -             (sshd?, (p|l)+) >
<!ELEMENT   sshd       - O             (#PCDATA) >
<!ELEMENT   p          - O             (#PCDATA) >
<!ELEMENT   l          - -             (lhd?, lit+) >
<!ELEMENT   lhd        - O             (#PCDATA) >
<!ELEMENT   lit        - O             (#PCDATA | (p|l)+)+ >
```

Summary

We took care in Chapter 4 to demonstrate that we could design a document type with highly intuitive mechanisms. That design and Table 4-1, our WAE Table of Element Types, functioned impressively well toward a structural markup of a real-world document in Chapter 5. But intuitive discussion can only go so far. A digital document requires more design and rule-based information than can be borne by informal descriptions and tables. The mechanisms of SGML offer us the precision, succinctness, and consistency we need (and the document needs) to express the document's structure adequately. Once again, SGML eases the writer's (and editor's) task, this time by reducing the verbiage necessary for describing the structure of the document.

CHAPTER 7

ENTITIES
Making Text Reusable

SGML terms introduced or reinforced:

content model, general entity, parameter, parameter entity, (parameter) entity reference open, parameter separator, reference close

Overview

SGML entities come in two varieties: parameter entities and general entities. Parameter entities are meant for the DTD itself and an understanding of them is therefore essential for us in order to read a DTD. Normally only a DTD designer or SGML specialist would *add and modify* entity declarations. An author or editor would normally only *read* parameter entities. In this chapter we will introduce the parameter entity as a means to simplify and condense our example WAE DTD.

General entities, on the other hand, are part of the everyday work of authors and editors. A writer will *use* general entities constantly. They serve as a shorthand for the writer who would otherwise need to insert the same text string repeatedly. In addition, character entities, a special case of general entities, allow the author to enter characters which do not exist on his or her keyboard. In this chapter we further modify our example DTD to introduce one general entity of the "author's shorthand" variety. Then we add one character entity that enables the author to insert an "extended" character into a document, a character that is not found on most standard keyboards. In addition we will create a character entity to represent a character that is normally reserved for use in tagging.

7.1 Parameter Entities and General Entities

The SGML DTD notation provides a shorthand for defining the structural components of a document. It allows us to write a DTD that clearly and unambiguously describes all the possible parts of a document and the relationships among those parts in a very compact form. The element

---

types we have chosen for our example DTD appear to describe a basic document rather well. And the DTD, as we left it at the end of Chapter 6, appears to be a concise and highly readable definition of the document type. But despite the economy of the notation and the readability of our DTD, we can still do better! Let us look again at the DTD as we left it at the end of Chapter 6:

```
<!--                    Writers And Editors (WAE) DTD                 -->

<!--          Element Type Declarations                               -->
<!--          ELEMENT    MINIMIZATION    CONTENT                       -->
<!--          =======    =============   =======                       -->
<!ELEMENT     manual     O  O            (ti?, au*, sec+) >
<!ELEMENT     ti         -  O            (#PCDATA) >
<!ELEMENT     au         -  O            (#PCDATA) >
<!ELEMENT     sec        -  -            (shd?, ((p|l)+ | ssec)+ ) >
<!ELEMENT     shd        -  O            (#PCDATA) >
<!ELEMENT     ssec       -  -            (sshd?, (p|l)+) >
<!ELEMENT     sshd       -  O            (#PCDATA) >
<!ELEMENT     p          -  O            (#PCDATA) >
<!ELEMENT     l          -  -            (lhd?, lit+) >
<!ELEMENT     lhd        -  O            (#PCDATA) >
<!ELEMENT     lit        -  O            (#PCDATA | (p|l)+)+ >
```

As you may notice, there is a single model group in the DTD which is repeated three times: "(p|l)+", shown in bold. In SGML (and programming) terms, we have "reused" the construct of "one or more paragraphs or lists" three times in the DTD. It would enhance the readability of the DTD if we could somehow *define* that construction once and then simply *reference* it whenever it is used.

SGML parameter entities allow the DTD designer to reuse a portion of DTD text, enabling more complex structures to be expressed in the DTD. They also aid in the maintenance of the DTD. If they are properly used, they can greatly improve the general readability and our understanding of the DTD. In our discussion we shall look at the benefits of parameter entities and at the mechanics of declaring a parameter entity.

General entities can also be declared by the designer of the DTD, but they appear in the author's actual document (document instance). General entities are also shorthand, but they are a shorthand and tremendous time saver for the author. Again, while parameter entities are for the DTD, general entities are for the author.

Character entities are a special variety of general entities, providing a method for including in our documents characters that cannot be expressed in the normal ASCII character set or for including characters that are normally reserved for use by SGML itself (the less-than sign "<", for example). Learning how entities are declared and used will introduce only a few additional grammatical marks to those we have already learned for elements.

7.2   The Need for Parameter Entities

Why should we think of trying to do better in designing a DTD? Our WAE DTD is admittedly a trivial example, consisting of only a few lines. We noted above the reused item (p|l)+, appearing three times in this DTD. A construct that is this short and with so few repetitions is likewise trivial, but we can imagine what repetition would mean for a construct such as the following, which occurs in the content model of the DocBook element type SetInfo:

```
Author | AuthorIntitials | Title | Copyright | CorpAuthor | CorpName | Date |
Editor | Edition | InvPartNumber | ISBN | LegalNotice | OrgName | OtherCredit |
PrintHistory | Product Name | ProductNumber | Publisher | PubsNumber |
ReleaseInfo | RevHistory | Subtitle | VolumeNum
```

If this content model were used in dozens or even hundreds of additional element type declarations throughout the DTD, it would make the DTD complicated almost to the point of unreadability!

Parameter entities address several issues that are related to DTD writing and DTD reading. The first issue is the method of handling a section of DTD code that is used in multiple places. In a very simple way, we could describe a parameter entity as a "wrapper" for a cluster of structural elements. If you look back at our WAE DTD above you will see that the code (p|l)+ appears in the sec element, the ssec element, and also in the lit element.

In Table 4-1, Table of Element Types, we used an entry of text-matter to allow us to avoid repeating the entire declarations for the paragraph and list elements each time they occurred. In fact, we isolated text-matter and gave it its own private table. And within the main table for the document, we simply said "See below." as a reference to text-matter's special table. This is the spirit behind using parameter entities to eliminate repeated DTD code. The text-matter item is a "wrapper" for the paragraph and list elements, allowing us to work with them as a single piece within the DTD. (Note, however, that this is a purely syntactic wrapper, for use in the DTD only, not a structural element.)

The second major issue addressed by the use of parameter entities is the one that most affects writers and editors, who are normally only readers of DTDs rather than creators of DTDs. Parameter entities can improve the readability of a DTD by allowing layers of detail to be "hidden" in the entity declaration. For example, if we were to create an entity called txm (for text matter), we would know that any place it was referenced (used) in the DTD, some sort of text matter could appear. And we would not have to worry about exactly what the valid text matter items were. Likewise, if we see a particular entity referenced in many places, we only need to go to one place to find out what it contains. Without the use of entities we might not even be aware that the contents were repeated.

For the DTD creator, parameter entities are especially useful. They simplify maintenance of the DTD by "normalizing" the DTD code. This means that any repeated piece of contents is *defined* only once (in the entity declaration) and is then simply *referenced* where it occurs (in the element type declarations). When writing a new DTD, this translates into a much shorter writing time and reduced possibility for errors, since many complex structures will only need to be written once, rather than wherever they may be used. As the designer continues to maintain an existing DTD, parameter entities require changes to be made in one place only. This assures that no occurrences get missed, and it greatly speeds up the modification cycle.

Before we look into the mechanics of parameter entities, here are some general considerations:

1. The declaration of an entity has its own syntax (manner of declaration). That declaration resembles in many ways the declaration of an element type, with its own structured subcomponents.

2. We do not use the parameter entity name as a GI. The name of the parameter entity is strictly for *internal DTD use only*. We only see the parameter entity name within the DTD. (We shall explain shortly how we use that name.)

3. Using parameter entities resolves some serious problems that could result if we had to rely solely on element type declarations.

    a. The reader may not even notice that the entire cluster (of a txm, for example) is recurring; we may tend to "miss the forest for the trees."

    b. The marker (who also is a reader of the DTD) may also miss the recurrences within the DTD and so may not mark accurately.

    c. The end result would be a highly verbose, cumbersome, and unreadable DTD.

4. ENTITY and ELEMENT both begin with the same letter, both have three syllables, and both are stressed on the first syllable. They are therefore extremely easy to confuse in conversation!

7.3   Defining and Using Parameter Entities

The basic syntax of a parameter entity declaration differs from that of an element type declaration, although they share certain similarities. A parameter entity is declared using the following general pattern:

```
<!ENTITY % name "replacement text">
```

As we saw with the element type declaration, each component of the pattern shown has a special significance, even the spaces. In order to simplify identifying the components and their meanings, we will rewrite the pattern into a tabular form (Table 7-1) similar to the one we used for element type declarations in the previous chapter.

Note that columns 1 and 9 serve only to identify and delimit the declaration itself. They don't actually tell us anything about the entity being declared. The real information, called the

Table 7-1: Entity declaration parts

	1	2	3	4	5	6	7	8	9
	opening delimiter and declaration name	separator	parameter	separator	parameter	separator	parameter	separator	closing delimiter
	<!ENTITY	one or more spaces	%	one or more spaces	*name*	one or more spaces	*replacement text*	zero or more spaces	>

"parameters" of the declaration, occurs in columns 3, 5, and 7 while the spaces in columns 2, 4, and 6 are merely "parameter separators".

There are several considerations regarding the mechanics of the parameter entity declaration that we need to be aware of. First, the percent sign (in column 3) is required to identify that this is a parameter entity, and not some other entity type. Second, note that there must be at least one space on either side of the percent sign. Third, the entity name parameter (found in column 5) is limited to seven (7) characters in length. Fourth, the replacement text parameter is enclosed in quotation marks (") and is the actual text that will be substituted whenever the entity name is referenced in the DTD.

In order to understand the meaning of "replacement text," it is helpful to know exactly how parameter entities work. In brief, whatever is in the replacement text is simply inserted into the DTD at the point where the parameter entity is referenced. The entity declaration can therefore be considered as a container for the replacement text, and when the entity is actually used (referenced), it is a pointer to the container. Note that the substitution takes place in the DTD when the computer is "parsing" (or "interpreting") the entire document: SGML declaration, document-type declaration (which includes the DTD), and author's document ("document instance"). This substitution is not something that the author does when writing (or is even really aware of). We can make this clearer by using an example from our WAE DTD from the previous chapter.

As mentioned above, there is a construct in the WAE DTD that is repeated in several places. It is the `text-matter` element types of *paragraph* and *list*, coded as `(p|l)+` in the DTD. If you look at Table 4-1, you can see "text matter" used as a container for this construct and then referenced in the table whenever those element types can appear. We can very easily rewrite this as a parameter entity as follows:

```
<!ENTITY % txm     "(p|l)+" >
```

Note first that we have preserved intact the structural content of the elements in the replacement text. Also note the entity name `txm`, which we will use in the DTD wherever it refers to this entity.

We now need to change the element type declarations to reference the entity. When we use a parameter entity in the DTD, the percent sign (the **parameter entity reference open**) is prefixed to the name and the name is followed by a semicolon ";" (the **reference close**). In general an element type declaration with a parameter entity reference within it might be written like this:

```
<!ELEMENT name  - - %entity;>
```

Or, to be specific, the WAE element type declaration for `sec` would be rewritten this way:

```
<!ELEMENT sec  - -  (shd?, (%txm; | ssec)+) >
```

From this example you may guess why these entities are called *parameter entities* - because they are referenced from the parameters of markup declarations. While in the WAE DTD we only use parameter entities in the content model parameter, they may also appear in the name parameter.

As with nested items in the element type declaration, we read entities from the inside out. It is quite simple; all we do is substitute the entity replacement text for the entity reference in the element type declaration. The `sec` element type declaration after the replacement of the entity reference would expand to this:

```
<!ELEMENT sec  - -  (shd?, ((p|1)+ | ssec)+) >
```

It is this expanded view of the element type declaration that you, as an author, will be dealing with. The use of entities in the DTD does not change the element types or their content models. When tagging a document, it makes no difference if the content models were written out in full or "streamlined" through the use of parameter entities. Entities simply allow for the removal of repeated text and the concentration of that text into a more convenient and readable format *in the DTD*.

To summarize our understanding of an *entity*, let us note the following:

1. Its pattern for declaration has its own "lay of the land," each parameter of the declaration having special meaning.

2. An entity name is *not* a GI, so we will not use it in tagging our documents.

3. An entity reference is a highly mobile "placeholder," functioning much like a *see* reference in an index or footnote. Its sole mission is to point to something else.

4. As a pointer or referencing device, a parameter entity reference points to items strictly within the DTD.

5. While we cannot use a parameter entity reference directly in marking up a document, it has several benefits we should be aware of:

   a. Having read the declaration of the entity once, the reader may "plug in" the replacement text everywhere that the entity is referenced.

   b. It is much easier to concentrate on central details of document structure where we have eliminated the verbose detail of a lengthy structure through entity references.

   c. For the maintainer of the DTD, he or she needs to make only a single change to the declaration of an entity, and the DTD will automatically apply that change to every reference to the entity throughout the entire DTD. There may be hundreds of such references, so this is a powerful motivation for the use of parameter entities.

Here is the entire WAE DTD rewritten to take advantage of parameter entities:

```
<!--                 Writers And Editors (WAE) DTD                -->

<!--        Entity Declarations                                   -->
<!ENTITY % txm       "(p|l)+" >

<!--        Element Type Declarations                             -->
<!--        ELEMENT   MINIMIZATION    CONTENT                      -->
<!--        =======   =============   =======                      -->
<!ELEMENT   manual    O O             (ti?, au*, sec+) >
<!ELEMENT   ti        - O             (#PCDATA) >
<!ELEMENT   au        - O             (#PCDATA) >
<!ELEMENT   sec       - -             (shd?, (%txm;  | ssec)+ ) >
<!ELEMENT   shd       - O             (#PCDATA) >
<!ELEMENT   ssec      - -             (sshd?, %txm;) >
<!ELEMENT   sshd      - O             (#PCDATA) >
<!ELEMENT   p         - O             (#PCDATA) >
<!ELEMENT   l         - -             (lhd?, lit+) >
<!ELEMENT   lhd       - O             (#PCDATA) >
<!ELEMENT   lit       - O             (#PCDATA | %txm;)+ >
```

Note that when we *reference* a parameter entity, we enclose the reference in a "%" (parameter entity reference open) delimiter and a ";" (reference close) delimiter.

7.4   The Need for Character Entities

We typically write a document in SGML using what is called ASCII (**A**merican **S**tandard **C**ode for **I**nformation **I**nterchange) text. The ASCII code contains all the letters (both upper- and lowercase), all the digits (0-9), some basic punctuation marks (comma, period, quote, etc.), and a few additional characters. But SGML is an international standard, and ASCII unfortunately does not support all the characters needed. For instance, it does not handle the diacritical marks used in most languages, such as the umlaut (Ä). We use character entities as our tool for addressing this issue. This is also the means of representing characters in our text which have special meaning to the SGML interpreter, such as the less-than sign "<", which indicates the start of a tag.

7.5   Declaring and Using Character Entities

Despite their similarity in name to the parameter entities described earlier, character entities are quite different. (Note: Character entities are a special case of general entities, as we noted above, meaning that we can reference them in places other than in declaration parameters.)

As an author you may (depending on the writing tools you are using) actually use character entities in marking your text. For example, if you wanted to mark the inequality expression, 5<7, you could use a character entity to represent the less-than sign. Fully marked, the same expression would then look like this:

```
5&lt;7
```

Note that we use the SGML delimiter characters "&" (called **entity reference open**) and ";" (called **reference close**) to *reference* (use) our declared general entity (including character entities).

In order to inform our DTD that "`lt`" is the name for the less-than sign, we need to declare it as an entity. Here is that declaration:

```
<!ENTITY  lt   "<" >
```

In the example, `lt` is the entity name and "<" is the replacement text.

Character entity declarations may also be used for characters that are not part of the standard ASCII set. Here is one such declaration:

```
<!ENTITY  smile    SDATA    "[smile ]" >
```

This is used to define a "smiley face." Notice the SGML keyword `SDATA`, which informs the computer that the replacement text is system-specific, that is, it will be processed differently for different types of systems. The author, however, does not need to worry about how it will be represented but can simply reference the entity when writing. The actual implementation of the character is the responsibility of the rendering system.

We may also expand the concept of character entities to handle longer pieces of text in general entities. Consider the situation where there is a particular phrase that is repeated many hundreds of times in a document. We would like there to be some minimum-keystroke shorthand to represent that phrase. The same procedure we use for declaring a single-character entity applies to an entity of a whole text string. In order to "store" the phrase *writers and editors* as an entity which we can reference with the code string "wae", we would add this declaration to our DTD:

```
<!ENTITY  wae   "writers and editors" >
```

And we would use the same means for referencing this entity as we did for the one above:

```
The popularization of SGML is of great interest to &wae; because it represents
a means of creating documents that are totally portable and highly reusable.
```

7.6   Summary of DTD Symbols

The shorthand that we developed in this chapter for our WAE entities is meant to make life easier: easier reading for us when we need to interpret a DTD and much easier work for us as writers, should we need to use a very "dumb" editor for marking up (tagging) a document. So far we have learned only a dozen grammatical marks that are used in a DTD, but these seem to cover nearly everything we need to interpret a DTD. Here is a list of those symbols:

<!	Opening delimiter string for a markup declaration
--	Comment delimiter string
ELEMENT	The SGML keyword for introducing an element type declaration
ENTITY	The SGML keyword for introducing an entity declaration
space	Delimiter for separating parameters of a declaration
()	Parentheses for delimiting content models and nested model groups, similar to parentheses in algebraic expressions. They force us to evaluate models from the inside out.
|	OR connector, denoting a choice between the items on either side
?	Denotes an item that is optional and may not be repeated
+	Denotes an item that is obligatory and may be repeated
*	Denotes an item that is optional and may be repeated
,	Connects two items that must appear in their stated order
#PCDATA	Keyword standing for plain text (any string of text)
SDATA	System-specific character data entity
>	Closing delimiter for a markup declaration

7.7   Modified WAE DTD

In this chapter we have enhanced our example in four ways:

1. We "collapsed" the DTD into a more readable format by declaring the entity txm.

2. We enabled the writer to use the less-than symbol by entering the name lt surrounded by the SGML entity reference open and close delimiters.

3. We encoded a frequently used phrase so that the writer need only enter a three-letter name to reference it.

4. We added a "smiley face" character to illustrate how characters outside the standard ASCII character set are implemented.

Now the WAE DTD, incorporating the entities described above, appears as follows (with the changes emphasized):

```
<!--              Writers And Editors (WAE) DTD              -->

<!--       Entity Declarations                              -->
<!ENTITY % txm              "(p|l)+" >
<!ENTITY   lt               "<" >
<!ENTITY   wae              "writers and editors" >
<!ENTITY   smile   SDATA    "[smile ]" >

<!--       Element Type Declarations                        -->
<!--       ELEMENT    MINIMIZATION      CONTENT              -->
<!--       =======    ============      =======              -->
<!ELEMENT  manual     O O               (ti?, au*, sec+) >
<!ELEMENT  ti         - O               (#PCDATA) >
<!ELEMENT  au         - O               (#PCDATA) >
<!ELEMENT  sec        - -               (shd?, (%txm; | ssec)+ ) >
<!ELEMENT  shd        - O               (#PCDATA) >
<!ELEMENT  ssec       - -               (sshd?, %txm;) >
<!ELEMENT  sshd       - O               (#PCDATA) >
<!ELEMENT  p          - O               (#PCDATA) >
<!ELEMENT  l          - -               (lhd?, lit+) >
<!ELEMENT  lhd        - O               (#PCDATA) >
<!ELEMENT  lit        - O               (#PCDATA | %txm;)+ >
```

Summary

Entities, as we studied them in this chapter, extend the writer's efficiency and the effectiveness of the document in significant ways. First, they enable us simply to create (declare) an entity once and then to reference it repeatedly within the DTD (parameter entities) or our own written text. Parameter entities dramatically simplify the appearance of the DTD, enhancing its readability.

Second, character entities allow us to enter virtually any printable character into our text, whether or not we find that character on our local keyboard. The SGML standard assures us that the rendering system (browser/viewer, typesetter, or whatever) will interpret the encoded special characters and simply make them happen. Again, the work of proper rendition has been redistributed from the writer to the particular presentation systems.

But perhaps the major benefit from entities is a longer-range one. Since entities are declared only once, this greatly lightens the writer's burden during the document's life cycle of revisions. With entities, the writer and editor need only to modify the language within each entity's replacement text parameter (in the declaration), and those changes will be instantly and automatically installed.

We will return to the topic of entities in Chapter 10, in which we investigate how to collaborate on SGML projects in writing workgroups. There we shall go beyond parameters, characters, and text strings to significant portions of large documents.

CHAPTER 8

ATTRIBUTES
Enhancing the Power of Markup

SGML terms introduced or reviewed:

attribute, attribute definition, attribute definition list, attribute definition list declaration, attribute list, content model, element type, element type entity, entity declaration, entity reference, generic identifier

Overview

Attributes are a means of specifying properties of elements. They constitute our third major topic of markup (after elements and entities). We consider both how to declare attributes formally and how we add attributes to the markup in order to convey a richer level of information about its elements. Much of the extended usefulness ("intelligence") of a marked-up document in fact lies in "value added" that we impart through attributes. We look closely at attribute markup as demonstrated both in our WAE example DTD and then in a real-world document. We suggest some notable benefits that attribute markup brings to the document.

8.1 Declaring and Using Markup

In declaring element types and entities to generate a minimal SGML-compliant document, we have clearly seen in the previous two chapters that there are really two "faces" of markup. We (acting as DTD designers) first *declare an element type or entity* within the document type definition (DTD). In Chapter 6 we dealt with the element type and looked in close detail at each parameter of its standard declaration. Its own syntax (writing rules) specifies the order of each portion of the declaration and what special standard symbols we may use. And in Chapter 7 we studied the entity and the standard syntax for its declaration.

Having declared these objects, we are then able to *use* them in adding markup to our text. We add this markup in order to convey information about the data[1]. Note once again that markup does

---

not intrude into the semantic content of the document itself. That is why we emphasize that markup conveys information *about* the data. It does not add information *to* the data. This rather subtle distinction is important for us to keep in mind because we aim always for the data of a document and the markup of a document to maintain their independence one from the other. The use of SGML enables us (and the computer), to keep the data and markup separate, even though both data and markup combine to make up the text of a document.

There are many kinds of markup declarations possible in SGML, 13 in all to be exact. Of these we have studied element type, entity and comment. True, a comment is a rather "degenerate case" of a declaration because it doesn't define anything, but it is a declaration nonetheless, following SGML rules for that declaration. We are about to study the attribute as our third major markup consideration. As with the element type and entity, the attribute also has strict syntactic rules both for declaration and for use in markup of the document instance.

In this chapter's discussion we need to reiterate a priority that should be shared by all writers and editors but which may get stifled or sidetracked among the details of syntactic formalism. Our assumption is that we focus throughout the entire writing process—creating text, declaring markup items, and adding and validating markup—on the *data* (i.e., the information content) of the document. In this book and in our exercises we tend to dwell on markup and on the various details of declaration. This is an author's natural reaction during this introductory study, inasmuch as SGML is somewhat novel, rather difficult at first, highly concise and totally rule-driven. So we are tempted to concentrate on becoming familiar and comfortable with SGML, mastering its precise rules so that we can apply all of this to productive work.

In addition to emphasizing our focus on data, we make a strong case in this chapter that our enhancement of the data through markup for attributes constitutes a significant added value to the data. But we must keep firmly in mind that all of this apparatus for markup is to convey explicitly certain critical information that *already exists in or about the data*. We add the apparatus because this sort of information is normally not explicit within the data itself but is derived from it. For example, the elements of a book's structure have been with us practically forever, although we have relied on human intuition to deduce that structure: front matter, body, end matter. We added the SGML apparatus of element types, declared and applied as markup, only to make that structure explicit. We are again emphasizing this in order to insist that we continue to focus on the data and that attributes are yet another way of making explicit what is already inherent in the data though somewhat imprecisely defined.

1. Remember that the term "data" used here means the information content of the document, that is, the part that you write. It does not include the markup.

8.2   How Attributes "Fit" with Elements

The elements of a document are, by classical definition, the structural building blocks of the document. We emphasized this in Chapter 6 in our discussion of structure. We noted that sections, headers, paragraphs, lists, list items, and the like are *structural* items. We also noted that a well-structured document is *indented*. That is, the various building blocks have a hierarchical or treelike relationship among themselves. Paragraphs belong within chapters, list items belong within lists, and chapters belong within sections, which in turn belong within complete books. SGML, with its syntactic formalism, offers a convenient and concise way to express those structural relationships among the elements of any type of document. The element then is purely structural, at least as we used it in Chapter 6.

The formal declaration of the element type (speaking now in the SGML sense) seemed to be minimal. The syntactic rule we presented in Chapter 6 allowed us to state the element type's formal name (in proper SGML form, which we would use in tagging the element), and told us whether start- and end-tags are required ("minimization"), the occurrence and order of all subelements ("content model"), and constraints (if any) to the occurrence of elements of that type.

So whether we consider the element in the rather intuitive (traditional) sense or in the formal (SGML) sense, an element seems to be a very minimal concept for describing a document. In fact, we were so emphatic about structure in earlier chapters that we may have led you to believe that SGML was only about structure.

But there are clearly more qualities that pertain to the elements of a document than simply how each element fits within the structural hierarchy of the document. And this is particularly true at higher levels of the document. For example, in the user's manual for a brand-new machine, the technical writers need to identify the revision or draft level of each chapter. For a sensitive document, the security level information—classified, restricted, secret, top secret, or unrestricted (released)—needs to accompany the document. If it is military related, then the document needs to bear the identification of the military branch to which it applies: army, navy, and so forth.

These examples remind us of the information that we fill in on paper cover pages that accompany hard-copy drafts through traditional authoring processes. This is essential information, not an *addition to* the data of the document itself, but *pertaining to* the data. And the element need not be a character-based element. A figure in a draft copy needs to bear information about where it is coming from ("line art from Graphics, file #3.1.4," or "photo from Communications file, Board members," for example). The point is that for electronic authoring and publication, we cannot rely on hard-copy cover pages and blue-line references to produce and deliver the document. All that essential information *about* these various elements must occur in the electronic document itself. And we must not invade or intrude into the data proper. So how are we to accomplish this?

SGML offers us a very straightforward and explicit means of adding this sort of information: the **attribute**. If you are a writer and if you related to the discussion in the preceding two paragraphs, then you already know what motivates the need for attributes in electronic markup and publication. The information the attributes bear about a document is the sort of information *about* the document that we have manipulated all along: revision and draft levels, security and clearance levels, and physical location of graphic materials, just to cite a few examples. So there is nothing revolutionary about the concept of attributes. There is, as you might expect, a standard method for defining attributes and then for using them in markup. But before we launch into formal discussion about the syntax of attributes, we need to emphasize two basic notions.

First, an attribute does not stand alone, but is always related to some object, usually an element. We hinted at that above; all of our examples dealt with some structural element: book, manual, chapter, for example.

Second, with SGML attributes we can accomplish far more than simply to transplant editorial procedures from hard-copy to electronic format. Defining and using attributes allows us to enhance the document in ways not even possible with traditional hard-copy. That is why we titled this chapter "Enhancing the Power of Markup," Marking the document with attributes is truly adding value to the document. In fact, a large part of the usefulness of an SGML document derives precisely from markup for attributes.

So let us move to attributes via two definitions: the formal one and an informal working definition. The SGML Standard 8879 says that an "attribute (of an element)" is "a characteristic quality, other than type or content" (ISO 8879, §4.9). This offers us a hint of how comprehensive the notion is, because it says that every quality of an element *besides its type or content* is an attribute. "Type," we recall, is simply its semantic role in the document ("article," "book," "manual," or "chapter," for example). And "content" is what we define formally in the content model parameter of the element type's declaration (an article's "(fm, bdy, appm?, bm?)," for example). So everything else we wish to *say about* the element we express through attributes. In a non-writing context, we might observe that "passenger car" is like our "manual," which we said was a document type and a topmost element. So a passenger car is a *type* of motor vehicle just as "manual" is a type of document. But there are attributes of a passenger car which we use to describe it in terms beyond its mere type and components. For example, "beige" would be one possible value of the *attribute* "color," and "automatic" might be a value for the *attribute* "transmission type."

So, to expand on the formal definition of an attribute, we say that an attribute of an element is a quality of that element which displays the following traits:

1. It attaches to its element type and persists in that relationship for all elements of that type throughout the document.

2. It bears some family relationship to the element.

3. It expands and enhances the functionality of the markup we use for the document.

4. It adds information about the particular element.

We should note first that when we use an attribute to *add information about* an element that we are not *adding meaning to* the data of the document. The internal content of the data, with all of its creativity, will forever remain the sole responsibility of the writer, regardless of any markup schemes or electronic technologies involved.

Second, we observe that it is tempting to co-opt attributes of an element for the purpose of specifying how the element should appear. We have emphasized in previous chapters that the author need not concern him or herself with presentation details (whether list items should be numbered, lettered, or bulleted, for example). And yet the attribute, by definition, seems to invite just this sort of "meddling" with the presentation or production of the text. After all, to specify certain presentation details does not really intrude into the author's domain of the text and its contents. And to add stage directions like reverse video to the title of a book indeed only adds information about the element. But the larger issue here is that the motivation for SGML in the first place is to assure *portability* of a document to as many presentation technologies and platforms as possible and *reusability* of a document for as many different functions as possible. So when we include any system-specific production or presentation instructions as attributes, we defeat the central purpose of SGML. Not every viewing device will even have reverse video. And there will be certain environments in which local style guides will dictate a list numbering scheme that the author may not have even considered. We raise this issue for two reasons: (1) Attributes are a handy way to specify presentation details, and some users of SGML exploit them for just this purpose, but (2) the standard strongly discourages the practice, for the reasons we just noted. Appendix B of the SGML standard, "Basic Concepts," expresses this warning in a more formal manner:

> A descriptive tag normally includes the element's generic identifier (GI) and may include attributes as well. The GI is normally a noun; the attributes are nouns or adjectives that describe significant characteristics of the [element described by the] GI. (The use of verbs or formatting parameters, which are procedural rather than descriptive, is strongly discouraged because it defeats the purpose of generalized markup.)
>
> — ISO 8879, §B.5 "Attributes"

So, however tempting it might be, you should avoid using attributes to specify presentation related information. We have stressed in this book the importance of structure rather than appearance so that you will be aware of the difference and how each relates to the philosophy of SGML. Because of the generalized nature of SGML, you will find areas (such as attributes) where you can specify processing or presentation related issues while still remaining *technically* SGML compliant. Unfortunately, every one of these items will make your document less portable, less scalable, and less reusable, thereby defeating the major benefits of using SGML.

8.3   How Attributes Are Used

Before we turn to the mechanics of understanding the formal definitions of attributes in a particular DTD, let us first consider a few specific examples of attributes—qualities or characteristics of a document's elements-which we might likely find or use in our day-to-day work. We shall then summarize our discussion by noting some significant payoffs or value added that result from enriching the marked-up text with attributes.

8.3.1   Figure or Table Identifications and References

Figures and tables are typically floating elements, which means that they are not tied to a specific location in the text, but only to a general location. The exact location of the figure or table is determined by the presentation system, and, because the position may change from system to system, the element is said to "float." In traditional cut-and-paste production we literally had to place physically the actual graphic or a dummy of the correct size onto the camera-ready page layout. And even with electronic page production software, the figure or table must appear precisely on the screen where it will be printed, with the related text wrapping or flowing around it. In SGML we associate a table or figure with its related text not by physical layout but by means of attributes. So within the running text we insert a referencing tag, whose "pointing-to" attribute would be the internal identification of a table. Conversely, the actual table itself, however it is marked up, will include an identification attribute. The value of that attribute will be that same internal identification that the running text needs in order to associate itself with the table.

8.3.2   Indexable Terms

Nowadays it is a rather trivial task for a computer to generate an index to a document. But indexes can be smart or dumb, depending on the effort put into design and markup of the document. If we rely solely on the computer to produce an index after the text is all prepared, then it will likely produce a "full-text index", in which nearly all of the substantial words of the document appear. However, if we use markup to identify each term that we think is important enough to appear in the index, then we might tag each such term and then include a reference point or locator for that item within the text. The identification of that reference would again be an attribute of the indexed item.

8.3.3   Type of Signature Authority

For a document that requires sign-off at various levels, it is necessary for the markup to indicate the type of sign-off that appears in the document. (This sign-off could even be electronic.) We would assign a value to a "signature-type" attribute, depending on whether the signer is the preparer of the document, an approver, a reviewer, one who concurs, or some other type of signature authority. ("sigtype" is the actual name of the attribute in MIL-M-28001A.)

8.3.4 Security

A document (or some portion of a document) may be marked for security levels, again by means of an attribute to which we assign a choice of values: unrestricted, classified, secret, and top secret, for example.

8.3.5 References to External Identification Schemes

Electronic documentation systems have traditionally relied on keywords as a means of categorizing documents and then of locating and retrieving them. It enhances the markup of the document considerably if we cite the authority we use in assigning a keyword. One such authority is the list of Library of Congress Subject Headings. So "LCSH" could be the value of an "authority" attribute for a keyword element.

8.4 Enhancing the WAE DTD with an Attribute

One of the most valuable contributions a writer can make to the management of a document is to note the date of last revision every time a change is made. With traditional hard-copy manuals this often takes the form of a date automatically printed in the page footer or header. Word processing software supports this well, since the date is usually stored in a code that is separate from the text of the document and automatically changes every time the document is resaved. If there is no printed document however, then we must ask how the revision date can "ride" along with the document if it is not hand-entered in the data of the document itself.

One readily available means of a separate-but-attached date is by storing the date as an attribute of the document. We would like to be able to mark a document so as to "date stamp" it. We also want to record who the last writer was to revise the document. And we want to do this without having to write the date and name in the data content of the document itself. Here is how we propose to mark the document, using a tag containing the GI of the element and two attributes:

```
<manual last-rev="12-DEC-1995" last-au="Mark Galioto">
```

Note that there is a space in the tag between the generic identifier and the attribute name "last-rev" and another space separating the two attributes. Note also that we assign each attribute's value to its attribute by means of the "=" sign. The value being assigned to the attribute is enclosed in quotation marks (" "). (This example should make it clear why we do not say that "tag" and "GI" are the same thing; the tag may contain many different kinds of information in addition to the GI.)

Let us now revisit the DTD for our WAE document to modify the document element type manual so that it will accept the markup we introduced above. We recall that a manual element is purely a container of subelements: title, author(s), and section(s). Moreover, we agreed that both the start-tag and the end-tag could be omitted. Here is the formal declaration of the element type manual from our DTD:

```
<!ELEMENT   manual   O O      (ti?, au*, sec+) >
```

We define attributes for an element type by means of an **attribute definition list**. In this case we need to create an **attribute definition list** containing two members, last-rev and last-au. Here is the formal **attribute definition list declaration**, which defines the attribute list for manual:

```
<!ELEMENT   manual   O O      (ti?, au*, sec+) >
<!ATTLIST   manual
            last-rev  CDATA     #REQUIRED
            last-au   CDATA     #IMPLIED          >
```

Note the following items in this markup declaration:

1. We use the keyword ATTLIST to identify the attribute definition list declaration.

2. The name that follows ATTLIST is the name of the element type to which the list of attributes belongs. The <!ATTLIST...> declaration does not need to appear directly below the element declaration because the name of the element type is what links the element type declaration to the attribute definition list declaration.

3. The next field of the attribute is the value or type of value that we may assign to a particular attribute. Both of these attributes take values that are simple character data.

4. The first attribute *must* have a value; that is the meaning of REQUIRED. Assigning a value for the second attribute last-au is optional. Although IMPLIED does not really mean "optional," we will assume for practical purposes that it does.

5. The order in which the attributes appear in the declaration does not dictate the order in which they may appear in the tag.

   This

   ```
   <manual last-rev="12-DEC-1995" last-au="Mark Galioto">
   ```

   is identical to this:

   ```
   <manual last-au="Mark Galioto" last-rev="12-DEC-1995">
   ```

At first it may seem like a lot of work to remember the attributes for each element type and what values might be assigned to them. The encouraging news is that most SGML authoring tools will present a list of the attributes for each element and prompt for values as required. In a less sophisticated environment the writer really just needs to remember the required attributes. Once again, the ability to read a DTD at the level we teach in this book has significant benefits for the writer.

Table 8-1 is a summary of the fields of an **attribute definition list declaration**, using our familiar numbered box notation.

Table 8-1: Attribute definition list declaration parts

1	2	3	4	5	6	7
opening delimiter and declaration name	separator	parameter	separator	parameter	separator	closing delimiter
<!ATTLIST	one or more spaces	*element type name*	one or more spaces	*attribute definition list*	zero or more spaces	>

Table 8-2: Attribute definition list parts

1	2	3	4	5
parameter	separator	parameter	separator	parameter
attribute name	one or more spaces	*declared value*	one or more spaces	*default value*

Look first at box 3, the *element type name* parameter. This is what ties the attribute definition list declaration to a particular element type. The name given here must match exactly the name in the element type declaration. In addition, note that the parameter in box 5 is an **attribute definition list**. The word "list" implies that there may be more than one item in this field. It needs to be broken down into separate nested parameters in order to understand how to interpret each attribute definition properly. We can see that breakdown in Table 8-2, "Attribute Definition List Parts."

So, using our new attribute definition list declaration as an example, we note that the declaration begins with <!ATTLIST, followed by a space, followed by the name of the element type to which the list of attributes (last-rev and last-au) belongs. Then follows the attribute definition list itself, each member of which is laid out just as the second box specifies: name of the attribute (last-rev and last-au), declared value allowed for the attribute (character data in this case), and the "default" value to be assigned to the attribute when the writer doesn't specify a value in the start-tag. In this simple example we see only two options, neither really matching our notion of "default"; we shall look shortly at another example in which "default" makes more sense. Here #REQUIRED means that the writer *must* assign a value to last-rev. A value for *last-au* is optional.

Having thus modified our WAE DTD, the full modified form now appears as follows:

```
<!--            Writers And Editors (WAE) DTD          -->

<!--      Entity Declarations                          -->
<!ENTITY % txm              "(p|l)+" >
<!ENTITY   lt               "<" >
<!ENTITY   wae              "writers and editors" >
<!ENTITY   smile   SDATA    "[smile ]" >

<!--      Element Type Declarations                    -->
<!--      ELEMENT   MINIMIZATION   CONTENT             -->
<!--      =======   ============   =======            -->
<!ELEMENT  manual    O O             (ti?, au*, sec+) >
<!ATTLIST manual
               last-rev  CDATA       #REQUIRED
               last-au   CDATA       #IMPLIED  >
<!ELEMENT  ti        - O             (#PCDATA) >
<!ELEMENT  au        - O             (#PCDATA) >
<!ELEMENT  sec       - -             (shd?, (%txm; | ssec)+ ) >
<!ELEMENT  shd       - O             (#PCDATA) >
<!ELEMENT  ssec      - -             (sshd?, %txm;) >
<!ELEMENT  sshd      - O             (#PCDATA) >
<!ELEMENT  p         - O             (#PCDATA) >
<!ELEMENT  l         - -             (lhd?, lit+) >
<!ELEMENT  lhd       - O             (#PCDATA) >
<!ELEMENT  lit       - O             (#PCDATA | %txm;)+ >
```

8.5   Markup for Attributes in a Workplace Document

Now that we understand the basics of reading the formal definition of attributes and marking according to that definition, let us finish the chapter with an example drawn from a more complex document.

Here is an attribute definition list declaration for the `doc` element type from a military DTD (MIL-M-28001):

```
<!ATTLIST doc
          service    (%service;)                    #REQUIRED
          docid      CDATA                          #IMPLIED
          docstat    (revision | change
                     | prelim | draft | formal)     "formal" ─ default value
          mantype    (standard | card |
                     decal)                          "standard"
          %secur;                                                      >
```

There is very little in this declaration that is new to us. We should note that in the "default value" position `docstat` has a value of "formal," meaning that if the writer does not assign a value to `docstat`, then it will take the value "formal" by default. Likewise `mantype` will assume the value "standard" if we do not assign some value from among "standard," "card," or "decal."

The other notable characteristic of this declaration is that the designers of the DTD have "hidden" certain items beneath entity references: `service` (for which branch of the U.S. military) and `secur` (for security attributes). By now we are well trained, when we see an entity reference, to go find the declaration of the entity. The two declarations we need are as follows:

```
<!ENTITY % service "af | navy | army | mc | dla | cg" >


<!ENTITY % secur
          "security   (u | c | s | ts)    #IMPLIED
          restrict    NMTOKENS            #IMPLIED
          release     NMTOKENS            #IMPLIED" >
```

The most effective way to read the attribute definition list is to "plug in" the replacement text of both of the entities, just as we did earlier in Chapter 7. When we do that, we find that the original declaration expands out to its full form as follows:

```
<ATTLIST doc
          service    (af | navy | army | mc | dla | cg)    #REQUIRED
          docid      CDATA                                 #IMPLIED
          docstat    (revision | change |
                     prelim | draft | formal)              "formal"
          mantype    (standard | card |
                     decal)                                "standard"
          security   (u | c | s | ts)                      #IMPLIED
          restrict   NMTOKENS                               #IMPLIED
          release    NMTOKENS                               #IMPLIED  >
```

Summary

The central notion of SGML attributes is simple enough: (1) Elements can have properties associated with them; (2) those properties can assume values. The designer of a DTD attaches those properties using attributes. And the writer of the document assigns values to those properties. For declaring properties and assigning values to them, we might have expected a significant amount of messy, verbose detail. But the formal SGML mechanisms of attribute definition and markup are highly consistent and concise, no matter what sort of properties we are handling. For attributes, more than for any other aspect of SGML, it is highly beneficial for the writer and editor to understand the underlying syntax and formalism in order to do markup effectively.

As we have tried to show, much of the liveliness and smartness we anticipated in Chapter 1 is in fact the product of attributes. Furthermore attributes are at the heart of hypertext documents, as we will see in Chapter 9. And finally, attributes, as we will see in Chapter 14, are among the chief enablers of HyTime. Therefore consider your time in this chapter to be well spent!

HYPERTEXT
Editing for Interactive Navigation

Terms introduced or reinforced:

anchor, attribute, attribute definition list, attribute specification, attribute specification list, content model, default value, generic identifier (GI), hyperlink, ID, ID reference value, ID value, IDREF, unique identifier

Overview

Earlier we stressed and then reviewed the important SGML baseline recommendation that you as an author should be concerned exclusively with the structure of your document and that you should practically disregard the final rendition (or presentation) of the document, be that rendition on page, screen, or multimedia CD-ROM. But for a hypertext implementation, while you may still ignore appearance, you are definitely not free to ignore the final presentation altogether. It is necessary for you to understand (1) the definition and behavior of a hypertext document type and (2) the preparation of a hypertext document using SGML tags.

You should be aware that in discussing hypertext we will be viewing different objects or different "faces" of hypertext. Sometimes we will be looking at the reader's computer screen, just as we have often considered the final rendition or representation of any SGML text. Sometimes we will view hypertext apparatus in the underlying SGML source document, just as we have done for other details in the previous three chapters. And sometimes we will look at how that apparatus is defined in the DTD. We will try to make it clear just which "face" of hypertext we are viewing at any particular moment.

The concept of hypertext is very straightforward. And so is the *basic* set of enabling SGML markup constructs. The issue becomes somewhat complex because there is a wide variety of designers' preferences in dealing with hypertext, and so there are differences among the various applications. Another complicating factor is the terminology of hypertext. Not only must we use SGML terminology accurately, but there is a separate set of non-standard terms that hypertext authors use. This non-standard set does not always bear a one-for-one relationship to the standard terms. Moreover there are occasionally overlapping meanings among the terms of the two sets. This mix of terminology makes it necessary for you to be alert to the "real" meaning when you hear hypertext terms used. In this book we use only the SGML terminology for hypertext. Our approach to learning hypertext will be the same as for the other topics in this book: a conceptual and intuitive discussion first, followed by the theoretic and formal mechanisms essential to making hypertext work.

9.1   Linear versus Non-linear Text

Hypertext is a variety of document representation whereby the author enables the reader to navigate through the document by means of built-in links: (1) links to go "out" to related text, tables, figures, and any other material, and (2) a mechanism that gets the reader "back" from that linked-to material to wherever he or she was located prior to the link. At least that is the way an on-line hypertext document appears to the reader.

But hypertext is a concept that is much older than electronic on-line documents. When we are seriously reading a print document of practically any variety, there is something at some point in the document that prompts us *go somewhere else*. It may be a definition of a word or phrase, a footnote, an endnote, or a cross-reference, even a reference to a separate book altogether. Or it may be a reference to a table or to a figure. If we choose to act on the prompt, we automatically do the following:

1. Insert a place holder in the current location of our reading. The place holder may be a finger, a bookmark, a paper clip, a sticky note, or just a mental note.

2. Go to the object that is referenced—the footnote, table, endnote, cross-referenced section or whatever—and read or examine that material.

3. Return to the original location, the one with the place holder.

One notable and familiar wrinkle in this sequence is that the referenced material—the cross-referenced section, for example—may in turn lead us to yet another footnote, endnote, and so on. This will require multiple fingers, sticky notes, or mental notes in order to get back to our original location in the original document.

This activity of marking a place, going somewhere else, and then returning is so common that we may not recognize that this type of navigation contrasts sharply with how we normally think of most traditional text. We think of most prose, particularly artistic prose, as being of the top-to-bottom variety. The reader is supposed to begin at the beginning and read in *linear* fashion to the end, page after page and chapter after chapter. But even to stop and look up an undefined word while reading a novel represents *non-linear* navigation.

Some print documents are non-linear by design. An encyclopedia, for example, is designed specifically for non-linear reading, as is most reference literature. Does anyone ever sit down to read all of the material from the "S" volume from start to finish, that is, in linear fashion? And the readers of most technical documentation read their material in a non-linear manner, even if the technical writers intend for it to be read cover to cover, start to finish.

So an electronic hypertext document is really only an extension of how we have been reading reference material all along. The most easily recognizable visual feature of a hypertext on-line document is the highlighted word within a block of text which, when "clicked on," causes a related block of text or table or figure to appear. A hypertext document, by definition then, is *interactive*. In a sense, the reader is present, even in the original design and composition of the document. The author anticipates all of the reader's possible choices, as he or she works through the final presentation on the screen. True, a page designer for traditional text also has the reader in mind, and that design certainly has impact on the composition of the manuscript. And the layout of each page should enhance the reader's understanding of the text. But that text, like practically all text from the dawn of writing, was meant to be read sequentially and "from the top."

The notable exception to this model is the reference book, which the user approaches with a specific piece of content in mind. Here the reader does not begin at the beginning but goes as directly as possible to the text block(s) of interest. Reference documents come in all varieties: telephone books, encyclopedias, price lists, parts manuals, city directories, and membership lists, to name a few paper-based examples. But they need not reside on paper. They may be electronic (paperless or on-line): airline reservation tables, CD-ROM encyclopedias, safety regulations, state legislative codes, legal cases. And as we have noted above, even the most traditional printed media may entail non-linear navigation.

Hypertext applies the reference book (non-linear) metaphor to all types of documents. The assumption is that the author will not lock the reader into linear, read-me-from-the-top navigation. The text, typically using intuitive visual cues, must invite the reader occasionally to hop over to some related text or graphic that does not physically happen to appear on the current screen. Moreover, once the reader lands in that target text or graphic, there may appear yet more possibilities for linking to yet other related portions of the document. Or the links may take the reader even into separate documents. The document thus is "intelligent," in the sense that we described "intelligence" in "Smart Document Architecture" in Chapter 1.

By means of its visual linking cues—typically, highlighted or reverse-video "hot" portions (words or phrases)—hypertext carries along with the document the intelligence necessary to open the document up, allowing the reader to navigate through the material precisely as he or she desires. The reader may be either a whimsical browser or a serious reference user with a well-defined question.

The other ingredient to intelligence for user-directed navigation is that the reader must always be able to return, backing up through the navigation path to return to precisely where he or she was before the first link was traversed. There are variations on this scenario of navigation, but virtually every hypertext product offers this model of link-to and return-back capability.

9.2   Anticipating Non-Linear Navigation

Structuring a hypertext document assumes first the same sort of design work that we do for any conforming SGML document. All of the usual structural elements like front matter, body, back matter, section, paragraph, list, and the like will apply to a hypertext document as well, and we will tag the document accordingly. We might refer to "structure" in this sense as "static structure." This structural definition of the document provides the SGML parser/validator and the rendering software with a map of how the various elements of the document fit together.

But the uniqueness of the hypertext document is that we must think not only of the *static* structure—how the elements are joined and how they are related—but also of its *dynamic* structure. This entails our anticipating how every possible reader of the document may choose to navigate within (and beyond) the document during a browsing/viewing session. In other words, a dynamic view of document structure introduces the notion of the reader's pathways—every possible pathway that he or she may elect to follow.

A good example of the importance of dynamic structure would be a government report, in which one of the primary user-accommodation problems is the treatment of acronyms. Traditional style books will dictate that each acronym should be fully spelled out first, with the acronym appearing parenthetically immediately after the full form: "Defense Advanced Research Projects Agency (DARPA)." Thereafter we are free simply to use the acronym DARPA. This is an adequate rule because in the traditional document the author expects the reader to begin at the beginning. In this case "DARPA" will be spelled out at first occurrence, so the reader had better start at the beginning or expect to flip back to the first occurrence as the need for re-definition arises.

The hypertext author, on the other hand, will anticipate that the document may be part of an on-line retrieval system and that the user may "land" anywhere in the document. This may be because only an internal portion of the document is of interest to the reader, or it may be the result of some hypertext link from somewhere that brought the user to this internal section of the document. Either way, the notion of "start of the document" (where we were supposed to have described our terminology in full) does not fit within the hypertext model. Thinking dynamically tells us to insert "hot links" (hypertext cues) at every occurrence of the acronym, so that the reader may optionally just "click and view" the glossary term and then return immediately to the running text.

The same concept applies to figures (including tables and graphics). In traditional page layout, we normally place the figure immediately next to the most prominent first occurrence of the text relating to that figure. Then we include a "back reference" if further running text alludes to material in the figure (or table). But the hypertext author is not concerned with physical proximity of the figure, and so there is no issue of first occurrence of allusion or of forward- or back-referencing. Again, such terms as "before," "after," "forward," and "backward" pertain to the linear (traditional) document. Hypertext, on the other hand, implies that *every* allusion to a figure (or table) in the text should bear some cue that prompts the reader to click at will and to link to the figure from anywhere in the document. And that applies across document boundaries as well; a figure or table may well support text in several books in a set, for example. That cue will likely be some "hot text" (highlighted text which alludes to material in a figure or table) that will take him or her immediately to the figure or table.

9.3   Some Essential Terminology

Now that we have discussed the overall concept of hypertext, we need to survey the underlying mechanics so that you can accomplish the two hypertext activities required of an SGML author: (1) read the text to locate all possible hypertext links and (2) use SGML markup to enable hypertext navigation. We need first to establish a working definition of two essential terms for discussing links.

We should point out that while we have frequently used the term "link" in discussing "hypertext links" there is a formal SGML keyword LINK which is absolutely unrelated to our informal use of "link" in this discussion. (The SGML link is a "processing link," which is of interest to systems specialists and advanced users of SGML.) When we say "link," we are using the term as an abbreviation for hyperlink, which is defined in the HyTime standard (see Chapter 14).

As we promised in the chapter overview, the basic mechanics of hypertext are intuitive and simple. In a traditional book, there is some location in the text at which we encounter some prompt which makes us pause, go to some other material, read that material, and then return back. The prompt may be an explicit footnote or endnote reference or a reference to a table or graphic. We call that prompt (at which we hold our place with our finger) one anchor of a hyperlink. The referenced object (the footnote, table, or graphic) is the other anchor. The relationship between the two is the hyperlink itself. In rather general terms we could say that a hyperlink is a connection between two objects at different places in a document, with those objects being any sort of thing contained in the document (including written material, tables, figures, etc.). Later in this chapter we will discuss and use *hyperlink elements*, SGML elements which we will insert at the locations of those prompts.

But *linking to* some other text represents only half the apparatus of hypertext links. If the link is to "know" where to find that paragraph, section, chapter or whatever, then that linked-to text must bear some sort of identification. We will look below at just how the mechanics of that identification work in SGML. Every portion of text, every table, every graphic to which a hyperlink points must have a name by which it can be designated as an anchor (another term defined in the HyTime standard).

So for now, let us use the term *hyperlink* to mean "pointer to something else in the document." And we will use *anchor* to mean "something that a hyperlink can point to." We will also continue to use "link" as an abbreviation for "hyperlink."

9.4 Designing for Hypertext

Our design task for installing hypertext links in a document is first *to identify where links should occur.* At first glance, this would seem to be trivial, since we can easily recall how references to figures and tables and "see page..." references to text look in a traditional document. But as we have noted above, the electronic medium allows for more buried "intelligence" in the text and more flexibility and interactivity with the reader. This opportunity in turn makes greater demands on the author. A document is typically loaded with "candidate links." The author's task is to identify those candidates. We find that there are three distinct classes of link "candidates," each requiring different levels of electronic authoring skill. We identify these three classes as explicit, implicit, and value added.

The second task, as we mentioned above, is to identify every linked-to item of text, and every table and graphic that a link may point to. That is, we must identify all of these as *potential referenced anchors* of the links.

9.4.1 Explicit Links

A document typically contains references and citations to items found elsewhere in the document or in some other document. There may be such cues as "see page...," "Table No....," "Figure No....," In addition, footnotes in a traditional text are best interpreted as explicit links in hypertext, inasmuch as there is no "foot" in an electronic display. The skill required for identifying explicit links is minimal. Even a robot could spot these candidates and insert hypertext links.

9.4.2 Implied Links

In every document there are items which do not explicitly prompt the reader to go look at some text or figure or table but which strongly *imply* linking. We mentioned acronyms above. In traditional editing we offer full spelling first and then expect the reader physically to turn pages back to that first occurrence for an explanation of the acronym. In an electronic hypertext document every acronym is ideally an implied link. It should contain a link to its fully spelled-out form or to a glossary entry. True, there is no "see" or "refer to..." in the running text, but the document's own conventions should enable the reader to spot these "implied" links easily. We call them "implied" because their very occurrence implies that they should contain a built-in link.

9.4.3 "Value-Added" Links

The most valuable contribution an author can lend to the intelligence of a document is to add links that are neither obvious to a robot (explicit) or readily obvious to a superficial reader (implied). These are links which are discernible only to a subject specialist, someone well versed in the material which the document treats. You may identify some phrase or word which would benefit greatly from a link to some background presentation located somewhere else in the text or in another document in the database. Or it may, for example, be some geographical name for which a map would be of great help. The map may be totally separate from the document. But the author or electronic markup editor inserts such links to add additional specialized intelligence and therefore extra value to the document.

9.5   Basic SGML Hypertext Linking Apparatus

This is a good place to remind ourselves of something that may seem startling: There is no SGML command or keyword or predefined method for *doing* hypertext linking. Recall that the philosophy of SGML is simply to *enable* whatever functionality we would like to see for a document. How that happens is up to the software and hardware which implement that functionality. In other words, hypertext linking, like page appearance, is a matter of the document's presentation or rendition. This is virtually the same discussion we had earlier about markup, structure, and rendition. This may seem like subtle trivia at this point, but we raise the point because we are tempted to try to find or define something simple like *link* and *anchor* directly as SGML element types, just as we would do for paragraph, section, and the other structural items.

The only bad news therefore is that there is no "canned" *link* and *anchor* in SGML. But the great news is that SGML offers us all the ability to enable links and anchors with only two basic items: ID and IDREF. There are two things to note about these terms:

1. They are SGML "keywords" (i.e., words that are reserved for their original intended use, which we shall examine shortly) and are therefore capitalized in this book.

2. They are not generic identifiers (GIs) of elements. That is, they are not used in tags in the way that "<p>" or "<doc>" or "<shd>" are now familiar to us in our SGML repertoire. But ID and IDREF are keywords used in attribute definition lists.

As you recall from Chapter 8, we use attributes to enable an element to bear additional "freight" of some sort. In this case the "freight" is the hypertext enabling apparatus.

Let us review just enough of Chapter 8 to understand the function of an attribute. If we think of an element type as a *noun*, then an attribute functions as an *adjective*, enhancing its meaning in some way. So in the markup of an element, an attribute is something that may be part of a tag, enhancing the meaning of the element in some manner. If the author of a DTD decides that you *must* insert a particular attribute with a tag, then you must insert the attribute when you tag the document. This, you recall, was the meaning of REQUIRED as applied to attributes.

We are about to enhance our WAE DTD yet again, this time to provide markup to enable hypertext linking. We are going to do this by adding a new element and two attributes to the DTD.

First we will add the element txt-link to function as a "link" in the hypertext sense, and also to locate the initiating anchor of the link. The element txt-link in turn includes an attribute linkend, which identifies the other anchor (the reference subject). Next we add id[1] to identify a potential "anchor." But id is not an element. Rather it is an attribute which we are about to add to the element type p (paragraph) and to other element types as well. As we redesign our DTD, we shall use the SGML keywords IDREF and ID for attribute types (declared values). And we must keep in mind the following relationship:

1. We shall use IDREF as the declared value of the "linkend" attribute of txt-link, whose value is a pointer (the "ID") to some other text (the anchor of the hyperlink).

    Remember: *IDREF is part of the "link."*

2. We shall use ID as the declared value of the id attribute, serving to identify elements that could be the anchor of a link.

    Remember: *ID is part of the "target."*

9.6 Enhancing WAE for Hypertext Markup

The following discussion really serves two purposes. First, it is a conceptual and procedural approach to the modification of a DTD, our familiar WAE DTD in this case. But of even more importance is that it serves as a wrap-up of the previous three chapters on elements, entities, and attributes. In particular, it provides an example of attributes that is easy to follow.

Again, bear in mind that in this development we are going to be switching between informal discussion, marked up text, formal SGML syntax, the WAE DTD, and screen representation.

9.6.1 What Is Needed for a Hypertext Link

This is equivalent to asking how cross-references work in a traditional document. In both cases the author must first insert some sort of *link to* the cross-reference at some appropriate point in the document. This serves to indicate the presence of the link and also is its initiating anchor. In the traditional document we typically use "see," "see also," or simply a page number or chapter or section reference in parentheses. For the electronic document a hypertext link also requires a similar *link-to* apparatus.

---

1. Note the use of "id" as the attribute name here. This is a correct usage even though "ID" is also an SGML keyword. You are allowed to do this because SGML keeps user defined names distinct from keywords. SGML knows which is which by where they are used. In a rather loose way you may consider id (the attribute name) and ID (the declared value) to mean the same thing: a unique identifier for an element.

But the other component of the hypertext linking differs to a greater degree from that of the print document. In the traditional document, we can locate everything not only by chapter and section number but by page number as well. We simply say "see," followed by the name of the chapter, section, page, or numbered paragraph, and the reader can then turn to that location.

In the electronic document, the issue of locating a particular object in text is not so trivial. That is because, for the most part, SGML tagging remains unaware of the data (semantic) contents of the text. So even if a chapter or section bears a title, we cannot use a "see..." or "cross-reference..." tag that will magically know the start of a section simply by reading the text we provide for the title of the section. In addition, page numbering really does not exist, so we surely cannot say "see page 92," at least not without some complex DTD design. All of this means that if we wish to link to some particular object in the text, we must somehow identify or label that object. Moreover we must identify it uniquely (i.e., so that its identification belongs only to that object and to no other).

So there are two parts of the hypertext process: a link-to mechanism, and a unique identifier. Note that while the identifier of a particular object must be unique, there can be two, three, or thousands of link-to pointers to that object.

9.6.2   An Element Type for Doing Link-To

We are about to do just that for our WAE DTD, but as we said above, there is slightly more apparatus to invent along with the element type itself. The name of our new element type is txt-link. We call it that because it links to elements in the text. It would be possible to define element types linking to other types of objects, such as tables and figures.

Note that txt-link, unlike all of the other element types in our DTD thus far, does not contribute to the *hierarchical structure* of the document (how the various subordinated pieces fit with one another in a hierarchy or nesting relation). Instead, it introduces an additional structural dimension involving non-hierarchical relationships. We could say that this is the heart of the whole concept of hypertext: It adds a new dimension to the structure of the document.

9.6.3   What That Element Type Accomplishes

We know that we will insert a txt-link element into the text wherever we wish to offer the reader an opportunity to traverse a link to some other element. And we know that the tag for the txt-link must also identify the referenced anchor element (target). With that much in mind, we will add the attribute linkend to the txt-link element type.

Here are two separate excerpts from the description of a program operated by the Department of Energy. Each passage is marked with our new txt-link tag:

A CRADA**<txt-link linkend="gl.CRADA">** is a contractual agreement in which a DOE laboratory and one or more partners outside the federal government agree to collaborate, share costs, and pool the results from a particular R & D program.

DOE has developed a Small Business CRADA**<txt-link linkend="gl.CRADA">** and a modular CRADA**<txt-link linkend="gl.CRADA">**, both of which facilitate negotiation, development, and timely approval.

9.6.4   How We Mark the Anchor Element

The anchor element in this document is the paragraph which introduces and defines the acronym "CRADA." The name of the attribute with which we have "enhanced" the paragraph <p> tag is id. Here is that passage, together with the markup that uniquely identifies it.

<p id="gl.CRADA">CRADA: Cooperative Research and Development Agreement. A CRADA is a collaborative tool for gaining access to DOE laboratories, technologies, and expertise. DOE is seeking to increase the number and scope of collaborative R & D agreements with U.S. industry through the use of CRADAs.

9.7   Modifying WAE for Hypertext Linking

First we add the "link-to" element type, or initiating anchor, which we call txt-link. At the same time we must define an attribute linkend for the element type:

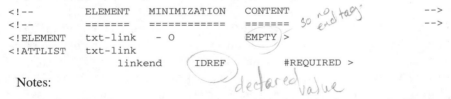

```
<!--        ELEMENT    MINIMIZATION    CONTENT                    -->
<!--        =======    ============    =======   so no end tag    -->
<!ELEMENT   txt-link    - O            EMPTY >
<!ATTLIST   txt-link
               linkend   IDREF              #REQUIRED >
                                                 declared value
```

Notes:

1. These elements do not *contain* any character data from the document, unlike the elements we have studied thus far. Its sole function is to locate one anchor and point to another. So there is no formal **content model** for the element. The SGML keyword EMPTY makes this fact explicit.

2. As an "empty" element, there can be no end-tag for its markup. So not only *may* the end tag be omitted, but there is also no end-tag even possible.

3. The keyword IDREF is SGML's built-in mechanism for saying "this is a reference to something out there." In formal terms we say that "the value of the attribute must be the ID of some element." In our examples it would be the ID of the referenced anchor (target) of the hyperlink.

4. The keyword REQUIRED as the **default value** for the attribute means that the author/editor *must* provide a value for the attribute, using an "=" sign. This is what we did in our markup in the example.

We will need to indicate in the DTD where the txt-link element may appear in the document. Our intuition tells us that it could appear virtually anywhere that character data appears. The simplest way to implement this is by defining a new parameter entity that will allow for repeating occurrences of PCDATA and txt-link elements. We will then reference that parameter entity from the content model of the declarations of the element types where we want to be able to insert txt-link elements. This is the entity declaration we will use:

```
<!ENTITY % lnkdta "(#PCDATA|txt-link)+" >
```

Next, the DTD must account for the referenced anchor, the destination of our hyperlink. We do this by expanding certain element types in our DTD to include the optional attribute id. Study the marked-up text above carefully to see how the start tag <p> now includes this attribute. This means that any paragraph in our document can now bear an id attribute which uniquely identifies that paragraph as a possible hypertext anchor. Moreover, we may also add that attribute to any other element types which might likewise serve as anchors: list, list item, section, and chapter. Here is the revised definition of the paragraph element type:

```
<!--        ELEMENT    MINIMIZATION   CONTENT                  -->
<!--        =======    =============  =======                  -->
<!ELEMENT   p          - O (#PCDATA)      >
<!ATTLIST   p
               id      ID        #IMPLIED  >
```

Notes:

1. The content model for the paragraph element type is unchanged from our original definition. Recall that the "PC" in #PCDATA means "parsed character." This tells the computer that there may be markup within the paragraph (such as general or character entities). Markup must be "parsed" - recognized, interpreted, and acted upon intelligently.

2. We *may* omit the end tag. For p it is common to do so.

3. The keyword ID is SGML's built-in mechanism for saying "this is the unique identifier of an element."

4. For practical purposes we may treat the keyword IMPLIED as meaning that the author/editor *may* provide a value for the attribute. We did provide a value for id in our markup in the example above.

5. The meaning of the value that we provide for the id attribute is absolutely arbitrary. It is only a string of characters used by a link to find its target. SGML does not "care" whether the value of that link actually matches a paragraph number or chapter or section title. Good sense dictates that it should, but that is only an issue of tidy editing.

6. The value that is assigned to `id` must be unique within the document. If we identify a section as "section_1" we cannot assign that value to the `id` attribute of any other element in the document.

Now return to the marked up text above. Look at each tag and see how its element type is defined in the revised DTD. Next, look very carefully at how a link "shakes hands" with its referenced anchor. The underlying "golden strand" is the unique identifier which you supply as the value of both of the attributes, the `IDREF` one in the `txt-link` element and the `ID` one in the anchor element.

Our remaining task in modifying the WAE DTD is to add the `id` attribute to each of the other elements types that might function as hypertext anchors. Here then is the fully modified DTD, now supporting hypertext links:

```
<!--            Writers And Editors (WAE) DTD                 -->

<!--       Entity Declarations                                -->
<!ENTITY % txm                "(p|l)+" >
<!ENTITY % lnkdta             "(#PCDATA|txt-link)+">
<!ENTITY    lt                "<" >
<!ENTITY    wae               "writers and editors" >
<!ENTITY    smile    SDATA    "[smile ]" >

<!--       Element Type Declarations                          -->
<!--       ELEMENT    MINIMIZATION    CONTENT                  -->
<!--       =======    ============    =======                  -->
<!ELEMENT  manual     O O             (ti?, au*, sec+) >
<!ATTLIST manual
              last-rev  CDATA        #REQUIRED
              last-au   CDATA        #IMPLIED  >

<!ELEMENT  ti         - O             (%lnkdta;) >
<!ELEMENT  au         - O             (#PCDATA) >

<!ELEMENT  sec        - -             (shd?, (%txm; | ssec)+ ) >
<!ATTLIST  sec
              id    ID    #IMPLIED  >

<!ELEMENT  shd        - O             (#PCDATA) >

<!ELEMENT  ssec       - -             (sshd?, %txm;) >
<!ATTLIST  ssec
              id    ID    #IMPLIED  >

<!ELEMENT  sshd       - O             (#PCDATA) >

<!ELEMENT  p          - O             (%lnkdta;) >
<!ATTLIST  p
              id    ID    #IMPLIED  >
```

```
<!ELEMENT   l          - -              (lhd?, lit+) >
<!ATTLIST   l
              id    ID    #IMPLIED   >

<!ELEMENT   lhd        - O             (#PCDATA) >
<!ELEMENT   lit        - O             (#PCDATA | %txm;)+ >
<!ATTLIST   lit
              id    ID    #IMPLIED   >

<!-- Hyptertext link, with attribute to identify anchor -->
<!ELEMENT   txt-link   - O  EMPTY        >
<!ATTLIST   txt-link
              linkend    IDREF      #REQUIRED >
```

9.8   Implementation Issues

Let us reiterate what this enhanced markup, supported by the revised DTD, really accomplishes. We insisted in earlier chapters that issues of final page and screen appearance are primarily issues of processing. As such, the writer need only be concerned with proper markup, leaving the processing to whatever viewer/printer/database software actually renders the document.

Including the mechanisms for hypertext raises processing issues of two varieties. First, unlike appearance (which the author is free to ignore), the author must be highly aware of hypertext links during the authoring process of how the document is going to "play," with regard to its navigation.

But there is another processing question which the alert reader might have asked during this development. We have referred to "hot spots" in the text, and most of us have used hypertext applications, such as the Microsoft Windows "help" utility, in which certain areas of text are highlighted, displayed in reverse video, or in some other way flagged as hypertext prompts. Yet the DTD and the markup says nothing about *what to highlight* as a hypertext prompt. Note that a robust hypertext authoring system offers options in specifying which word(s) get highlighted. The DTD for the hyperlink would include more attributes in the attribute list, including the actual character string to be highlighted. But in our presentation and in the software for SGMLab (which accompanies this book) we have chosen to limit the writer to specify only *where* the link is to occur. And the software, as our implementation of the hyperlink, will highlight only the preceding word when it displays your document.

Summary

SGML, to be sure, offers the most formal and consistent means for implementing hypertext links in an interactive document. But while all of the "pieces" required for building hypertext are present in SGML, it nevertheless requires the author to be knowledgeable about how to use those pieces. Specifically, the writer and editor should understand how `ID` and `IDREF` as basic SGML linking apparatus can be used to create the navigational anchors for hypertext. And as we have mentioned repeatedly, this understanding is important even for work groups that use advanced hypertext authoring tools (which may hide much of the underlying mechanisms).

A quality hypertext document does not happen automatically, even with the best of authoring tools. The most important factor in achieving that quality—more important than properly using SGML or buying the smoothest authoring tools—is the author's knowledge of the document's subject area and his or her intimate sense of the reader's need for navigation within the document.

CHAPTER 10

ENTITY MANAGEMENT
Managing Reusable Text

SGML terms introduced or reinforced:

entity, entity declaration, entity reference, entity set, general entity reference, parameter entity reference, public identifier, replacement text, specific character data entity.

Overview

Using parameter entities benefits the designer and human reader of a document-type definition, as we saw in Chapter 7. And general entities simplify the writer's task. But entities accomplish far more. Because an entity is declared *once* to be read *many times*, we can use entities containing large sections of a document to (1) free the writer from concern over the specifics of computer storage of the many parts of a large document, (2) ease the writer's task of incorporating disparate types of media, and (3) enhance the reusability and longevity of a document. We have distinguished between (1) the markup representation of *element structure* (enabled by markup during the authoring process) and (2) the *visual (or perceivable) representation* of the document. We now propose a third layer: the *storage representation*. This layer provides yet more relief to the writer, since all of the system-specific detail can be isolated to entity declarations separate from the body of the document.

10.1 Entities

The SGML term "entity" is strikingly simple in its formal definition and highly pervasive in its actual usage. We studied two varieties of SGML entities in Chapter 7: **parameter entities** and **general entities**. There we hinted at benefits of entities and made some distinction between who benefits from each type. The designer or editor or reader of a DTD benefits from parameter entities, we said, while general entities benefit the author. We also distinguished between the objectives of each type of entity, that is, what sort of text each type of entity refers to and where each type of entity reference is used. Finally, we studied some examples of how we declare and use those two types of entities.

In this chapter we will expand on that why-who-what-where-how discussion in order to gain a larger view of entities in general. That will make it quite easy to introduce entity management. If you have been waiting for even more proof of the benefits and payoff of using SGML, then this discussion should help convince you that the SGML claims of document portability and reusability are indeed attainable. And entity management is, as we shall find, neither subtle nor revolutionary. It merely formalizes the way writers and writing groups have manipulated large documents all along.

10.1.1   Formal Definition

The definition of "entity" is simple:

> **entity:** A collection of characters that can be referenced as a unit.
> — ISO 8879: §4.120

While we do not intend for this chapter to be an exhaustive commentary on the ISO definition, we need to look closely at some important aspects of entities that the definition conveys.

There are two distinct activities implied by the formal definition. "Collection of characters" implies that someone points to or specifies or gathers or delineates some portion of text. For every type of entity we are discussing, SGML enables us to "collect" an entity by means of an entity declaration. To declare an entity then means to collect some string of characters. The declaration is the formal *means* that SGML offers to make collection possible.

The *purpose* of declaring an entity is likewise explicit in the definition. The whole point is to enable us simply to *refer* to the collected text and not to be forced to repeat all of the same text string every time we use it.

The underlying principle of an entity declaration—reference rather than repeated inclusion of text—is common to many activities in computer programming. The entity declaration enables us simply to point to (reference) the entity. The enabling mechanism for "pointing to" an entity is similar to pointing to (or addressing) data in computer storage in general. The entity bears a *name*, and this name is the pointing apparatus for the entity. The ISO 8879 definition for entity declaration highlights the importance of the entity's name:

> **entity declaration:** A markup declaration that assigns an SGML name to an entity so that it can be referenced.
> — ISO 8879: §4.121

In addition to "collection" and "reference," there is a third significant property of entities that the definition only implies but that is the most powerful of all: declare *once* and reference *many times*.

What we have said so far about entities applies to entities in general. The difference between the various varieties of entity usage become clear when we ask the various "wh—" questions: Why? who? what? and so forth.

10.1.2 Parameter Entities

What sort of text does the declaration for a parameter entity collect? (A more formal way to phrase the question is "What is its replacement text?") As we saw in Chapter 7, the text for a parameter entity is a string of characters which itself is part of yet another declaration. We declared a parameter entity txm which was our name for the string "(p|l)+".

We said in Chapter 7 that both of our reasons for using parameter entities had to do with economy. First, by declaring the entity txm to replace the fully spelled-out text string, we cut the length of each occurrence by 50 percent. This saving of three characters would not seem to justify the complication of using a parameter entity declaration and references. But in Chapter 7 we also cited a five-line string of parameter text which was replaced by a mere seven-character entity name. So there is most definitely an economy possible with real-world DTDs. This is an economy that applies at the time of creating the document type definition.

The other economy is one of maintenance. Even in our tiny WAE DTD we found three occurrences of "(p|l)+". If, for example, a DTD designer or an author should wish to alter the content model of a very complex DTD (but one which used parameter entities extensively), then it would be a simple matter to change only the parameter entity declaration rather than having to search for and edit the same string throughout the entire DTD. So for our WAE DTD we may wish to change "(p|l)+" in the content model to "(p|l|blkq)+". We would only need to change it once in the declaration in order for the change to take effect for the entire DTD. This economy therefore applies over the entire life cycle of the document.

From our discussion it should be clear that parameter entities operate only within markup declarations. Their "collections of characters" comprise strings that belong only in declaration parameters. Since in typical documents, most markup declarations occur in the DTD, it follows that the beneficiaries of parameter entities are people who deal directly with the DTD. These include designers of DTDs, but they may also include writers and managers who must simply make slight modifications to a DTD.

But the greatest benefits of parameter entities come to the *human reader* of the DTD. This is most often the writer or editor who is seeking to understand the structure of a particular document type. A well-designed DTD that uses parameter entity declarations and references is far more readable than one that repeats long and complicated strings of parameter text.

The mechanics of declaring an entity (repeating our exhibit from Chapter 7) is as follows:

```
<!ENTITY % name "replacement text">
```

When we reference a parameter entity in a content model we enclose its name within a "%" (defined in ISO 8879 as parameter entity reference open or PERO) and a ";" (reference close), as follows:

```
<!ELEMENT    sec       - -      (shd?, (%txm;  |  ssec  |  txtref)+) >
```

10.1.3   General Entities

The "collections of characters" referenced by general entities are of even more immediate concern to the writer, since these entities occur in the body of the document itself. As with all entities, the benefit is economy of some kind, and here again the benefit is at least twofold. First, a general entity could replace a character string that is long, difficult to type, and occurs frequently throughout the document. For instance, using the general entity reference "cob" for the replacement text "Chairman of the Board Linius Phelan Bennington III" clearly represents a "creation-time" benefit for the author, particularly if it is referenced 150 times in the document.

The additional creation-time benefit which we discussed in Chapter 7 is to enable the writer to incorporate foreign symbols that are not on the keyboard. Because an entity name merely *references* the character by some standard name, the author only needs to key in that name. So the Byelorussian "capital U" character, which is a non-Russian Cyrillic character, can be represented by the entity reference "Ubrcy," which the writer enters as "Ў" (without quotes). That character is defined as part of a standard character *entity set* known as ISOcyr2. We will discuss entity sets shortly.

Like parameter entities, general entities offer immense life-cycle (maintenance) benefits as well. Suppose, to everyone's horror, that research of company dossiers revealed that the distinguished chairman is actually Bennington IV and not Bennington III. Just one change in the replacement text of the entity declaration would repair the entire document.

As for the mechanics of declaring a general entity, here is the declaration of the Byelorussian character we cited above:

```
<!ENTITY ubrcy SDATA "[Ubrcy ]"--=capital U, Byelorussian-->
```

This declaration defines a character whose representation is likely to be dependent on system-specific output devices. So the ISO definition includes the SGML keyword SDATA, which informs the computer that this is a specific character data entity. By definition, the text (the single character referenced here) is system-specific:

> **specific character data entity:** An entity whose text is treated as *character data* when referenced. The text is dependent on a specific system, device, or application process.
>
> NOTE—A specific character data entity would normally be redefined for different applications, system, or output devices.
>
> — ISO 8879: §4.304

In other words, the entity replacement text will be (probably) rendered differently on different types of systems.

10.2 Benefits

To summarize, we find entities to be beneficial in two respects. First, an entity has direct and immediate benefits to the portion of the document to which it applies. A parameter entity makes for more concise and readable entity declarations and content models within a DTD. And a general entity declaration dramatically reduces keystrokes for the writer. Furthermore, a general entity enables the writer with only a standard keyboard to include characters from any written alphabet on earth. Entity declarations for many such characters have been collected into ISO standard character entity sets; we shall cite an example shortly.

The second general benefit of entities is that they enhance the maintenance task and hence the life cycle of the document. A parameter entity declaration allows a designer easily to modify a complex DTD at a single location without perturbing and perhaps "breaking" a complex definition. For the writer with a maintenance task in a large document, that task is immensely simplified if some string of characters (like a complicated list of current addresses that is repeated throughout a long document) is represented by a general entity.

10.3 Entities in Pre-Electronic Writing and in SGML

We turn now to entity management, in which the "collection of characters" is within the body of the document and typically applies to larger portions of a document. While a single-character entity is theoretically treated identically to an entity of several million words, in practice there can be significant differences when dealing with entities whose texts are large chunks of a document, which will probably all be stored on a computer under different file names. For the remainder of this chapter we will be (1) examining what some of those differences are and then (2) determining how SGML helps us formalize the process of concurrent authorship of multiple portions of large documents.

A large documentation project will be fragmented, in the sense that several writers will be working simultaneously on different portions of the document. This is not bad... not even undesirable and certainly not uncommon. Instead of a writer's doing an entire set of chapters, a single writer may be assigned to create sidebar, tabular, or other specialty material for the entire book. And within multiple-author projects, those authors may be geographically scattered across multiple continents.

The document itself, even a traditional publication, will be fragmented if it incorporates deliverables other than hard-copy print media. Some of this heterogeneous material is pure running character text, some is graphical, some is tabular, and some is not page-oriented text at all. Again, this is not at all peculiar to electronic documents. Even for something as common as a typical college textbook product (which includes the textbook and its ancillaries), the variety of deliverables for the final package is mind-boggling: running character text, graphics (line, greyscale, photo), tables, lists, indexes, glossaries, test item booklets, test generation software, spreadsheet software and templates (for an economics textbook), instructor's manuals, overhead transparencies, accounting forms (for an accounting book), plus cover and promotional art. True, the editors would not consider this to be a single document, but with proper entity management and document markup techniques such a "package" can indeed be a "document."

Producing such a package is quite routine in major college textbook divisions, and it represents all of the problems that SGML can help to ease. The various editors, graphics specialists, software providers, and media producers somehow make it all come together. And this happens in spite of how separated all of the specialists (many of them third-party providers working in different countries) and components may be.

We urged in our early chapters that the author of an electronic publication be relieved from details of presentation. We are arguing here that the author should also be relieved from needing to know the actual file location of every storage unit (entity) of the entire document and its ancillaries. In slightly more formal terms, the writer and his or her document need system and device independence.

10.4 Layered Activity

All of the above has been true of documentation projects even without electronic tools. In a traditional publication environment, the central focus of all of the participating groups is on the final printed product (plus the non-print ancillaries). On the other hand, we have insisted for electronic publishing that as writers we disengage our focus on final presentation and concentrate rather on structure. We have therefore formalized a distinction between writing and editing on the one hand and production on the other. By disengaging these layers, we can theoretically guarantee that our product will potentially "play" on any device or medium, known or yet to be invented.

We have insisted on an authoring process whose output (marked-up text) is what we may call the markup representation of the document's *abstract* (or *"logical"*) structure. How to do this is of course the focus of this book. On the other hand, we recognize a *perceivable* (*visual* or *audio*, normally) *representation* (perhaps as data access and retrieval). But simply to formalize the activities of traditional publication into these two representations is not sufficient, because we still do not have an adequate mechanism for accomplishing what traditional publishers have done along. For a document of any magnitude we still must somehow pull together a large number of components in order to create the final unified document. We need therefore to formalize this activity of pulling it together.

The most critical problem in a highly decentralized document (many entities of many types in the hands of many authors in many places) is at all times to know what is where, so in addition to our *visual representation* layer, and our *markup representation* layer we need a *storage representation* layer. This needs to be a totally separate layer because it is wrong for a marked-up document (the representation of element structure) to incorporate system-specific data about locations of text and data. It is wrong for the same reason that a document should also not specify details of visual presentation, as we have insisted throughout this book. Any system-specific information is bound to change, so the document should contain nothing that is system dependent or device dependent.

Note that the layered representations do not necessarily represent sequential stages in a document's production. On the one hand, a marked-up manuscript (representing the abstract or "logical" structure of the document) may indeed first be an SGML document and later be transformed to a non-SGML representation for rendition as hard copy. But in a retrieval system, all of the layers may coexist simultaneously.

10.4.1   Markup Representation

An SGML document, with its element structure properly marked and validated, represents the document's abstract or logical information. We call this "abstract" because within this layer we do not account at all for the external realities of (1) how the document is to be rendered (the perceivable representation) or (2) where the various portions (entities) of the document may physically reside (the storage representation). The actual body of the document—the textual material that the writer creates—is of course anything but abstract. But we are talking now only about the SGML representation of structure of the document's elements.

10.4.2   Perceivable Representation

In the earlier chapters of the book, we used various terms to describe the document's existence beyond its abstract representation: rendition, presentation, appearance. And while we have urged the writer to postpone concerns about appearance (page or screen layout, for example), we certainly do not ignore that final deliverable of the SGML document. In fact, because of SGML and the pervasiveness of the standard, there is not one but theoretically an infinite variety of renditions, presentation media, and appearances possible for a single SGML document.

And not all of the representations are necessarily visible. Postscript may be a means of representing the document for hard-copy typesetting or for specialized screen display. But the same document may be rendered as a database, to be visualized with a retrieval engine that matches the database. Or the SGML document may be rendered as Braille or as video or audio. Whether visible or not, these are all viable as perceivable representations.

10.4.3   Storage Representation

If we really want the abstract representation to remain abstract—even for large documents comprising hundreds of entities and residing on far-flung computers and storage devices used by dozens of co-authors—then the authors and editors need help. The document's system dependence (what kind of computer?) and device dependence (what file structure?) must be handled elsewhere. So SGML enables us to manage these concerns through entity structure. We therefore confine all of the system and device dependencies (specifics of computers and file structures) to the *storage representation*.

Just as for the entities we studied in Chapter 7, these larger document entities enjoy the benefits of "declare once reference many times." We declare an entity once, including all of the specifics needed to display, retrieve, print, or otherwise play the document later on. A photograph of a newly released circuit board may reside now on a particular computer with the following file specification:

```
/catalog/mod002/grafs/fig03.gif
```

And we could include this specific file structure in the entity declaration as the location of the picture.

The newly released board presumably replaced an obsolete board whose photo may have had the following "address" in real storage (compare the two addresses carefully!):

```
/catalog/mod001/grafs/fig03.gif
```

Fortunately for the writer, the entity's *name*—for both graphics—is "Fig-03," and he or she only needs to *reference* the photo by that name. When the product was modified and the photo retaken and filed within a different directory structure on the computer, only the entity declaration needed to be changed. So we might declare that entity with a system-dependent storage location as follows:

```
<!ENTITY  Fig-03    SYSTEM  "/catalog/mod002/graf/fig03.gif" >
```

Note that the SYSTEM keyword indicates that the replacement text in the entity declaration is not to be inserted into the document itself but is the system storage location of the actual image. Exactly what the browser, viewer, or printer does with that image is system-dependent; it may be printed on a page, displayed on screen, or even simply referenced. This construct is known as a "system identifier," one of the two types of "external identifier" we are going to discuss. They are called "external" because they are identifying something outside of the current entity.

We would store that entity declaration in some area separate from the document body, probably in a file containing the document's **entity set** (an entire list of entity definitions). Within the document content, the author would use the particular linking element type that is defined within the DTD to reference the graphic. It may be a special link for figures called `figref`:

```
… as you can see in Figure 3<figref name="Fig-03">, the set screw is located
just beneath the flange…
```

That same marked-up text can remain untouched regardless of the modified photo and the revised location for its storage, because only the entity declaration would have changed.

10.5 Lessons from Software Engineering

Some 30 years ago software engineers recognized a similar commingling of information among portions of large programs. They referred to this unhealthy commingling as "modular glue." This was bad programming practice because it made it difficult for a programmer to make changes within a single module when troublesome side effects were sure to follow elsewhere. So software engineering prescribed that modules should be isolated from one another as much as possible. "Hide something at every level" is one of the mandates of structured programming. Similarly, entity management (the discipline we are introducing in this chapter) prescribes that we isolate ("hide") or confine messy system-, device-, and file-specific details of an entity to its entity declaration. The result: A visible "virtual" storage structure, comprising entities on top of a concealed "actual" storage structure, comprised of system storage objects, such as files.

10.6 Examples

There is no single prescribed way to enable entity management in an SGML document. The point of this chapter is simply to survey the resources that SGML offers to add a *storage representation*. Precisely how entity structures are defined is a matter of the designer's choice. We close this chapter with two different examples of entity structuring. The first one demonstrates the ease with which SGML (including an adequate *entity manager*) enables a physically segmented document to exist as a logically unified one. In showing this we see how a document designer uses the entity declaration plus an entity set to hide system-specific details from the document instance, enabling all of the benefits that we have detailed in this chapter. Finally we see how the writer uses entity references rather than system-specific file names to refer to entities outside his or her current work space.

10.6.1   A Document Type Definition in a Separate Entity

One common use of entity management is for sharing and reusing the declarations of a document-type definition. One way of attaching the DTD to your document is by including the declarations between square brackets in the document type declaration—what is called the "internal declaration subset"—like this:

```
<!DOCTYPE manual [
```

```
    <!ELEMENT manual . . .>
    <!-- all the rest of the declarations here -->
]>
<!-- your document goes here -->
```

However, there is an alternative to repeating all the declarations in every instance of a WAE document, as we illustrated but did not explain earlier. Instead of declaring the DTD internally, you can put it in an entity of its own—once—and reference it from the DOCTYPE declaration of each WAE document instance, like this:

```
<!DOCTYPE manual SYSTEM "C:\pub\dtds\wae.dtd">
```

As in the earlier example, the keyword SYSTEM introduces a system identifier that locates an entity in a system storage location—in this case "C:\pub\dtds\wae.dtd". But because this is a DOC-TYPE declaration, rather than an entity declaration, it references the entity immediately rather than declaring a name for it for later reference.

For documents that are used in several different computer systems, system identifiers typically need to be localized in each system, because real storage structures can differ. In such cases, another type of external identifier, called a public identifier, can be used:

```
<!DOCTYPE manual PUBLIC "+//ISBN . . .//DTD Writers and Editors DTD//EN">
```

Here, the public identifier uniquely identifies the DTD itself, rather than its real storage location. SGML systems that support public identifiers maintain a catalog that allows them to locate the local storage address for each public identifier.

10.6.2   One Logical Document With Several Physical Entities

Suppose a work group of five writers is to produce a maintenance manual. They wish to divide a document *physically* so that each writer can edit within his or her separate directory area of the computer. But the manual itself of course is *logically* a single document. Here is the marked-up document instance for an entire maintenance manual with the file name "WDGTMMAN.SGM":

```
<!DOCTYPE manual SYSTEM "C:\pub\dtds\wae.dtd" [
<!-- We "hide" the details of how the document is physically divided by placing
the entities into an entity set, which in turn resides in some file of its own
-->
<!ENTITY % MEnts SYSTEM "e:\sgmlab\MaintMan.ent" >
      %MEnts;
]>
 <manual last-rev="01/01/2000" last-au="Ron Turner">
 &fm;
 &ch01;
 &ch02;
 &ch03;
 &bm;
```

```
</manual>
```

Notice that the document type for the manual is our familiar "WAE," the declarations for which (the external "declaration subset") are stored at the system storage location "WAE.DTD." Written into the internal declaration subset (between the square brackets) there are declarations that apply only to this instance of a WAE document: a comment declaration, entity declaration, and an entity reference to still more declarations.

Note carefully that "MEnts" (the entity which we declare and reference here) is actually a reference to a system-specific file name. The external identifier parameter of the entity declaration is the only place in the document that we specify that actual file location and name: e:\sgmlab\maintman.ent. If we move or rename that file in the future, we only need to alter the name in the declaration.

You should also note that there are no clues at this level (except for the comment) that the purpose of the file is to contain the declaration for the physically separate entities that comprise the document instance. That is only clear within the entity set file itself "maintman.ent", which contains the following:

```
<!-- Entity Set for Maintenance Manual -->

<!ENTITY fm SYSTEM "e:\sgmlab\ron\front.doc" >
<!ENTITY ch01 SYSTEM "e:\sgmlab\tim\ch001.doc" >
<!ENTITY ch02 SYSTEM "e:\sgmlab\audrey\ch002.doc" >
<!ENTITY ch03 SYSTEM "e:\sgmlab\cameron\ch003.doc" >
<!ENTITY bm SYSTEM "e:\sgmlab\beth\back.doc" >
```

The quoted strings in the entity set file represent actual physical addresses of each of the five entities that comprise the document instance of the SGML document "wdgtmman.sgm".

It is not required for us to imbed these system-specific declarations in a separate entity set file ("maintman.ent" here). We could have declared the five entities directly and in full within the internal declaration subset itself:

```
<!DOCTYPE manual SYSTEM "C:\pub\dtds\wae.dtd" [

    <!ENTITY fm SYSTEM "e:\sgmlab\ron\front.doc" >
    <!ENTITY ch01 SYSTEM "e:\sgmlab\tim\ch001.doc" >
    <!ENTITY ch02 SYSTEM "e:\sgmlab\audrey\ch002.doc" >
    <!ENTITY ch03 SYSTEM "e:\sgmlab\cameron\ch003.doc" >
    <!ENTITY bm SYSTEM "e:\sgmlab\beth\back.doc" >
]>
<manual last-rev="01/01/2000" last-au="Ron Turner">
&fm;
&ch01;
&ch02;
&ch03;
&bm;
</manual>
```

But while this accomplishes the same purpose of identifying all the physically separated entities, it perhaps does so at the expense of cluttering the SGML document unnecessarily. As we have emphasized throughout the chapter, we are striving to separate the *storage representation* of the document from the other layers of the document's existence. That is the reason for the extra apparatus of an entity set file.

Finally, here are the contents of the remaining entities (other than the DTD) that make up the maintenance manual document. The SGML parser uses the DTD and entity list to thread its way through the document. The parser (as well as whatever application will render or represent the document) treats the document as a single *logical* object, regardless of the number of entities in which it is stored:

e:\sgmlab\ron\front.doc:

```
<ti>The Greatest Maintenance Manual Ever</ti>
<au>Ron Turner</au>
<sec>
<p>This is the entire text for the front matter of the manual</p>
</sec>
```

e:\sgmlab\tim\ch001.doc:

```
<sec><shd>Section 1: Parts List</shd>
<p>Here is the list of parts for the widget</p>
</sec>
```

e:\sgmlab\audrey\ch002.doc:

```
<sec><shd>Section 2: Principles of Operation</shd>
<p>Here's the very ample discussion of how the widget works.</p>
</sec>
```

e:\sgmlab\cameron\ch003.doc:

```
<sec><shd>Section 3: User's Guide</shd>
<p>Here are the crystal-clear, no-fail instructions for the user.</p>
</sec>
```

e:\sgmlab\beth\back.doc:

```
<sec><shd>Appendix: Where we hide all the good stuff</shd>
<p>The back matter typically contains what the user REALLY needs to know!</p>
</sec>
```

The complete list of the files that make up this document is:

1. `wae.dtd`: the DTD itself

2. `wdgtmman.sgm`: top level document instance entity

3. `maintman.ent`: entity declarations for external entities

4. `front.doc`: front matter entity text file

5. `ch001.doc`: chapter one entity text file

6. `ch002.doc`: chapter two entity text file

7. `ch003.doc`: chapter three entity text file

8. `back.doc`: back matter entity text file

10.6.3   Details Isolated from the Body of the Text

Segmenting the physical entities of the document is not the only reason for maintaining a separate entity set file. This mechanism for separation allows us to "hide" declarations for other entities as well. Suppose that the actual titles for the various sections of our maintenance manual are yet to be determined. But the various authors need to refer to those chapters *by name* from anywhere in the document. And those references need to remain valid no matter how often or how drastically the titles are changed.

To accomplish this we again use SGML's facility for *indirection* through **entity references**. And again we use the mechanism of an entity set. But now the items within the entity set in which we are interested are character strings, the names of each chapter in the document. Here is a revised version of our entity set (file "maintman.ent"):

```
<!-- Entity Set for Maintenance Manual -->

<!-- File locations for each chapter -->

<!ENTITY fm SYSTEM "e:\sgmlab\ron\front.doc" >
<!ENTITY ch01 SYSTEM "e:\sgmlab\tim\ch001.doc" >
<!ENTITY ch02 SYSTEM "e:\sgmlab\audrey\ch002.doc" >
<!ENTITY ch03 SYSTEM "e:\sgmlab\cameron\ch003.doc" >
<!ENTITY bm SYSTEM "e:\sgmlab\beth\back.doc" >

<!-- Chapter titles -->

<!ENTITY cht01 "Section 1: Parts List" >
<!ENTITY cht02 "Section 2: Principles of Operation" >
<!ENTITY cht03 "Section 3: User's Guide" >
```

With the chapter titles now declared in the entity list as general entities, the various authors do not need to be concerned about the precise wording of each chapter title. Instead the text for the three chapters would now read as follows:

```
e:\sgmlab\tim\ch001.doc:

<sec><shd>&cht01;</shd>
```

```
<p>Here is the list of parts for the widget</p>
</sec>
```

e:\sgmlab\audrey\ch002.doc:

```
<sec><shd>&cht02;</shd>
<p>Here's the very ample discussion of how the widget works.</p>
</sec>
```

e:\sgmlab\cameron\ch003.doc:

```
<sec><shd>&cht03;</shd>
<p>Here are the crystal-clear, no-fail instructions for the user.</p>
</sec>
```

So if the editor should decide finally to change "Section" to "Chapter" in each of the titles, it would take only a single revision to each of the three corresponding items in the entity set. The actual file with the text of the chapter would remain untouched.

Cross-referencing the various chapters by their titles is also smoothed considerably with an entity set. The author of Chapter 3 needs to refer to Chapter 2. A general entity reference accomplishes this very nicely:

e:\sgmlab\cameron\ch003.doc:

```
<sec><shd>&cht03;</shd>
<p>Now that we have an idea of how the widget functions (see "&cht02;"), here
are the crystal-clear, no-fail instructions for the user.</p>
</sec>
```

With the replacement text fully expanded ("resolved"), the marked-up paragraph would read as follows:

```
<sec><shd>Section 3: User's Guide</shd>
<p>Now that we have an idea of how the widget functions (see "Section 2:
Principles of Operation"), here are the crystal-clear, no-fail instructions for
the user.</p>
</sec>
```

Summary

We have reviewed some essentials of entity structure in order to discover how SGML and the various SGML systems might help us to manage the separate entities of a major document. The character-only portions are typically parceled out among several writers, and the various non-character entities (graphics) are also separate. This is the way writing projects have always been. SGML's entity structure allows us to manage these distributed entities in a standard and highly efficient manner. Whether the entity is a file-sized portion for which a single writer is responsible or whether it is a short character string of system-specific data, SGML entity management saves work for the writer, eases the editor's task, and enhances the life cycle of the document.

CHAPTER 11

MARKED SECTIONS
Labeling for Special Purposes

SGML Terms introduced or reinforced:

entity, marked section, marked section declaration, status keyword

Overview

An SGML document is *portable* and *scalable*, able to be processed on variety of dissimilar platforms of variety of sizes. And because of the standard, that document is *reusable*, able to be processed in ways both known and yet to be invented. Most of that portability, scalability, and reusability relies on the separation of intrinsic information—described in the document with SGML markup—from information that applies only to use of the document in a particular processing system (typesetter, viewer, or other device). But the author can easily build other kinds of flexibility into the document itself using marked sections. Marked sections enable the writer, for example, to label version-specific portions of a document. With that added markup, the processing system can create entirely different versions of the same document. The mechanisms for employing marked sections efficiently entail only a small number of SGML keywords, plus parameter entity declarations and references.

11.1 Extending the Notions of Portability and Reusability

We have emphasized that an SGML document is *portable*, achieving that portability thanks to the ability of SGML to allow permanent, intrinsic information about the document to be distinguished from instructions for a particular *processing program*. The latter software is in the typesetter or retrieval system or workstation browser or whatever else reads and processes the marked-up document. And ideally the size and power of the computer which processes the document are irrel-

---

evant. In other words, in addition to being portable (across different types of processing machinery), the SGML document is *scalable*, runnable on computers of differing speeds and sizes.

The third promise for marked-up SGML text is that it can be *reused* in ways other than that for which it was first written. So a document, for example, that is now typeset and printed as hard copy may in the future be viewed as on-line hypertext. And perhaps years later, the same text may be incorporated into a database retrieval system.

 On a less dramatic scale, SGML enables us to reuse a document in a manner that otherwise beleaguers writers and editors of technical documents. Suppose, for example, that we generate a user's manual for a portable software application that *internally* functions identically across several popular operating systems: MS-DOS, UNIX™, Windows, VMS™, and Macintosh®. This commonality means that the bulk of the manual set will be identical for every version of the software, but the installation instructions will be different for each of the operating systems. Likewise, there will need to be system-specific keystroke instructions and screen illustrations for each description of user interaction.

The alternative approaches (and editorial dilemmas!) for producing the manual set to cover all of these operating systems are as follows: (1) entirely separate versions of the manual for each version of the software product (costly and difficult to revise), (2) a cumulative list of system-specific instructions and screen illustrations at each juncture in the manual where they occur (resulting in a bloated and cumbersome manual), or (3) separate appendices for each block of system-specific material (forcing the exasperated user into endless page flipping).

The preference on the user's part is clear. It would be most satisfying simply to follow a custom-written manual that includes no alternative instructions and no messy other-system disruptions of any kind. But the costs of producing such separate version-specific hard copy can be prohibitive. If there were some way that one document could do it all, marked up such that the typesetting device could automatically receive its four or five alternative editions, then we might be able to satisfy everyone.

A similar case occurs with college textbooks programming languages. One of the headaches for publishers is that different universities have selected different campuswide computing systems. And a number of the students will do not do their homework on the university mainframe at all but on their own personal computers. And these computers will likewise not be the same. So the tutorial help and examples in the textbook must again somehow match the installation and keystroke (and mouse) instructions and the screen illustrations of each student's particular computer or terminal. In the face of this set of permutations, the textbook publisher needs a cost-effective method of producing system-specific versions of the textbook in order to secure adoptions at the largest number of universities possible. Once again, if the manuscript of the textbook could be written just once—including all of the variant installation instructions, keystroke sequences, and screen illustrations—then the cost and effort of the entire editing, production and subsequent revision cycles would be eased dramatically.

Finally consider the case of an intelligent on-line operation and maintenance system for a sophisticated multiacre physical plant. In this system, the "duty cycles" (intervals of time between maintenance and replacement tasks) for each motor, valve, and machine subassembly are stored in a database. The computer automatically prompts the maintenance technicians at the precise scheduled time for each task: replacement, lubrication, inspection, recertification, pressure testing, or whatever. If this is a large complex of buildings, then it is likely that for every subsystem (air conditioning, for example) there will be different configurations for each building or department. Furthermore, within subsystems there could be different models of the same devices (slightly different control panel keypads for scheduling the air conditioning, for example).

For an on-line retrieval system such as this we clearly would not even consider forcing the user to look at the instructions for all the different models of some device every time there is some version-specific detail. We might consider hypertext for enabling the user to branch to the pertinent text only. But using hypertext as a version manager could require the user to reiterate his or her choice of system configuration at each branch point, thereby creating a document that could be a nightmare to maintain and still not satisfy the user.

For all of these cases the optimum solution—from a writing, editing, revision, and production standpoint—would be to insert all the variants of a text at the location where they occur. So for software installation instructions, the writer could draft a list of the version-specific sections, something like the following:

DOS Version:
```
At the C:> prompt insert your disk into Drive A: (or B:) and type A:INSTALL (or
B:INSTALL). When you are asked for the drive name on which you would like
MegaBudget to reside, type the drive name followed by a colon (C:, D:, and so
forth) then press the <ENTER> key.
```

Windows Version:
```
Pull down the File menu under the Windows Program Manager and select Run. At the
Command Line field in the Run box, type in A:INSTALL or B:INSTALL, depending on
your floppy drive. Press the Enter key or click on OK.
```

UNIX Version:
```
Create a directory of your choosing for MegaBudget, such as the following:
    /Mybudget/MyPrograms/MegaBudget
Change to the MegaBudget directory and "tar" the files into your directory,
using the command:
    tar -xvf /dev/fd0
```

(We concede that these example instructions do not represent a highly user-friendly installation process, but they happen to resemble a great deal of actual commercial software installation instructions!)

Using the above "alternative texts," let us see how SGML (1) enables the writer to include all the variants at the same location of the document and (2) enables the presentation device (typesetting system, on-line viewer, or whatever) to output only the pertinent variant and to hide all the rest.

11.2 Declaring an SGML Marked Section

The mechanism of SGML for marking such variants is known as **marked sections**. They allow us to write a multipurpose document with no redesign of our DTD, minimal additional markup, and with all the related text grouped together for easy revision and republication.

The writer's list of alternative installation instructions for MegaBudget, as you recall, looked something like this (We've paraphrased the actual text for convenience):

DOS Version: Do DOS install.

Windows Version: Do Windows install.

UNIX Version: Do UNIX install.

If the writer wishes, for a specific processing run, to generate the DOS version of the manual, he or she can mark those alternative sections as a series of SGML marked sections in the following manner:

```
<![ INCLUDE [Do DOS install.]]>
<![ IGNORE [Do Windows install.]]>
<![ IGNORE [Do UNIX install.]]>
```

The effect of processing these sections of the document (e.g., printing or displaying to screen) is that, while all three of the sections are present in the source document, only the DOS marked section will appear (i.e., be processed).

For the Windows version, the writer would edit the marked section markup as follows:

```
<![ IGNORE [Do DOS install.]]>
<![ INCLUDE [Do Windows install.]]>
<![ IGNORE [Do UNIX install.]]>
```

And when it is time to process the document for the UNIX version of the manual, he or she could again modify the marked sections as follows:

```
<![ IGNORE [Do DOS install.]]>
<![ IGNORE [Do Windows install.]]>
<![ INCLUDE [Do UNIX install.]]>
```

11.3 Syntax of Marked Sections

Our examples above illustrate an "edit-then-process" sequence for using marked sections. Before we turn to refining that procedure for treating real documents in a more efficient manner, let us identify the formal syntax for marked sections.

This entire string of characters is a marked section declaration:

```
<![ IGNORE [Do DOS install.]]>
```

It fits the general form:

```
<![ status keyword [content]]>
```

The formal syntactic description of a marked section in our familiar table format is found in figure 11-1:

One item of particular interest to us is the **status keyword** (field 3). This is what tells the system how to process the marked section. We will use only two of these in this example: IGNORE and INCLUDE. Other keywords (CDATA, RCDATA, and TEMP) enable other varieties of processing, which will not be covered in this book. In the particular example of a marked section shown above, the status keyword is IGNORE.

Field 6, the *content* parameter, contains the actual text of the marked section. The content may be of any length and may contain any element tags and entity references that would be allowed if the marked section declaration did not exist. We might best visualize this by considering the document as completely written and tagged first (with all the variant portions included), then the marked section declarations simply bracket the variant portions of the existing text. In our example above, the content of the marked section is "Do DOS install."

As always, we have considerable flexibility in how the marked-up text may appear. For example:

```
<![ IGNORE [Do Windows install.]]>
```

is functionally the same as:

```
<![ IGNORE [
Do Windows install.
]]>
```

11.4 Using Entities with Marked Sections

The example given in Section 11.2 is certainly realistic enough… for installation instructions. And it does indeed accomplish what we had promised that marked sections could accomplish: (1) collecting all of the variant text at a single location in the document and (2) hiding all but the pertinent text at the time of processing. But a document could include hundreds of such clusters of variant text. And as the procedure now stands, the writer must change the status keywords IGNORE and INCLUDE for every such cluster throughout the document for each version of the product for which he or she is to produce a manual. We have evidently gained our document portability at an enormous expense to the writer or editor!

Just as we observed in Chapter 7 ("Entities: Making Text Reusable") for other purposes, declaring and referencing entities provides the preferred way out of our dilemma. Here is our same cluster of system-specific variant marked sections, this time with entities declared (once) and then referenced (many times) and with the full text inserted:

```
<!-- Here is the set of declarations for each of the versions. Note that the
editor will change "INCLUDE" to "IGNORE" (and vice versa) in these declarations
only -->
```

Table 11-1: Marked section declaration parts

1	2	3	4	5	6	7	8
markup declaration open (MDO) delimiter	declaration subset open (DSO) delimiter	parameter	separator	DSO delimiter	parameter	marked section close (MSC) delimiter	markup declaration close (MDC) delimiter
<!	[	*status key-word*	zero or more spaces	[	*content of marked section*	]]	>

```
<!ENTITY % DOSVersion       "INCLUDE"     >
<!ENTITY % WindowsVersion   "IGNORE"      >
<!ENTITY % UnixVersion      "IGNORE"      >

<!-- And here is the cluster of marked sections, which the editor no longer has
to touch in order for the document to be processed. Note that these marked
sections represent just one set of perhaps many such version specific variants
that could occur throughout the document. Also note that the content of each
marked section can be short or many pages in length. -->

<![ %DOSVersion; [
<shd>DOS Installation:</shd>
<p>At the C:> prompt insert your disk into Drive A: (or B:) and type A:INSTALL
(or B:INSTALL). When you are asked for the drive name on which you would like
for MegaBudget to reside, type the drive name, followed by a colon: C:, D:, etc.
Then press the <ENTER> key.</p>
]]>

<![ %WindowsVersion; [
<shd>Windows Installation:</shd>
<p>Pull down the File menu under the Windows Program Manager and select Run. At
the Command Line field in the Run box, type in A:INSTALL or B:INSTALL, depending
on your floppy drive. Press the Enter key or click on OK.</p>
]]>

<![ %UnixVersion; [
<shd>UNIX Installation:</shd>
<p>Create a directory of your choosing for MegaBudget, such as the
following:</p>
<code>/Mybudget/MyPrograms/MegaBudget</code>
<p>Change to the MegaBudget directory and <q>tar</q> the files into your
directory, using the command:</p>
<code>tar -xvf /dev/fd0</code>
]]>
```

Summary

As we have noted, there are other uses for marked sections besides managing multiple versions of a document. But the power of the marked section to solve this headache alone for documentation managers with minimal editing and practically no rewriting at all makes it well worth the investment to learn and use.

CHAPTER 12

READING *A DTD*
A Brief Walkthrough

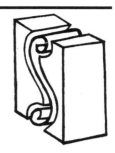

SGML Terms introduced or reinforced:

attribute, element, entity, entity declaration, entity reference, generic identifier, PCDATA, reference concrete syntax, replacement text

---

Overview

Is the ability to read a DTD with moderate fluency something of the *need-to-know* variety, or is it merely *nice to know*? A rather lengthy argument attempts to convince you that being able to approach and navigate intelligently through a DTD is useful and in fact essential to your professional work with SGML. We then suggest some simple rules for a "DTD walkthrough," based loosely on the classic "structured walkthrough" from software engineering. Finally we confront a small portion of an industrial strength DTD (DocBook) in order to recognize that the same SGML syntactic rules we have seen at work in our much simpler WAE DTD operate precisely the same here. Our walkthrough takes us from a high abstract level ("Book" in the DocBook DTD) to that of PCDATA (actual character data). The chapter, in other words, is a confidence builder, providing you with the courage to attack any DTD and recognize at least its most salient features.

12.1 DTD Fluency
Nice-to-Know or Need-to-Know?

There is a frequently expressed wish among some members of the community of SGML hopefuls (novices or yet-to-be's) that SGML software products will eliminate the need for knowing anything about SGML internals. With falling prices, greater popularity of the standard, and friendlier software (the reasoning goes), we will never even need to see a DTD. There is enough truth in that statement to deserve some serious discussion. For if all of the apparatus of SGML is to be hidden from the writer and editor, who now only need to select an "SGML output option," then this chapter, as well as much of the previous 11 chapters, is rather pointless.

The designer of electronic documents (which you probably are not) surely *must* understand the mechanics of document-type definition well enough to be able to make significant modifications to the DTD in use at his or her site. And in a great deal of the publicity for SGML training, there is a tacit assumption that it would be *nice* also for the writer or editor to know the internals of the DTD to some depth. But in order to set honest and realistic expectations for the reader of this book, we need to state clearly why the writer or editor *must* also know some DTD internals.

1. *Only an appropriate level of fluency is necessary.* While the designer must obviously have mastered the syntax and other mechanics of the DTD thoroughly, we do not claim that the writer/editor need attain that level of mastery. Instead, we maintain that the writer/editor must be able to navigate within a DTD with good understanding, and not be able to redesign or modify the DTD. That is, he or she should achieve *reading fluency.* That fluency should be sufficient to guarantee that he or she will be able to confront a particular document's unfamiliar DTD for the first time and be able to understand the formal definition of markup for that document.

2. *"The truth is in the code."* While it may sound daunting to say it aloud, the SGML document—which by definition includes the DTD and the marked-up text—is in many respects like a computer program. The "programming language" in this case is the tagging system which the writer/editor uses to mark up the document. And that system is defined by the DTD. So, consciously or not, the writer/editor is constantly referring to the DTD of the document whenever he or she applies tags to the document. Of course that "reference" to the DTD is almost always subconscious. But no matter how straightforward and intuitive a particular DTD and its tagging system may be, the writer is bound to find him- or herself with a question that demands an authoritative answer. The practical issue now is how to get help, *if* there is no SGML document designer available and *if* there is no documentation that speaks to the specific problem. The answer is the same as for any other computer program: The truth is in the code. In this case, "code" means the document's markup plus the formal definition of the markup—the DTD, in other words.

So at the moment of any ambiguity or other problem with markup, the writer/editor's relationship with the DTD definitely becomes *need-to-know* as opposed to simply *nice-to-know.* Without that knowledge the writer is virtually helpless.

3. *Inadequacy of secondary documentation.* Fortunately for the writer, those responsible for setting SGML application standards (DocBook, AAP, ATA, Patent Office, FDA) have done an admirable job of documenting their DTDs for their various user communities. The *Guide to the DocBook DTD* (available via anonymous ftp on the Internet[1]) is an example of ample documentation for a complex, production-level DTD.

Unfortunately for the writer, a DTD and its documentation are separate objects, often written and maintained by different people or groups. This can be unfortunate because the writer is now doubly dependent, relying on some wobbly assumptions: (1) The documentation is well structured, lucid, accurate, and totally appropriate for the users (writers and editors *primarily*) and (2) the documentation is absolutely current, matching precisely the most current release level of the DTD.

Once again, the writer, as a professional, cannot allow him or herself to be wholly dependent on secondary information (the documentation) when the primary source of information (the DTD itself) is within reach.

4. *Non-existence of reliable documentation for highly customized environments.* Even with an industry-standard DTD, a writing group (ourselves included!) will likely be using an enhanced or modified version, and such modifications may or may not be well documented for the user. The writer's only recourse for help may be the customized DTD itself.

5. *Generic (textbook-level) tutorial help cannot address specifics.* Textbooks—this one included—by definition address only broad and general concepts. If the user finds an example in the textbook that fits, then that is fortunate. If not, there will probably be no more detailed help available. In that case the most economical way of solving a problem will be for the writer to access the DTD directly.

6. *Reading a DTD directly is often easier and faster than reading documentation about the DTD.* As incredible as this sounds to an SGML newcomer, the formalism of SGML guarantees fast and direct access to every aspect of electronic document markup. The only proviso of course is that the writer/editor must master the syntax (rules for composition) of SGML. Once that hurdle is passed, all DTDs read much the same, because all of the standard ones use the reference concrete syntax (i.e., the syntax defined in the ISO standard). The design of the various DTDs varies indeed, and a particular design may lead you through considerable page flipping, as we shall see. But the syntax of a DTD is consistent and totally predictable. The payoff for the user's becoming an active DTD reader is that he or she is liberated from dependence on documentation, which has no guarantee of consistency across the various DTDs and their various revisions.

7. *You will readily understand revisions to your DTD.* The DTD will evolve with use, particularly within a broad user community. This means that enhancements and revisions and the documentation for those revisions will typically refer directly to the DTD itself.

All of the above arguments urge the writer not to become overly dependent on user documentation but to exercise appropriate professional energy and initiative for accessing the DTD directly. But there are significant product developments in the SGML arena which would

---

1. Try the ftp site at: ftp.ora.com in the directory /pub/davenport/docbook. Additional information is also available via World-Wide Web at: http://www.ora.com/davenport/README.html

seem to free the writer almost entirely from needing to know any SGML internals whatever. Several word processing and documentation tool suppliers speak of "SGML filters." We are tempted therefore to think of such filters in the same way that we think of simple word processing import and export filters.

In fairness to the suppliers, we can say generally that you get what you pay for. Expensive, intelligent workstation environments come with inference tools that go a long way toward automatic conversion to and from SGML, as well as high quality authoring environments for creating native SGML documents. But even in the most powerful tools, the DTD is still present, and the user who understands the DTD will enjoy increased productivity. Knowing the whole picture gives you a distinct advantage when creating conforming documents, regardless of the tools in use. It may be likened to the difference between the computer repairman who simply swaps parts and the one who understands exactly what every component does and how they work together. Either one can repair your computer, but there is little doubt which one you would prefer to call when it malfunctions.

The reality for writers who must use more modest utilities—add-on utilities to word processors, for example—is that they must be highly disciplined writers and must think for themselves. So the remaining items in the list contain some points to consider regarding the need for using SGML tools intelligently and professionally.

8. *You still must understand a document's structure.* Any time you tag a document, you are making explicit statements about the hierarchical structure of the document. Even with a highly automated structural markup product and with very intuitive visual clues on the screen, you must have a clear idea of the structure of the document. And as we demonstrate in this book, the syntax of SGML is the most concise and consistent manner for expressing that structure.

9. *Structure is not the only thing.* In spite of how we emphasize structure in this book, we need to remember that markup can be used to add value to the document in ways that no automaton could ever provide. For marking attributes in particular (Chapter 8), the writer must exercise skill and bring external knowledge *about* the document to bear. Again, high-level visual representation can assist the writer in assigning values to attributes, but the writer is responsible for doing it right. And doing it right in SGML means to do it according to the DTD of the particular document.

10. *The skill requirement of an SGML user must always be far greater than that of a typical software user.* The manager of a large writing organization would like to believe that the details of SGML software can be so hidden that the writer can function somewhat like the user of a payroll program: simply entering data and then clicking on "CALCULATE". This analogy between data processing software and its users, on the one hand, and SGML software and writers, on the other, is highly suspect. It is a tempting analogy, because the user of even a large industrial payroll program does not need to know COBOL (a language in which the program may have been written). But when errors or glitches occur during a payroll run,

there are well-defined avenues of recourse: highly refined documentation and established support services (whether in-house or contracted). For electronic authoring, the weakness of the analogy is that a "user" of a DTD (1) is far more creative than a data entry clerk, by definition; (2) will constantly push a DTD to its limits; and (3) handles data that is far more complex than the well-defined financial and biographical information which a payroll program expects to see.

In summary, we suggest that DTD reading fluency for the writer and editor is not only a "nice-to-know" skill but is "need-to-know," in spite of all the emerging SGML tools and technologies.

12.2 Ground Rules for the Walkthrough

We have borrowed the term "walkthrough" from software engineering methodology developed in the seventies. This refers to an exercise in which programmers and managers would look at a segment of computer code, letting the code itself guide them through its operation. This exercise helps to flush out bugs during a stage in which it is still cheap to modify the code.

While a DTD is not, strictly speaking, the same as a computer program, it is like computer code because it is the only means by which the computer can interact intelligently with your document. So we choose the walkthrough as a means to let a DTD "speak for itself." That is, rather than trying to plow through a complex, industrial-strength DTD from beginning to end, we shall use the three constructs we have studied in this book—element, entity, and attribute—as signposts to direct our "walk."

This purpose of this particular walkthrough is important to note. We are not examining the DocBook DTD in order to understand the DTD's particulars. That would be far too ambitious for us at this stage. Rather we move into this DTD in order primarily to discover first-hand that all DTDs have certain generic features and that we are able to spot those features with confidence. So this is an exercise in basic reading fluency, mostly to build your confidence.

Confidence in what? We hope to empower you as an SGML practitioner to be able to get the "lay of the land" of *any* DTD or revision of a DTD that you may encounter on the job. And since DocBook is both (1) unfamiliar to you (we assume) and (2) as complex as about any DTD you will encounter, you should certainly feel confident, rewarded, and empowered at the close of this exercise.

Here then are some suggestions for letting the DTD "speak for itself":

1. Go for the first element type, the document element.

2. Use the content model of an element type to lead you to subordinate elements. This is the DTD's manner of expressing the particular treelike structure of a document.

3. Use your basic definitions of the parts of an element type declaration to paraphrase (perhaps even out loud) what the DTD is "doing."

4. Where there is an entity reference, place your finger (or sticky note or whatever) there and go to the entity declaration.

5. When you have found the entity's declaration, use that declaration to say (aloud) what it says within the content model where the entity reference appears.

6. When you encounter an attribute definition list, say what that attribute means for marking up the document. If it is REQUIRED, say "must enter a value." If it is IMPLIED, say "it is not required."

7. Continue threading your way down the "element type tree" until you reach a greater level of detail than you need for basic understanding of the most prominent aspects of the document.

8. You may find other tricks that help you—such as drawing a diagram of the document structure—as you go. There are no hard and fast rules for doing a DTD walkthrough, as long as the end result is a clear understanding of the basic structure that the DTD was designed to reflect.

12.3 A Short DocBook DTD Walkthrough

The following pages contain an excerpt from the DocBook DTD that we will use for our walkthrough. In the remainder of this chapter we are departing from the expository style we have used throughout the book. We are now going to be much more interactive, inviting you to follow the discussion actively. For your convenience we have included, on the SGMLab diskette which accompanies the book, the entire DocBook DTD as well as this excerpt. You might choose to print out the DocBook excerpt as separate hard copy to help you follow along in the walkthrough. There will be a significant amount of flipping forward and backward through the DTD, so you will probably mark locations with bookmarks, sticky notes, fingers, felt-tip highlighter, and the like.

Note that we have numbered the lines to make it easier to refer to particular sections in the discussion that follows. *The line numbers are not part of the DTD itself.*

```
1    <!--======================================================================= -->

2    <!--

3        DocBook DTD $Revision: 2.1 $

4        $Date: 1993/12/17 19:44:30 $

5        Copyright 1992, 1993 HaL Computer Systems International, Ltd., and
```

```
6        O'Reilly & Associates, Inc.

7        Permission to use, copy, modify and distribute the DocBook DTD and
8        its accompanying documentation for any purpose and without fee is
9        hereby granted, provided that this copyright notice appears in
10       all copies. If you modify the DocBook DTD, rename your modified
11       version. HaL Computer Systems International, Ltd., and
12       O'Reilly & Associates, Inc., make no representation about the
13       suitability of the DTD for any purpose. It is provided "as is"
14       without expressed or implied warranty.

15       The DocBook DTD is maintained by HaL Computer Systems
16       International, Ltd., and O'Reilly & Associates, Inc. Please
17       direct all questions, bug reports, or suggestions for changes to:
18       davenport@ora.com or by postal mail to either: Terry Allen, O'Reilly &
19       Associates, Inc., 103A Morris Street, Sebastopol, California,
20       95472; or Conleth O'Connell, HaL Computer Systems, 3006-A
21       Longhorn Blvd., Austin, Texas, 78758.

22       Please note that an SGML declaration is provided for this DTD.

23       Public Identifier:
24          "-//HaL and O'Reilly//DTD DocBook//EN"

25       -->

26  <!-- ================================================================== -->
27  <!-- ################################################################## -->
28  <!-- ================================================================== -->

29  <!-- EXTERNALLY DECLARED CHARACTER ENTITIES -->

30  <!-- Uncomment the ENTITY sets needed for your application. -->

31  <!--
32  !ENTITY % ISOchars PUBLIC
33       "-//ENTITIES Public ISO Character Declarations//EN"
34       "iso-public" >
35  <!ENTITY % ISOchars PUBLIC
36       "-//ENTITIES System ISO Character Declarations//EN"
37       "iso-system" >
38  <!ENTITY % ISOchars SYSTEM "iso-public">
39  <!ENTITY % ISOchars SYSTEM "iso-system">
40  -->

41  <!-- ================================================================== -->
42  <!-- ################################################################## -->
43  <!-- ================================================================== -->

44  <!--
```

```
45          PARAMETER ENTITIES to allow inclusion of local modifications.
46          To include your local terms, table content model, graphics
47          format, or other local item,
48          At the head of your instance, after the DOCTYPE line, include
49          a reference to an external entity file that includes all
50          the local terms, table content models, and (or) graphics
51          formats you are using:

52          <!DOCTYPE Chapter SYSTEM "/yourpath/docbook.dtd" [
53          <!ENTITY % localmods SYSTEM "/yourpath/localmodfile" >
54                  %localmods;
55          ]>

56          You may need to set up attributes for your local elements.

57   -->

58   <!-- CONTENT MODEL LOCALIZATIONS -->
59   <!ENTITY % local.admonitions   "" >
60   <!ENTITY % local.appendix      "" >
61   <!ENTITY % local.book          "" >
62   <!ENTITY % local.chapter       "" >
63   <!ENTITY % local.cptrterms     "" >
64   <!ENTITY % local.equations     "" >
65   <!ENTITY % local.examples      "" >
66   <!ENTITY % local.index         "" >
67   <!ENTITY % local.links         "" >
68   <!ENTITY % local.lists         "" >
69   <!ENTITY % local.notations     "" >
70   <!ENTITY % local.refclasses    "" >
71   <!ENTITY % local.nav           "" >
72   <!ENTITY % local.ndxterms      "" >
73   <!ENTITY % local.synopsis      "" >
74   <!ENTITY % local.tables        "" >
75   <!ENTITY % local.terms         "" >

76   <!-- ================================================================= -->
77   <!--
78          ATTRIBUTE LIST for a set of common attributes.
79   -->

80   <!ENTITY % commonatts
81              "Id        ID              #IMPLIED
82              Lang       CDATA           #IMPLIED
83              Remap      CDATA           #IMPLIED
84              Role       CDATA           #IMPLIED
85              XRefLabel CDATA            #IMPLIED"
86   >
```

```
87  <!-- ===================================================================== -->
88  <!-- PARAMETER ENTITIES -->
89  <!-- ===================================================================== -->

90  <!-- Book Contents -->

91  <!ENTITY % appendix.gp    "Appendix %local.appendix;" >

92  <!ENTITY % book.gp    "Book %local.book;" >

93  <!ENTITY % chapter.gp    "Chapter %local.chapter;" >

94  <!ENTITY % index.gp "Index | SetIndex %local.index;" >

95  <!ENTITY % bookcontent.gp "%appendix.gp; | Bibliography | %chapter.gp; |
96      Glossary | %index.gp; | LoT | Preface | RefEntry | Reference | ToC " >

97  <!-- ===================================================================== -->

98  <!-- Contents that can appear almost anywhere -->

99  <!ENTITY % ndxterm.gp "IndexTerm %local.ndxterms;" >

100 <!ENTITY % xref.gp "FootnoteRef | XRef" >

101 <!ENTITY % links.gp "Link | OLink | ULink %local.links;" >

102 <!ENTITY % basechar.gp "%ndxterm.gp; | #PCDATA | Anchor | BeginPage" >

103 <!ENTITY % phrase.gp "%basechar.gp; | Comment | Subscript | Superscript |
104     %links.gp;" >

105 <!-- ===================================================================== -->

106 <!ENTITY % bookinfo.content.gp "Author | AuthorInitials | Title | Copyright |
107     CorpAuthor | CorpName | Date | Editor | Edition | InvPartNumber | ISBN |
108     LegalNotice | OrgName | OtherCredit | PrintHistory | ProductName |
109     ProductNumber | Publisher | PubsNumber | ReleaseInfo | RevHistory |
110     Subtitle | VolumeNum" >

111 <!-- ===================================================================== -->

112 <!ENTITY % docinfo.content.gp "Author | AuthorInitials | CorpAuthor | ModeSpec
113     | OtherCredit | RevHistory" >

114 <!-- ===================================================================== -->

115 <!ENTITY % words.gp "Abbrev | Acronym | Character | Charset | Citation |
116     CiteTitle | CiteRefEntry | Emphasis | FirstTerm | Font | ForeignPhrase |
```

```
117        GlossTerm | Glyph | Footnote | Markup | Quote | SGMLTag | Trademark |
118        WordAsWord" >

119 <!-- ================================================================ -->

120 <!ENTITY % inlinechar.gp "%phrase.gp; | %computerterms.gp; |
121        %docinfo.content.gp; | %words.gp; | %xref.gp; %local.terms;" >

122 <!-- ================================================================ -->

123 <!-- Contents of Table -->

124 <!ENTITY % tblcontent.gp "(Graphic+ | TGroup+ %local.tables;)" >

125 <!-- All the varieties of lists -->

126 <!ENTITY % list.gp "ItemizedList | OrderedList | SegmentedList | SimpleList |
127        VariableList %local.lists; " >

128 <!-- ================================================================ -->

129 <!-- Para elements -->

130 <!ENTITY % para.gp "FormalPara | Para | SimPara" >

131 <!-- ================================================================ -->

132 <!ENTITY % component.gp "Abstract | Anchor | AuthorBlurb | %admonition.gp; |
133        BridgeHead | Comment | Epigraph | %formalobject.gp; | Highlights |
134        %ndxterm.gp; | %list.gp; | %object.gp; | %para.gp; | MsgSet | Procedure |
135        Sidebar" >

136 <!-- ================================================================ -->

137 <!-- The sect1.gp parameter entity is used in Chapter, Preface, and Appendix
138 -->

139 <!ENTITY % sect1.gp "((%component.gp;)+, (Sect1* | RefEntry*)) | Sect1+ |
140        RefEntry+" >

141 <!-- ================================================================ -->
142 <!-- ################################################################ -->
143 <!-- ================================================================ -->
144 <!-- ELEMENTS -->
145 <!-- ================================================================ -->

146 <!-- ================================================================ -->
147 <!-- GENERAL BOOK STRUCTURES -->
148 <!-- ================================================================ -->
```

```
149 <!--

150        A Set contains at least two books. A Book, which could be a
151        journal or an anthology, must have a Chapter or Reference or
152        Part, and may contain other contents as required. We believe
153        this model accommodates the order of contents for English,
154        French, German, and Japanese books.

155        A Part contains at least one book content element. A
156        Preface, ToC, LoT, Bibliography, Glossary, or Index can be a
157        chapter-level component, while ToC, LoT, Bibliography,
158        Glossary, RefEntry, and Index may also appear within
159        chapter-level components.

160 -->

161 <!-- A model for a Set of Books -->

162 <!ELEMENT Set - - ((Title, TitleAbbrev?)?, SetInfo?, ToC?, (%book.gp;),
163        (%book.gp;)+, SetIndex?) >
164 <!ATTLIST Set
165          %commonatts;
166          FPI        CDATA          #IMPLIED
167 >

168 <!ELEMENT SetInfo - - ((%bookinfo.content.gp;)+) >
169 <!ATTLIST SetInfo
170          %commonatts;
171       -- Contents points to the IDs of the book pieces (from
172          book.gp) in the order of their appearance --
173          Contents  IDREFS         #IMPLIED
174 >

175 <!-- A prescriptive model for a Book -->

176 <!ELEMENT Book - - ((Title, TitleAbbrev?)?, BookInfo?, ToC?, LoT*, Preface*,
177        (((%chapter.gp;)+, Reference*) | Part+ | Reference+ | Article+),
178        (%appendix.gp;)*, Glossary?, Bibliography?, (%index.gp;)*, LoT*, ToC? ) >
179 <!ATTLIST Book
180          %commonatts;
181          FPI        CDATA          #IMPLIED
182          Label      CDATA          #IMPLIED
183 >

184 <!ELEMENT BookInfo - - (BookBiblio, LegalNotice*, ModeSpec*) >
185 <!ATTLIST BookInfo
186          %commonatts;
187       -- Contents points to the IDs of the book pieces (from
188          book.gp) in the order of their appearance --
189          Contents  IDREFS         #IMPLIED
```

```
190 >

191 <!ELEMENT BookBiblio - - (Title, TitleAbbrev?, Subtitle?, Edition?,
192      AuthorGroup+, ((ISBN, VolumeNum?) | (ISSN, VolumeNum?, IssueNum?,
193      PageNums?))?, InvPartNumber?, ProductNumber?, ProductName?, PubsNumber?,
194      ReleaseInfo?, PubDate*, Publisher*, Copyright?, SeriesInfo?, Abstract*,
195      ConfGroup*, (ContractNum | ContractSponsor)*, PrintHistory?, RevHistory?)
196      >
197 <!ATTLIST BookBiblio
198           %commonatts;
199 >

200 <!-- Most of the book component elements -->

201 <!ELEMENT Appendix - - (DocInfo?, Title, TitleAbbrev?, (%sect1.gp;)) >
202 <!ATTLIST Appendix
203           %commonatts;
204           Label           CDATA           #IMPLIED
205 >

206 <!ELEMENT Chapter - - (DocInfo?, Title, TitleAbbrev?, (%sect1.gp;), (Index |
207      Glossary | Bibliography)*) >
208 <!ATTLIST Chapter
209           %commonatts;
210           Label           CDATA           #IMPLIED
211 >

212 <!ELEMENT DocInfo - - (Title, TitleAbbrev?, Subtitle?, AuthorGroup+, Abstract*,
213      RevHistory?, LegalNotice*) >
214 <!ATTLIST DocInfo
215           %commonatts;
216 >

217 <!ELEMENT Part - - (DocInfo?, Title, TitleAbbrev?, PartIntro?,
218      (%bookcontent.gp;)+) >
219 <!ATTLIST Part
220           %commonatts;
221           Label           CDATA           #IMPLIED
222 >

223 <!ELEMENT Para - - ((%inlinechar.gp; | %list.gp; | %object.gp;)+) >
224 <!ATTLIST Para
225           %commonatts;
226 >

227 <!ELEMENT SimPara - - ((%inlineobj.gp;)+) >
228 <!ATTLIST SimPara
229           %commonatts;
230 >
```

The first thing to do when confronted with an unfamiliar DTD, such as the one above, is to attempt to get the general "lay of the land." By this we mean to identify the major sections of the DTD and to try to grasp how the DTD designer organized things.

Let us look first at the header comment block (lines 1-25). This provides much background information about the DTD: copyright language protecting the DTD; who wrote it; what group uses it; and who is responsible for maintaining it. In addition, note that the DocBook DTD itself can be publicly declared and then referenced in the user's document, just as with other PUBLIC entities (lines 22-24).

The character entity declarations in lines 29-40 are provided as an alternative means of including ISO standard entity lists special characters.

The comment block in lines 41-57 accomplish the entity management that we discussed in Chapter 10. All of the local (i.e., specially defined by this writer or writing group) entities are grouped together into a file on the local system. Here it is located in the directory path /your-path/localmodfile.

In the DTD, the content model for various elements includes such "generic" subelement types as "book," "chapter," "appendix," and "tables." However we wish to allow the user of the DTD to modify these and other element type declarations in such a way (1) that the DTD remains relatively intact and (2) that the modifications remain grouped in one central location for easy maintenance. That is the spirit of lines 58-75, "Content Model Localizations." The declarations in line 59-75 are all empty. But if the designer chooses to expand on the concept of Book to include ShopManual and PartsCat as well, then line 61 might be rewritten as follows:

```
<!ENTITY % local.book     "| ShopManual | PartsCat" >
```

The section "Parameter Entities" (starting in line 87) demonstrates how these "local" declarations are used to extend the basic entity declarations that come with the DTD. Note that each of the names of the entities declared in lines 87-140 ends with the suffix ".gp" (standing for "group"). So rather than limit these entity declarations, which are referenced in content models, strictly to Appendix, Book, and Chapter, they allow for the addition of whatever the "content model localizations" (lines 58-75) may contain. Because of our local declaration for local.book above, the expanded replacement text (the portion of the entity declaration inside quotes) for book.gp will be:

```
<!ENTITY % book.gp   "Book | ShopManual | PartsCat" >
```

We will see later how properly selected entity names can help in hiding unnecessary levels of detail while preserving the readability of a DTD.

Now locate where the element type declarations begin (line 141). The comment block in lines 149-160 describes in a very helpful manner the relationship between Set, Book, and Chapter, the three element types of greatest interest in our short walkthrough. Since we have decided to begin our walkthrough with the element type declaration for book, we should now go there (lines 175-183) to examine it closely.

```
<!ELEMENT Book - - ((Title, TitleAbbrev?)?, BookInfo?, ToC?, LoT*, Preface*,
        (((%chapter.gp;)+, Reference*) | Part+ | Reference+ | Article+),
        (%appendix.gp;)*, Glossary?, Bibliography?, (%index.gp;)*, LoT*, ToC? ) >
```

While we notice that there are attributes associated with this element type, we will ignore them for now. The first thing to examine is the generic identifier (GI) "Book." Note carefully the spelling (not too hard in this case, but sometimes it may be rather unusual) so you will recognize it when used in tagging. In many cases the GI will make clear the function of the element type (such as book or paragraph), but in other cases it may take some thought to determine what it means.

Second, notice the tag minimization section for the Book element type. Neither the start-tag nor the end-tag may be omitted.

Third, let us examine the content model to determine what this element type contains. A quick read-through of the content model shows 14 explicit element types and 3 parameter entity references. We also note that there are several pairs of left and right parentheses. The easiest way to deal with nested parentheses is always to locate the matching closing (right) parenthesis when we find an opening (left) one. Another approach is to number each opening parenthesis and then use the same number on the closing parenthesis that goes with it. Remember, of course, that the entire content model is enclosed in the outermost set of parentheses. Regardless of the method we use for matching parentheses, we always read what they contain *from the inside out*. This is the first nested grouping:

```
(Title, TitleAbbrev?)?,
```

We should be able to read this fairly easily: "a Title element, followed by an optional TitleAbbrev element, with the entire construct being optional." Next, we note the comma indicating that these objects (if they even appear) are followed by:

```
BookInfo?, ToC?, LoT*, Preface*,
```

We read this as follows: "An optional BookInfo element, followed by an optional ToC element, followed by zero or more LoT elements, followed by zero or more Preface elements." We should be able to identify the purpose (the "semantic role") of each of these element types by its name. BookInfo is obviously additional information about the book, ToC is table of contents, and LoT is list of tables. If an element type name is unclear (LoT, for example) we could either look elsewhere in the DTD itself for a description, or refer to the documentation (if any) for the DTD.

The next section of the content model at line 177 is also nested, as we can see by the three opening parentheses. As before we go directly to the innermost level to begin reading.

```
(((%chapter.gp;)+, Reference*) | Part+ | Reference+ | Article+),
```

The innermost group is (%chapter.gp;)+, which we can read in one of two ways. We could simply read it as "one or more occurrences of whatever is in the chapter.gp entity." On the other hand, we could choose to "drill down" here to get to the meat of the DTD (i.e., the full replacement text for the entity). For the purposes of illustrating how to walk through a DTD, we will go ahead and drill down at this point.

In Chapter 7 (concerning entities), we learned that a parameter entity reference has the effect of inserting the entity's replacement text at the point of the reference. This means that we can find the entity declaration for `chapter.gp`, read the replacement text from the declaration, and then simply continue our walkthrough, as though we had never stopped looking at the `Book` element type declaration.

A quick look back at the DTD listing shows the `chapter.gp` declaration to be on line 93. It has a very short replacement text, consisting of just the `Chapter` element type and a reference to the `local.chapter` entity. We know from our earlier observation of lines 58-75 that these "local" entity declarations are empty in this application. So we know that we can ignore the "`%local.chapter;`" entity reference in line 93 and concentrate just on the `Chapter` element type. We find the declaration of `Chapter` on lines 206-207:

```
<!ELEMENT Chapter - - (DocInfo?, Title, TitleAbbrev?, (%sect1.gp;), (Index |
    Glossary | Bibliography)*) >
```

Once again we could start by reading aloud through the content model, saying "`Chapter` consists of an optional `DocInfo` element, followed by a required `Title`, followed by an optional `TitleAbbrev`, followed by whatever the `sect1.gp` entity replacement text contains, followed by zero or more of the following in any order: `Index`, `Glossary`, or `Bibliography`." Most of this is fairly self-explanatory, except for the entity reference. So once again we will go back to the entity declarations to find out what goes in that place.

The `sect1.gp` entity is declared on lines 139 and 140. Moving directly to its declaration and replacement text, we find that it is more complex than the ones we have seen so far. In order to make it clear it may help to "plug in" the replacement text for `sect1.gp` to the `Chapter` content model:

```
(DocInfo?, Title, TitleAbbrev?, (((%component.gp;)+, (Sect1* | RefEntry*)) |
Sect1+ | RefEntry+), (Index | Glossary | Bibliography)*)
```

A careful study of the parentheses shows that for `sect1.gp` there are really three components in this portion of the content model. We can diagram them this way:

```
One of the following:
    ((%component.gp;)+,
    (Sect1* | RefEntry*))
OR
    Sect1+
OR
    RefEntry+
```

To continue our walkthrough, we should next look up the `component.gp` entity declaration, which is on lines 132-135. At first glance this may seem extremely large and impenetrable, but a few moments of closer study will show that it is simply a long list of element types (or references to them) that can appear in a chapter. These include an abstract, a comment, lists of some type, and so on. In order to continue our "drill down" in pursuit of actual character data, we decide to look at the `para.gp` entity. This would seem to move us closer to actual written text based on our intuition that written text is most generally associated with paragraphs. The declaration of `para.gp` is found on line 130, and we can see that there are three options for paragraph element types: `FormalPara` or `Para` or `SimPara`. Continuing (for now) to look for where we will actually find author-level writing, we will go to the `Para` element type declaration, found on line 223:

```
<!ELEMENT Para - - ((%inlinechar.gp; | %list.gp; | %object.gp;)+) >
```

From here the `inlinechar.gp` entity seems to be the place that gets us closest to actual writing, so we will look for that declaration, finding it on line 120. What we find is that it contains still more entity references, such as `phrase.gp`, `computerterms.gp`, and `words.gp`. If we go to the `phrase.gp` declaration on lines 103 and 104, we find this:

```
<!ENTITY % phrase.gp "%basechar.gp; | Comment | Subscript | Superscript |
    %links.gp;" >
```

Like the `component.gp` entity, `phrase.gp` consists of a set of alternative objects. Since we are looking for some place to start writing our paragraph, it seems as if we should check out the `basechar.gp` entity, assuming that it means "basic characters." We find the `basechar.gp` entity declaration on line 102:

```
<!ENTITY % basechar.gp "%ndxterm.gp; | #PCDATA | Anchor | BeginPage" >
```

This appears to be the one we want. It gives us the option of inserting PCDATA (parsed character data)—the actual written data content of the paragraph. We have now "drilled down" from the book level to the actual writing level. It seems like a lot of layers, but a bit of study will reveal that we traversed only three elements to get here: `Book`, `Chapter`, and `Para`.

It may seem to you that there are many more entity references than are really necessary, since we were only trying to discover the structural relationship between written character data—the PCDATA which we as authors create—and `Book` as a whole. But that apparent complexity yields some significant payoffs, especially for the DTD reader. It provides the ability to cluster large groups of related detail and then to "hide" that detail in an orderly fashion. The advantage is that once we have "drilled down" through an entity, the `para.gp` entity for example, to reach all of the underlying replacement text at every level, we will never need to repeat our reading to that level of detail again. For `para.gp`, we know that it contains various types of paragraph and related element types declared for this document type. From now on, any time we see a reference to `para.gp` we will not need to follow it any further, unless we really are interested in one of the underlying items. Just to illustrate how much confusion of detail the use of entities hides, here are the `Book`, `Chapter`, and `Para` element type definitions with part of the entity replacement text inserted. Note that we are inserting only the replacement text for the entity references we have followed in this discussion.

```
<!ELEMENT Book - - ((Title, TitleAbbrev?)?, BookInfo?, ToC?, LoT*, Preface*,
    (((Chapter %local.chapter;)+, Reference*) | Part+ | Reference+ |
    Article+), (%appendix.gp;)*, Glossary?, Bibliography?, (%index.gp;)*,
    LoT*, ToC? ) >
```

```
<!ELEMENT Chapter - - (DocInfo?, Title, TitleAbbrev?, (((Abstract | Anchor |
    AuthorBlurb | %admonition.gp; | BridgeHead | Comment | Epigraph |
    %formalobject.gp; | Highlights | %ndxterm.gp; | %list.gp; | %object.gp; |
    FormalPara | Para | SimPara | MsgSet | Procedure | Sidebar)+, (Sect1* |
    RefEntry*)) | Sect1+ | RefEntry+), (Index | Glossary | Bibliography)*) >

<!ELEMENT Para - - ((%ndxterm.gp; | #PCDATA | Anchor | BeginPage | Comment |
    Subscript | Superscript | %links.gp; | %computerterms.gp; |
    %docinfo.content.gp; | %words.gp; | %xref.gp; %local.terms; | %list.gp; |
    %object.gp;)+) >
```

Again, contrasting this with the simplicity of the original declarations at lines 176, 206, and 223 should serve as a convincing demonstration of how entities hide detail in a useful fashion and ease our task of navigating through a DTD.

Now that we have done a bit of wandering around in the DTD, there are a number of strategies we could use to study the document's structure even further. As an illustration of one approach, we will expand all of the entity references in the Book element type declaration and then make a chart of the structure. We recall that parentheses represent the SGML syntactic manner of describing document structure in a formal manner, such that even a computer can deduce that structure. The following indented chart approach, while less formal, may help you to view that structure more clearly.

Here is the fully expanded (i.e., no entity references) declaration of Book:

```
<!ELEMENT Book - - ((Title, TitleAbbrev?)?, BookInfo?, ToC?, LoT*, Preface*,
    (((Chapter)+, Reference*) | Part+ | Reference+ | Article+), (Appendix)*,
    Glossary?, Bibliography?, (Index | SetIndex)*, LoT*, ToC? ) >
```

(As a side observation, you might be surprised to note that this document type allows for lists of tables and the table of contents to appear either as front matter or as back matter. This is one instance of the type of information you can find most efficiently from a direct reading of the DTD.)

The first step in charting the structure is to sort out the sequential objects. That will give us the following list. Each line is to be treated as a separate object, with the objects all appearing in sequence. You will note that each comma at the outermost level terminates a line. Refer to the expanded declaration for Book above as you read each item in this list.

```
(Title, TitleAbbrev?)?,
BookInfo?,
ToC?,
LoT*,
Preface*,
(((Chapter)+, Reference*) | Part+ | Reference+ | Article+),
(Appendix)*,
Glossary?,
Bibliography?,
(Index | SetIndex)*,
LoT*,
ToC?
```

Next we will break out the lines that contain more than one element type. Here we use indentation to indicate shared membership within a parenthesized grouping. You might note that this sort of indentation scheme is in fact quite common among commercial SGML editing tools as a way of representing document structure on the user's screen.

```
(       Title,
        TitleAbbrev?
)?,
BookInfo?,
ToC?,
LoT*,
Preface*,
(       (       (Chapter)+,
                Reference*
        ) |
        Part+ |
        Reference+ |
        Article+
),
(Appendix)*,
Glossary?,
Bibliography?,
(       Index |
        SetIndex
)*,
LoT*,
ToC?
```

By this point the structure should be fairly clear. Again, the indentation levels here are equivalent to levels of nesting among the parenthesized groups.

Summary

In this brief walkthrough, we have "drilled down" from the structural level of Book to PCDATA, which represents a large portion of the actual character text which we write, mark up, and edit. In this exercise we have allowed the DTD itself to lead us—through element type and entity declarations and references—from highest to lowest structural levels of the document. Having once studied the full replacement text for an entity, we then recognize what that entity reference hides. Thereafter we are free to navigate at whatever level of refinement we wish, "descending" to full replacement text only when we need to pursue a particular entity to its fully expanded form. Furthermore by recasting a document's content model from DTD syntax to an indented list, we can readily visualize the underlying DTD and the document's structure.

CHAPTER 13

HTML
SGML for the World Wide Web

Terms introduced or reinforced:

anchor, browser/viewer, hypertext, Internet, reference anchor, referenced anchor, World Wide Web

Overview

HyperText Markup Language (HTML), an SGML application, represents a distinct mode of authoring and publication. It is a markup language whose tagging repertoire is extremely limited and whose primary purpose is to prepare hypertext documents for viewing on the World Wide Web (WWW). Our focus in this chapter is to examine the simplicity of HTML as it is defined by its DTD. We offer instructions for accessing the WWW and viewing not only the documents but also the underlying HTML markup "behind" the documents.

13.1 Warning to Two Kinds of Readers

If you are an aspiring World Wide Web author who purchased this book *primarily* to grasp enough WWW fundamentals to get something written, viewable, and ready for the Web, fine. This book offers you precisely that set of survival-level facts and how-tos. Moreover, we also offer you pointers in the literal sense: names, e-mail addresses, and other such references to which you should go next. The WWW, by definition, is a rapidly evolving organism, and trying to find simply what to do next is sometimes a daunting task for the authoring newcomer. Our warning to you is that, because we are viewing HTML in its role as an SGML application, there will be occasional references to previous chapters in this book, material that we assume you have read.

If, on the other hand, you bought the book to learn about the more general universe of SGML, and if HTML is not your primary concern, then we have a warning for you as well. HTML, unlike many SGML applications, defines a total publication, transmission, retrieval, and viewing *environ-*

---

ment. For this reason some of the designers and users of HTML view the markup tags as procedural commands, an unfortunate circumstance that has partly affected both the DTD and the HTML documentation. In this book we will continue to use correct SGML terminology so that you can more easily see how HTML relates to SGML and to other SGML applications.

13.2 The Universe of the World Wide Web

The most generic and lowest-level DTD for HTML is extremely minimal. To understand why this is so as well as what is the motivation for the popularity of HTML, we need to digress to (1) a short survey of the World Wide Web (WWW) infrastructure, (2) the type of WWW documents available, and (3) the viewing mechanisms available to users.

13.2.1 World Wide Web Infrastructure

The World Wide Web is possible only because of the existence of the Internet. The WWW is to some degree an abstraction, because there is no physically separate network or transmission devices for WWW information. Rather it is enabled and sustained by a combination of standards: Internet (and other) communications protocols, viewing device standards, retrieval standards, and a document preparation standard (HTML). It is the latter which is of immediate concern to us.

The person credited with starting the World Wide Web project is Tim Berners-Lee. He launched the WWW because of a need he felt for an appropriate delivery system for hypertext. That project began in 1989 at the Conseil Européen pour la Recherche Nucléaire (CERN) in Geneva, commonly known by English speakers as the European Organization for Nuclear Research. Note that the *primary* motivation for the WWW was not to exploit the Internet or to enable a greater professional community but to *enable a consistent means of delivering hypertext for transporting research and ideas effectively throughout the organization.*

13.2.2 WWW Documents

Three primary features distinguish most documents on the WWW: (1) They are written using HTML markup; (2) they are relatively short (or at least each individual piece is); and (3) they contain hypertext links.

We should not assume that these "documents" are character text only. In fact, hypertext on the WWW now includes various media: character text, sound, video, and live database query and access, to name a few. But the requirement of the WWW that documents be first and foremost *on-line* means that we are witnessing the evolution of an unprecedented communications genre. It is unprecedented because it presupposes a reader who is retrieving and viewing the document on a computer monitor. So the WWW is not just an alternative venue for delivering traditional documents. It would be inappropriate (though not impossible) for a reader to expect to be fed entire chapters of linear text from a historical novel during a viewing session, for example.

But the WWW document is not only usually short. It also offers the reader the possibility to link to another document, to query a database, to view a video, to hear a musical passage, or to return back to whatever document he or she came from. This user-driven navigation is at the heart of hypertext on the WWW.

13.2.3   WWW Viewers

By "viewer" we refer to the computer and software that enable the user to fetch and view a document. The term "browser" has become more frequent, because it connotes the unpredictable "liveliness" and interactive nature of a viewing session. The two terms are often combined and the software referred to as a "browser/viewer." WWW browsers represent the fulfillment of the electronic document dream, because a properly marked-up HTML document will run on *every* WWW browser device that exists. This is remarkable because browser software is now available for every popular computer and operating system, no matter how small or large. But the overriding factor in helping the WWW to expand so dramatically is that, no matter what the computer platform, a browser is probably available *free of charge*, either as shareware or as public domain software. (There is also an increasing number of more sophisticated browsers available for a price from commercial sources.)

A WWW-conforming browser hides all of the ugly detail of linking to hypertext documents and moving them to the user's computer for viewing, no matter where on the Internet (i.e., where on the planet) they are stored. Furthermore, as the accompanying illustration (Figure 13-1) shows, a browser such as NCSA Mosaic[TM1] automatically presents the document in as pleasant a page format as the computer will allow: properly selected fonts and font sizes for headings, full bit-mapped graphics, proper highlighting of hypertext "hot" links, proper spacing and indentation of paragraphs, proper arrangement and numbering (or bulleting) of items in lists, proper colors for everything, and probably more, depending on the particular platform and browser software. For computer users with GUI (graphical user interface) expectations, the WWW browser is a dream come true.

---

1. NCSA Mosaic was written at the National Center for Supercomputing Applications at the University of Illinois, Urbana-Champaign. The Board of Trustees of the University of Illinois holds the copyright to the software and the trademarks for "NCSA Mosaic", "Mosaic", the Mosaic logo and the spinning globe logo.

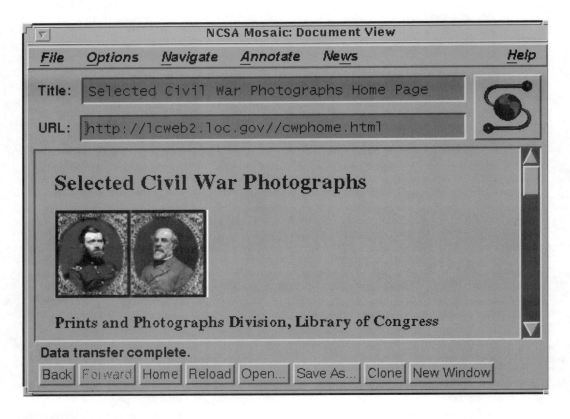

Figure 13-1. Sample Mosaic screen

13.3 The Core Enabling Technology of the Web

Among the total dynamic of the document revolution on the WWW, one would expect that there would be some trade-offs. Certain browsers may be free for the downloading, but nothing as delectable as total GUI access to a planetary knowledge base can be without cost. (We are ignoring the obvious cost of a user's getting connected to the Internet and the WWW in the first place, not to mention the cost of operating the Internet itself.) What might that trade-off be?

In order to assess the cost that enables the dream of the WWW, let us summarize the characteristics of the universal information technology:

1. It supports documents (including images, sound, databases) with an infinite variety of content.

2. It expects virtually no computing skills from its users.

3. It offers viewing and navigation of those documents on practically every computer platform in existence.

4. It automatically locates and transports those documents to the user's computer via the Internet through every networking protocol available.

The "cost" for achieving all of the above is borne by the document. This sort of universality truly demands a very low common denominator of document complexity in order for the mission of the World Wide Web to succeed. So the WWW document, written in HTML, allows a very limited array of structural features. In terms of our SGML examples in the previous chapters, there is practically no possibility of logical indentation of structure, except in the case of lists.

But structural simplicity is only one of HTML's characteristics. Its name suggests the hallmark of navigational method on the WWW: totally user-driven and non-linear linking to any object in any document that offers hypertext links. Every document on the WWW is a hypertext document by definition. Links therefore are more than just an add-on feature of the HTML document; they are its distinguishing characteristic. Hypertext links in HTML documents are defined using methods based on the standard SGML methodologies that we surveyed in Chapter 9. In this chapter we will see how the HTML manner of defining those links has itself evolved into a standard.

The two features of the HTML document which truly enable all of the universality in the above list are therefore (1) utter simplicity of structure, and (2) ample inclusion of links.

During our hypertext survey in Chapter 9, the issue of identifying the "referenced anchor" of a link to which the reader might traverse was rather simple, since the document was self-contained (i.e., no links to anything outside the current file). We simply named an element in the document with an ID and then linked to that named object from hyperlink elements elsewhere in the document through the use of an IDREF. But with HTML the domain is not only the current document but it also extends beyond to thousands of different computers in homes, offices, and institutions on every continent. The author of an HTML document, unlike most SGML authors and editors, will therefore typically be more concerned with hypertext links than with other aspects of document structuring.

Since HTML and the WWW are about document navigation and document locating, the "language" shares many of the concerns that we will study in HyTime, a standard extension of SGML whose primary focus is on locating and linking to data of all types. The most notable difference between HTML and HyTime however is that HTML is very minimalistic in its locating mechanisms, while HyTime can be as complex and abstract as necessary to meet real-world user requirements.

This chapter assumes that you have understood the general SGML topics of (1) generic identifiers and tagging, (2) the difference between a document's preparation and its presentation on a viewing device, and (3) the notion of hypertext linking, as expressed in an SGML document.

13.4 HTML Background

HTML, like other SGML applications, did not arise spontaneously. It was inspired by the need for a markup standard that would ensure the portability of hypertext documents on the World Wide Web. So unlike most other SGML applications, HTML arose not out of the needs of a particular industry but out of the need for making documents viewable anywhere on the Internet.

Standards for HTML therefore are tightly linked to (1) standards for computer viewing software and (2) standards for World Wide Web networking communications. The group who maintains these standards includes mainly people at the CERN high-energy physics laboratory in Switzerland and at the Massachusetts Institute of Technology (MIT) in Cambridge, Massachusetts, although there is extensive WWW/HTML development occurring all over the world.

13.5 HTML's Targeted Environment

What elements of the World Wide Web can the HTML document always expect to find? In other words, what is the targeted environment the writer and editor should keep in mind when preparing documents for deployment on the WWW?

The primary enabler of the document's portability is the set of standards for viewing devices, most often called "browsers." Just as in authoring for SGML in general, the writer need not—in fact, *should not*—be concerned with the *appearance* of the output. Not only are there major family differences between types of computers (PC, VAX™, UNIX™ workstation, Macintosh®), but the quality of terminals and monitors is so varied as to be impossible to anticipate. So the saying among HTML authors is just as important as for authors of other on-line SGML documents: leave rendition details to the browser (the reader's viewing system).

The other starring actor in the HTML realm is the WWW's mechanism for locating and transporting documents. So when a WWW user selects a particular "hot" portion of text (highlighted in some way to indicate a link to yet another document), the locating/transporting infrastructure of the WWW makes that new text magically appear on the user's screen. And once again, the user will see yet more "hot" links to explore. Again, the author is totally free from knowing how the viewer locates and fetches the document. So instead of dwelling on those mechanics, he or she will concentrate on document design. As we shall see later, designing and writing hypertext occupies a significant portion of authoring and editing activity. But the simplicity of HTML's own document locating schemes makes even that process very straightforward.

In relation to our discussion it is important to consider that the HTML application is intended primarily for informal, everyday communication. This does not require a large number of structural constructs, so the DTD is correspondingly simple. In fact, because of its simplicity, it is easy to get caught in the trap of considering HTML as markup for presentation only. We may find ourselves thinking: "An H1 element will produce large, bold type, so I will use it to emphasize this." But we must avoid getting trapped in the mindset of the document as a series of presentation-related device control codes and remember what the element types really represent. HTML's element types are designed to represent structures common in verbal communication: paragraphs, lists, headings and so forth. These are so common that we tend to take them for granted, not really recognizing them when we use them. However, by explicitly marking them through the use of HTML, we make them understandable to the browser software so that it can produce aesthetically pleasing and understandable renderings on a wide variety of output devices.

13.6 HTML and Other SGML Applications

Differences

Comparing HTML to other SGML applications is not a clean point-by-point process. This is partly because of the different histories of the applications and their user communities. But this is true mostly because HTML is a very special-purpose application, as we have noted. So the following list includes items that are not parallel among themselves. A further warning: Some of the differences and deficiencies in HTML may go away with future enhancements of the HTML standards and viewer specifications.

1. Level 1 HTML's element types are severely limited, offering only a fraction of the structural GIs available under most SGML applications. Just learn the "Basic Eight," as we shall soon see, and you're on your way.

2. The processing possibilities of an HTML document are very narrow: on-line viewing under the WWW plus *maybe* downloading and storing on the user's local computer (possibly for printing).

3. Practically every HTML document is peppered with interdocument links, while many other SGML documents do not contain such links.

4. An HTML document's size will ideally be short, often only a page or two, something that a user can view comfortably on a screen with not many Page-ups and Page-Downs. In other SGML applications, the length of a document most frequently conforms to a workgroup's tradition and practice.

5. HTML does not provide the level of sophisticated data indexing or retrieval capabilities that may be available in other SGML applications.

6. We might almost consider HTML in a broader sense to be a part of an architecture rather than simply an application or language. This is because HTML as an SGML application is closely tied to the viewing technology, the locating strategies, and the transporting mechanisms used on the World Wide Web.

13.7 HTML and Other SGML Applications

Similarities

1. HTML, as an SGML application, has an SGML DTD. An HTML document can be validated against that DTD using common SGML validating parsers.

2. Someone who is familiar with the concepts of SGML can readily read and understand any existing HTML document or easily create new HTML documents.

3. The author creating marked-up text need not dwell on the appearance of the final presentation.

13.8 Basic HTML Markup

We are now going to discuss a minimal set of HTML element types to enable you to mark up a document for viewing on the WWW.

Our discussion is based on a document provided by the National Center for Supercomputing Applications in Illinois. NCSA's "A Beginner's Guide to HTML"[1] is found at the following Web address (URL):

```
http://www.ncsa.uiuc.edu/General/Internet/WWW/HTMLPrimer.html
```

We have selected eight groups of element types that provide an adequate starting point for creating HTML documents. Here is our "survival kit" of element types, each with the exact spelling of its GI (uppercase used here, although lowercase is also acceptable), associated attributes, and usage:

1. *Title* of the document: `<TITLE>`

2. *Headers* (of six levels of significance: `<H1>`, `<H2>`, and so forth

3. *Paragraph*: `<P>`

4. Hyperlink *anchor*: `<A HREF=`{the address of the target (or "referenced") document} `NAME=`{an ID for this anchor, used to link to this point in the document}`>` Note that this element type, unlike the "txt-link" element type in Chapter 9, may be used to define both the reference ("initiating") anchor and the referenced ("target") anchor.

5. In-line *images*: `<IMG SRC=`{the computer file name of the graphic}`>`

---

1. Note that NCSA (like many others in the HTML community) refers to HTML element types as "tags." These are actually SGML element types, like those we discussed in Chapter 6, and so we will call them element types in this book.

6. *Lists*

    a. Unordered (i.e., unnumbered): `<UL>`

    b. Ordered (i.e., numbered or lettered): `<OL>`

    Each *item* in the list: `<LI>`

7. In-line elements:

    a. Emphasized: `<EM>`

    b. Stand-out emphasis: `<STRONG>`

    c. Citation of a source `<CITE>`

    d. "Typewriter Text" style (normally monospaced): `<TT>`

8. *As-is* ("preformatted") text block: `<PRE>`

Most of these element types are self-explanatory and require little discussion simply to *view* them in a Web hypertext source document (the tagged form that underlies the browser screen representation). But in order for you as a writer to *use* even these basic element types accurately, you should be aware of certain subtleties. Our approach in this discussion will be as follows:

1. A discussion of the element type.

2. Example(s) of the GI's usage in an HTML document.

3. The formal description of the element type, based on the HTML DTD itself.

We are going directly to the Level 1 HTML DTD for some purely practical reasons. First, that particular DTD is short, shorter than any other DTD that is of any great usefulness in the workplace. Second, you can always refer back to this DTD the way you would with a quick-reference card, since the DTD-style definition is by far more concise and unambiguous than any prose descriptions. (If you really want ample and profound discussions of HTML, consult the Web itself, join the WWW-HTML newsgroup, buy a textbook on HTML, or all of the above!). Third, studying HTML strictly in the context of the HTML DTD offers us an excellent opportunity to practice the DTD fluency skills we have been developing throughout the book. And unlike the DTD walkthrough in Chapter 12, in which we simply looked at generic mechanical features of the DTDs, we are here reading for the precise HTML detail.

In order to make the survey, discussion, and walkthrough as seamless as possible, we have reproduced here the HTML Level 1 DTD. As we did in the DTD walkthrough, we have numbered the lines in the left margin. We have also highlighted the eight basic groups of generic identifiers where they occur. *Note: The line numbers are not part of the DTD itself.*

```
1   <!-- Jul 1 93 -->

2   <!-- DTD definitions -->

3   <!ENTITY % heading "H1|H2|H3|H4|H5|H6" >
4   <!ENTITY % list " UL | OL | DIR | MENU ">
5   <!ENTITY % literal " XMP | LISTING ">

6   <!ENTITY % headelement
7          " TITLE | NEXTID |ISINDEX" >

8   <!ENTITY % bodyelement
9          "P | HR | %heading |
10         %list | DL | ADDRESS | PRE | BLOCKQUOTE
11         | %literal">

12  <!ENTITY % oldstyle "%headelement | %bodyelement | #PCDATA">

13  <!ENTITY % URL "CDATA"
14         -- The term URL means a CDATA attribute
15         whose value is a Uniform Resource Locator,
16         as defined. (A URN may also be usable here when defined.)
17         -->

18  <!ENTITY % linkattributes
19         "NAME NMTOKEN #IMPLIED
20         HREF %URL; #IMPLIED
21         REL CDATA #IMPLIED -- forward relationship type --
22         REV CDATA #IMPLIED -- reversed relationship type
23                         to referent data:

24                              PARENT CHILD, SIBLING, NEXT, TOP,
25                              DEFINITION, UPDATE, ORIGINAL etc. --

26         URN CDATA #IMPLIED -- universal resource number --
27         TITLE CDATA #IMPLIED -- advisory only --
28         METHODS NAMES #IMPLIED -- supported public methods of the object:
29                              TEXTSEARCH, GET, HEAD, ... --
30         ">

31  <!-- Document Element -->

32  <!ELEMENT HTML O O (( HEAD | BODY | %oldstyle )*, PLAINTEXT?)>

33  <!ELEMENT HEAD - - ( TITLE? & ISINDEX? & NEXTID? & LINK*
34                         & BASE?)>

35  <!ELEMENT TITLE - - RCDATA
36         -- The TITLE element is not considered part of the flow of text.
37         It should be displayed, for example as the page header or
```

```
38          window title.
39          -->

40  <!ELEMENT ISINDEX - O EMPTY
41          -- WWW clients should offer the option to perform a search on
42          documents containing ISINDEX.
43          -->

44  <!ELEMENT NEXTID - O EMPTY>
45  <!ATTLIST NEXTID N NAME #REQUIRED
46          -- The number should be a name suitable for use
47          for the ID of a new element. When used, the value
48          has its numeric part incremented. EG Z67 becomes Z68
49          -->
50  <!ELEMENT LINK - O EMPTY>
51  <!ATTLIST LINK
52          %linkattributes>

53  <!ELEMENT BASE - O EMPTY -- Reference context for URLS -->
54  <!ATTLIST BASE
55          HREF %URL; #IMPLIED>

56  <!ENTITY % inline "EM | TT | STRONG | B | I | U |
57                      CODE | SAMP | KBD | KEY | VAR |DFN | CITE "
58          >

59  <!ELEMENT (%inline;) - - (#PCDATA)>

60  <!ENTITY % text "#PCDATA | IMG | %inline;">

61  <!ENTITY % htext "A | %text" -- Plus links, no structure -->

62  <!ENTITY % stext -- as htext but also nested structure --
63                      "P | HR | %list | DL | ADDRESS
64                      | PRE | BLOCKQUOTE
65                      | %literal | %htext">

66  <!ELEMENT BODY - - (%bodyelement|%htext;)*>

67  <!ELEMENT A - - (%text)>
68  <!ATTLIST A
69          %linkattributes;
70          >

71  <!ELEMENT IMG - O EMPTY -- Embedded image -->
72  <!ATTLIST IMG
73          SRC %URL; #IMPLIED -- URL of document to embed --
74          >

75  <!ELEMENT P - O EMPTY -- separates paragraphs -->
```

```
76   <!ELEMENT HR - O EMPTY -- horizontal rule -->
77   <!ELEMENT ( %heading ) - - (%htext;)+>

78   <!ELEMENT DL - - (DT | DD | %stext;)*>
79   <!-- Content should match ((DT,(%htext;)+)+,(DD,(%stext;)+))
80        But mixed content is messy. -Dan Connolly
81    -->

82   <!ELEMENT DT - O EMPTY>
83   <!ELEMENT DD - O EMPTY>

84   <!ELEMENT (UL|OL) - - (%htext;|LI|P)+>
85   <!ELEMENT (DIR|MENU) - - (%htext;|LI)+>
86   <!-- Content should match ((LI,(%htext;)+)+)
87        But mixed content is messy.
88   -->

89   <!ATTLIST (%list)
90        COMPACT NAME #IMPLIED -- COMPACT, etc.--
91        >

92   <!ELEMENT LI - O EMPTY>

93   <!ELEMENT BLOCKQUOTE - - (%htext;|P)+
94        -- for quoting some other source -->

95   <!ELEMENT ADDRESS - - (%htext;|P)+>

96   <!ELEMENT PRE - - (#PCDATA|%inline|A|P)+>
97   <!ATTLIST PRE
98        WIDTH NUMBER #implied
99        >
```

Note the date of the DTD text presented above (`<!-- Jul 1 93 -->`, line 1). This is not the most current HTML DTD available but is rather a minimal DTD that is functional, yet still easy for us to study and understand. There have been many changes to the HTML DTD since this version, but this DTD should be supported by any available browser. Some of the more significant changes are noted in the discussion below. A copy of the HTML level 2 DTD is included on the disk that accompanies this book.

13.8.1   Title

```
<TITLE>
```

This is the title of the entire document, including all of the various hypertext references you may choose to imbed in the document. There can be only one title for a document. On a browser, the title will typically appear in a special title box or area of the screen, perhaps with the caption "Title".

If we were to create an HTML hypertext version of this chapter, we might write the title as follows:

```
<TITLE>HTML: SGML for the World Wide Web</TITLE>
```

Note that there is an end-tag, just as we would expect from the DTD. Not all element types in HTML have an end-tag however.

DTD Reference: Line 35

The two minus signs in the minimization parameter of the element type declaration tell us that both the start-tag and the end-tag are required. The contents of a "TITLE" is RCDATA (replaceable character data). This is character data that can contain general (e.g., character) entity references, such as >, the HTML definition of the ">" ("greater than") sign, should we wish to include that sign in the title. This would prevent the symbol's being erroneously interpreted as part of a tag.

13.8.2   Headers

`<H1> ... <H6>`

This is one of the few HTML element types that represents hierarchical document structuring in the sense that we have been discussing structure in this book. But the HTML DTD does not define a real hierarchical relationship where subordinate headings could only appear inside a higher-level structure. In most browser/viewers, however, the hierarchical relationship is expressed visually. Each successive type of heading is typically indented more from the left margin of the screen, with different font properties and varying amounts of vertical spacing between itself and surrounding text.

Example:

```
<H1>Unpacking your new MegaMytee Home Computer</H1>
…{General discussion about unpacking}…
<H2>Checking for Parts</H2>
…{Discussion of the parts list}…
<H2>Plugging in Cables</H2>
…{Instructions, diagrams about connecting}…
<H2>Warranty and User Support</H2>
…{Encouraging user to register for support}…
<H1>Starting up your MegaMytee</H1>
…
```

Note, however, that unlike most SGML applications, HTML heading types are not truly hierarchial levels. You are entirely free to combine types of headers in any order you please. The SGML validator for your document will not flag any errors, from a *correctness* standpoint.

However, if you choose to use, say, "H1, H3, H2," the results on the screen may be somewhat surprising to the reader as the headers will not be nested properly, as they were in our example above.

DTD References: Lines 77, 3, 61, 60

The declaration of headings (line 77) leads us immediately to two entities. In the generic identifier parameter, we find the entity "heading" which is defined at line 3 in our listing. This entity "expands" to the six types of heading tags: H1, H2, H3, H4, H5, and H6.

The content model for headings contains the parameter entity reference "htext" defined at line 61. The DTD tells us there that htext is either an "A" ("anchor," which we shall discuss below) or "text," the entity defined at line 60.

The entity "text" we find to be either character text (PCDATA for "parsed character data"), an image, or various in-line specialized elements, which we shall visit shortly.

13.8.3 Paragraph

```
<P>
```

This element type is deceptive for SGML-aware writers, because it does not mean quite the same thing in this HTML DTD as it does in most other SGML applications. As you will see in the DTD's comment for the element type at line 75, an HTML <P> is a *paragraph separator*. Elsewhere in this book "p" is a paragraph itself, bounded in the markup by a <P> start-tag and </P> end-tag, thereby situating the paragraph within the structure hierarchy. When we omit the </P> end-tag (something that most SGML applications allow), it is possible only because the end of the paragraph is implied by some other tag. In HTML, on the other hand, the function of <P> is to separate two pieces of text, which HTML therefore considers to be paragraphs. (As a result, users may tend to insert the <P> in order to force a vertical space during the browser's presentation of the document, thereby weakening the structure and reusability of the document.)

Example:

```
<H1>World's Most Brilliant Example of the Paragraph Tag</H1>
This is all you need to see. And this is the extent of the first
paragraph.<P>This is the second paragraph. Note that how (or whether) we format
paragraphs in our source text is immaterial in HTML.<P>
```

DTD Reference: Line 75

The SGML "declared content" designation of EMPTY tells us that the tag does not *enclose* any text but rather simply *marks a point* in the text. EMPTY is an SGML way of saying "use only a start-tag, because there is no end-tag."

The comment here reminds us that <P> "separates paragraphs." To belabor the message we have stressed throughout the book, it is not your concern as a writer *how* the various browsers will represent paragraph separation, only that you add the markup correctly.

Note: Newer versions of the HTML DTD (2.0 and above) support paragraphs with text and additional markup in the content model, and so allow for start- and end-tags bracketing the paragraph. *This newer approach is the preferred one for all new development.*

13.8.4 Anchor

<A>

The most notable characteristic of the Web HTML document is the "anchor", that point within a document (the "reference" anchor) from which it is possible to link to some other document or location in a document (the "referenced" anchor). It performs the same function as the "txt-link" element type of Chapter 9 in that it represents both a hyperlink and its reference (initiating) anchor. Unlike txt-link, however, instead of a "linkend" attribute that can point only to an identified element in the same document, the "A" element has an "HREF" attribute that can locate any document in the World Wide Web. So if we wished to point to the NCSA HTML "Quick Reference" document, we would insert an "anchor" as in this example:

```
<A HREF="http://www.ncsa.uiuc.edu/General/Internet/WWW/HTMLQuickRef.html">
HTML Quick Reference</A>
```

In addition, the "A" element type may be used to define a referenced (or target) anchor through the use of the "NAME" attribute. The techniques for defining and referencing named anchors are described in detail in Appendix A. Also in Appendix A is a complete discussion of "uniform resource locators," which are the methods HTML uses in hyperlinks for locating and retrieving documents.

DTD References: Lines 67-70, 60, 18-30, 13-17

The definition for "A" at line 67 is simple, implying that the usage for anchors and hypertext linking is consistent and straightforward. The element type declaration for "A" tells us that (1) both start- and end-tags are required, (2) the content is "text" at line 60 (which we saw earlier), and (3) the tag includes a hypertext reference.

The third item above deserves close attention. The attribute list (ATTLIST) for A is represented by an entity reference which is defined at lines 18-30. The only one of the attributes that concerns us is "HREF" (hypertext reference). The content for an HREF is a URL (uniform resource locator) represented by an entity reference that is defined at lines 13-17. The content of a URL is character data, according to that definition. Our discussion of URLs in Appendix A explains precisely what that content must be.

An important detail to emphasize is that while the anchor is a point in the text, it also serves to present some clue to the user that there exists some underlying hypertext at that point. Between the start-tag and the end-tag we must include "text" (see line 67). This text is the actual "hot" text, which the user will see marked in some way on the screen.

13.8.5 Images

`<IMG>`

Like the markup for anchors, the markup for images entails only (1) locating where in the text the image link should occur and (2) the location (i.e. what the source is) for the particular graphic.

Example:

```
<IMG SRC="http://WWW.ourserver/area_1/area_1_2/image005.gif">
```

DTD References: Lines 71-74, 13-17

The declared content of the element type IMG is EMPTY, which tells us that there is only to be a start-tag; the tag is to be placed at the location of the image within the text. The attribute SRC is used to indicate the location of the image by the use of a URL.

13.8.6 Lists

`<UL>`, `<OL>`, `<LI>`

The various list features of HTML, though only a subset of those in some other SGML applications, represent a "productivity bonanza" for writers and editors. *All* of such rendition details as bullet shapes, numbering, lettering, columns, indentations, and wrapping are handled automatically by the browser. The writer needs only to mark up the document with a minimal number of tags. We have chosen to discuss only two HTML list types: UL ("unordered list," whose list items will appear simply as a bulleted list) and OL ("ordered list," whose list items will each appear with an automatically assigned number or letter). Having tagged for one list type or another, the writer tags each list item with `<LI>`. You will note from the DTD that list item, like paragraph, has a content model of EMPTY. List items are therefore tagged only with the `<LI>` at the start of the item.

Example:

```
<H1>World's Classiest Example of HTML Lists</H1>
<OL>
<LI>Classy list item #1
<LI>Classy list item #2
<LI>Last of the classy list items
</OL>
```

DTD References: Lines 84, 61, 92

The two element types UL and OL, defined at line 84, allow for a sequence of three content types in any order: list items (LI), paragraph separations (whose presentation bears no bullets, numbers, or letters), and anchors for hypertext linking ("htext" at line 61 allows for those text items containing anchors). And the LI identifier at line 92 describes the simple no-content list item element type.

Note: Newer versions of the HTML DTD support list items with text and additional markup in the content model and so allow for start- and end-tags.

13.8.7   In-line Element Types

<EM>, <STRONG>, <CITE>, <TT>

We mentioned above that some HTML designers view it as a processing language. For this reason, the DTD *does* allow the writer to mark for B (bold), I (italic), and U (underlined), directly, as *physical* specifications for presentation. This, however, is not recommended because it may result in unpredictable and unintended results with certain browsers, as well as diminishing opportunities to reuse the document. Instead, we emphasize that HTML markup ideally should only indicate the *reason* for opting for some special treatment of a portion of text. Those *logical* options are only a few of the allowable element types: EM (emphasis), STRONG (strong emphasis), CITE (citation of a source), and TT ("typewriter text" style characters such as would be used for computer code). These options leave the appearance of the final output to the discretion and physical capability of the browser hardware: boldface, italics, underscore, fixed-width typewriter font, and whatever else.

Note that, unlike most other instances of markup, these specialized text portions can occur anywhere within the running text. HTML therefore refers to this sort of markup as "in-line."

Example:

```
We have all but <STRONG>preached</STRONG> in this section on the benefits of
confining ourselves to <EM>logical</EM> identificaton of meaning rather than
<EM>physical</EM> specification of style. This position is well substantiated
by such notable publications as <CITE>The SGML Handbook</CITE><P>
```

DTD References: 59, 56-58

The element type declarations for the in-line element types at line 59 tell us first that both start- and end-tags are required. We next find that the content of the text being so marked is #PCDATA (parsed character data). This keyword means parsed character data is allowed. Markup such as general entity references can be included, but only the parsed result will be treated as data for application processing.

The actual list of available GIs is in the entity definition for "inline" at lines 59-58. The series of options, each separated by the "or" symbol, tells us in DTD terms that we may select any one we wish. Note however that there are no semantics attached to this DTD definition; nothing in lines 56-58 hints at which ones we *ought* to select and which ones we *should avoid* using or *why* it makes any difference. This is just another instance of how SGML, functioning at its native level of description, deals only with description and validation and does not deal in semantics. Such is the mission of an architecture and of more external environments: comments in the DTD, an architectural standard (of which the DTD is only a part), or other such conventions.

13.8.8   Preformatted Text

```
<PRE>
```

We have added this element type to our basic repertoire because it is so frequently required for technical documentation. We have emphasized that browsers automatically exercise a very broad variety of rendition options: color, special effects, font styles, font sizes, and placement. That is all well and good for the sake of attractiveness of the final presentation. And that browser functionality indeed relieves the writer almost completely from the responsibility for formatting detail. But there are many instances among documents in which we do not wish for *any* mechanism to tamper with the way we have laid things out. The primary example of this is forms, in which we need to position our text precisely as we wish. And we need that "hardwired" format (normally with fixed-spaced font) to remain as-is across all delivery platforms. In other words, we have *preformatted* a block of text, and we want that text to remain so formatted.

Example:

```
<H1>Sample of some "preformatted" text</H1>
This is text that was prepared by the author for display with everything to
remain in exactly the same format<P>
<PRE>
```

```
 _____
|                                                 |
|     Name _____  Order Form for |
|                                   Cyber-Veggie Kitchen Tool |
|     Address_____                 |
|                                   Enclose check or money |
|     City _____  order in the amount of |
|                                   $159 in U.S. funds |
|     State_____ ZIP _____               |
|                                   Allow 6-8 weeks for delivery |
|_____|
```

```
</PRE>
```

DTD Reference: 96-99

In our example there are no HTML tags within the preformatted text element. However, note that the DTD definition of "PRE" allows for a limited amount of markup: in-line elements, hypertext anchors ("A"), and paragraph separators ("P"). So while the intention of PRE is to preserve the *layout* of the text segment intact, we can still invite the browser to enhance overall appearance to a limited extent. There is also an allowance for specifying the value of a width attribute, so that the browser can select a font and indentation to match the text block. However, since we cannot assume that all browsers will support WIDTH, it is best simply to assume an 80-character screen and then format accordingly.

Our example here happens to be a form. You should be aware that HTML has evolved (in level 2) to support a FORM element type, which allows the Web publisher to present a form with fill-in areas (like our name, city, state, and zip above) for the user to complete for a "live" data capture.

13.9 Basic HTML and Beyond

We have hinted throughout our discussion that HTML follows the spirit of the SGML tradition by being minimalist and simple. The DTD (which is SGML conforming) is so brief and straightforward that we were able to cover most of its significant statements just in our survey of eight basic "element type groups." This approach clearly supports the popular SGML notion that authors are most productive when they concern themselves as little as possible with presentation, leaving rendition details to the browser.

But HTML will not stay this simple. There are currently three distinct levels of HTML. The version we included in this book is HTML level 1, the one that is mandatory for all browsers (or "clients" as the standards people refer to the delivery systems).

HTML level 2 includes all of level 1 with the addition of fill-in forms.

HTML level 3, known as HTML+, is still under development at the time we are writing. It may include additional features such as tables, figures, and mathematical equations.

Further information about the ongoing advances in HTML can best be found on-line or in specialized books. Some places to begin looking are listed in Appendix A.3.

Summary

HTML has grown from its original concept of merely enabling hypertext on the Web to being the preferred method of presenting on-line information in a user-friendly manner. For the SGML savvy user, however, it has even greater benefits as that user can recognize that HTML documents are not tied to the World Wide Web but can also exist in the much broader world of all SGML applications. Knowing this, we can create HTML documents that comply with not just the letter of the DTD, but also with the spirit of SGML and so have all the benefits available through the use of SGML: portability, scalability and reusability.

CHAPTER 14

HyTime
SGML for Hypermedia

SGML terms introduced or reinforced:

architectural form, attribute, attribute form, element, element form, external entity, hypermedia

Overview

SGML, as we have seen, provides a document with flexibility and portability that is impossible with word processing or page description utilities. Nevertheless, limiting our discussion just to structured character text (with occasional graphics) and to explicit navigational locators (tags with ID attributes) does not begin to treat the electronic document in the ample sense that SGML promises to address. Hypertext linking, which we demonstrated earlier, is only single-medium linking, in contrast to the broader realm of hypermedia. And we have alluded many times to media beyond text and graphics (video, audio, and databases) and seen them at work in the SGML-based World Wide Web. But we have not discussed specifically how SGML may be a standardizing agent for multimedia. Our ambitious proposal in Chapter 1 for a "smart document architecture" (incorporating multimedia and interactivity) clearly requires more elaborate tools than we have seen thus far. This chapter discusses how HyTime responds to those requirements.

We survey the architectural forms of Hytime, the formal SGML markup declarations that define the HyTime standard. We use one of those architectural forms, `clink`, to demonstrate the HyTime version of a task from Chapter 9: establishing a point-to-point cross-reference link within a document.

This book began with a list of questions that writers and editors ask about SGML in general. We conclude the book by structuring this chapter as a series of questions about HyTime as an extension of SGML.

14.1 Why HyTime?

In Chapter 1 we listed some aspects of a "smart document," primarily that it would be non-linear (i.e., hypertext), highly interactive, and offer the user direct access to live data. And we added that it should handle multimedia. Two of those properties—multimedia and interactivity—characterize *hypermedia* rather adequately. It is not possible to say *how* much multimedia should be present and *how* interactive a particular document should be in order for us to call it hypermedia. It is more accurate to say that hypermedia incorporates all varieties of documents, no matter the quantity of hypertext or the level of interactivity.

We have alluded to non-character (multimedia) data in our discussions, but so far we have offered no specifics on how SGML might deal with graphics, audio, and video material in a document. And we offered examples in Chapter 9 of point-to-point cross-reference links. But neither in the case of multimedia nor of links did we resolve issues of treating hypermedia in a standard manner. HyTime, in a word, was invented to offer a standard for accomplishing the creation, life-cycle maintenance, and even rendition of hypermedia documents.

14.2 Does Hypermedia Require the Power of HyTime?

HyTime, like SGML itself, incorporates a certain discipline and formalism that require extra learning. But, as with SGML itself, the payoff is in hypermedia that is portable and whose life span is potentially infinite. So what is it about hypermedia that requires this extra sophistication?

A full discussion of hypermedia is beyond the scope of this brief chapter, but we suggest three aspects that clearly indicate a need for something beyond the simple SGML apparatus we have used thus far. First, the concept of "links" in the hypermedia sense extends far beyond point-to-point cross-reference linking in hypertext. In hypermedia we speak of *relationships* between objects. And those relationships may be of virtually any kind or of any variety we wish to define: spouse-to-spouse, part-to-whole, class-to-member, leader-to-organization. HyTime offers the flexibility to handle this open-ended notion of relationships among items in a document. And it offers a standard way of defining such relationships. (Later in the chapter we will "translate" our navigation link from Chapter 9 to a HyTime link.)

Second, a hypermedia document typically incorporates objects that are widely scattered one from the other. In Chapter 10 we referred to components of a document that might be distributed among the writers in a work group. And we discussed entity management in SGML to maintain that document as a logical whole. But in hypermedia, we really mean *scattered*: different countries, highly disparate platforms and formats, modules that come and go, and data that is highly volatile. Our discussion of Chapter 10 investigated using SGML entity structures for a more flexible document. HyTime extends that concept even further, offering a standard methodology for searching, locating, and addressing objects, even those whose whereabouts may be unknown until the user actually "plays" (renders) the hypermedia document.

Third, HyTime deals directly with time-based (video and audio) media. It offers all of the mechanisms necessary for scheduling (i.e., starting and stopping) portions of time-based media. This capability is clearly beyond the basics of SGML that we have seen thus far.

14.3 Is HyTime Different from SGML?

In a word, no. HyTime is an *application* of SGML that extends its functionality. HyTime covers the broad areas we listed above and solves the diverse problems that hypermedia presents to authors and editors. If you know the syntax of SGML, you know the formal declarations of HyTime **architectural forms** (described below). And you will add HyTime markup to a hypermedia document in exactly the same manner as you do it for basic SGML character-based documents. HyTime capitalizes on the power of **attributes** in SGML, as we shall discuss shortly. So your ability to understand and use attributes is your best preparation for mastering HyTime.

14.4 How is a HyTime Document Presented?

We have insisted that the final rendition or presentation of an SGML document is not the primary concern of the author or editor. In addition, we have noted that the flexibility of SGML guarantees that there is never any single rendition for a document, but that it will always be open-ended. The same is true for HyTime documents. While such a document might be viewable and playable on highly exotic hardware (virtual-reality machines, for example), the same document should typically be representable as a plain paper document. In other words, just as for SGML in general, we enable rendition on a variety of platforms and with various media, but we do not limit the authoring and editing process in doing so.

14.5 How Does HyTime Extend SGML?

The HyTime standard (ISO/IEC 10744:1992) consists partly of descriptive text, just as the ISO Standard 8879 of SGML contains text. In addition there are six sets, or modules, of **architectural forms**. An architectural form highly resembles an element-type declaration, as we shall see. But since the purpose of HyTime, as an application architecture, is to shape a document type, these architectural forms are intended as templates and therefore are not totally predefined element types.

The six HyTime modules (collections of architectural forms) are as follows, including a description of what each module makes possible:

1. Base: Element and attribute architectural forms common to the other five modules and also usable independently (e.g., attributes for controlling the location and type of referenced elements).

2. Measurement: Expression of size and position of objects using application-chosen measurement units (e.g., seconds, inches, words, virtual units).

3. Location address: Assignment of IDs to non-SGML objects and to elements in other SGML documents (useful for hyperlink anchors).

4. Hyperlinks: Relationships among information objects, in the same or multiple documents.

5. Scheduling: Description of "finite coordinate spaces" and scheduling events to occur within those spaces.

6. Rendition: Presentation of objects in finite coordinate spaces.

14.6 What Does an Architectural Form Look Like?

We promised earlier that your knowledge of SGML attributes will help you to understand HyTime architectural forms. That is because HyTime deals significantly in attributes. As you study the HyTime architectural forms more closely, you will be impressed by the dense population of ATTLISTs. The method of declaring attributes, assigning them values, and then interrogating those values is central to HyTime because HyTime expands in a major way on the *properties* of elements. A "property" of an element is commonly represented as being the value of some attribute of that element.

For HyTime properties of elements are a primary means of locating those elements, linking to them, querying about them, retrieving them, processing them, and formulating dynamic (i.e., on-the-fly, run-time) relationships of all kinds among the elements of a hypermedia document. These properties can be personality traits of an individual, characteristics of a species, hierarchical relationships among items in a tree structure, or formal parameters of a hypertext document itself.

The HyTime standard uses SGML element type declarations and attribute definition list declarations to specify formally the HyTime architectural forms. These declarations, unlike the declarations of document type definitions, are never actually processed by an SGML system; they are just a documentation technique. By convention, we emphasize that fact by showing the declaration names in lowercase, rather than the uppercase used for real declarations.

As an example of a very simple architectural form we turn now to "contextual link," called clink. This is a point-to-point link within a document whose function is precisely that of the txt-link we declared for our WAE DTD in Chapter 9. Here are the declarations for clink:

```
<!element clink     - O        (%HyBrid;)* >
```

```
<!attlist clink
          HyTime      NAME      clink
          id          ID        #IMPLIED -- Default: none --
          linkend     IDREF     #REQUIRED
    >
```

We observe the following regarding these declarations:

1. The keywords "element" and "attlist," unlike the usual practice, are in lowercase. This is to remind us, as we mentioned above, that these are not true declarations but are instead architectural form declarations.

2. All of the words in the declaration of the **attribute form** are standard. Unless you use a formal method for assigning alternative names to attributes, this is the wording as it must appear in ATTLIST declarations of element types that conform to the architectural form.

3. The attribute "id" is optional, just as one might expect for a one-way cross-reference link.

14.7   Architectural Form Versus Element Type

The architectural form declaration serves as a template which we adopt and tailor if necessary. We are free to name the element type anything we wish that our organization's conventions allow.

To create a clink form element type, we declare an element type and an attribute definition list declaration, using the corresponding architectural form declarations as templates. Here is one possible pair of declarations for doing a cross-reference link:

```
<!ELEMENT LinkTo     - O       (#PCDATA) >
<!ATTLIST LinkTo
          HyTime      NAME      #FIXED      "clink"
          linkend     IDREF     #REQUIRED
    >
```

Again, some items worth noting:

1. Here the name of the element type is arbitrary, just as we have learned throughout the book.

2. The attribute "HyTime" with its fixed name value of "clink" is the mechanism by which HyTime recognizes the element type LinkTo as a HyTime clink (that is, as being of the HyTime form clink).

3. The LinkTo attribute "linkend" is a copy of the "linkend" attribute of the form declaration for clink.

4. Using the GI "LinkTo" for markup will be exactly as it was without HyTime.

Note once again that by simply adding the `HyTime` attribute to the LinkTo declaration, a HyTime engine will recognize each LinkTo as a HyTime element. There is no need for the user to do anything extra when tagging the elements.

14.8 HyTime Just for Hypertext Linking?

Our first reaction to the above—conformance to still more standards apparatus—is that this is overkill for something as trivial as a cross-reference link within a single document. To which we respond that `clink` is indeed a very simple hypermedia construct and, like any other good computer language, HyTime lets you do simple things simply. But much of hypermedia is far more powerful and correspondingly more complex. And HyTime offers standardized ways to represent those constructs as well.

Our second observation is that, in preparing a document to be HyTime compliant, we guarantee maximum reusability and longevity for the document. If in the future someone enhances this document with multimedia and hypermedia functionality, because it is already HyTime conforming, the simple cross-reference links we originally wrote will continue to function without change.

14.9 Review

Standardizing a Hypertext Link with HyTime

To recap this overview of HyTime, let us revise our sample link from Chapter 9 to become HyTime compliant. Here is our original definition of the link:

```
<!--        ELEMENT    MINIMIZATION    CONTENT        -->
<!--        =======    ============    =======        -->
<!ELEMENT txt-link    - O             EMPTY          >
<!ATTLIST txt-link
              targ-txt  IDREF         #REQUIRED      >
```

In order to make this into a conforming (HyTime) contextual link, we first add the `HyTime` attribute:

```
HyTime    NAME   #FIXED      "clink"
```

So the revised contextual link would be declared as follows:

```
<!--        ELEMENT    MINIMIZATION    CONTENT        -->
<!--        =======    ============    =======        -->
<!ELEMENT txt-link    - O             EMPTY           >
<!ATTLIST txt-link
              targ-txt  IDREF         #REQUIRED
              HyTime    NAME          #FIXED       "clink"
```

>

Note that we do not have a `linkend` attribute although one is required by the `clink` architectural form. Of course, we do have a `targ-txt` attribute that serves the same purpose, but there is no way for HyTime to know this. HyTime gives the document type designer two ways to handle this situation:

1. We can simply change the attribute name from "`targ-txt`" to "`linkend`". This approach is most viable when no documents conforming to the DTD exist as yet. Otherwise it would be necessary to change all the start-tags for `txt-link` elements.

2. We can use a special HyTime attribute called "HyNames" to tell HyTime that we are using a different name for an architectural form attribute.

```
HyName CDATA    #FIXED "lnkend targ-txt"
```

The HyNames attribute tells a HyTime-aware system that the attribute it is expecting called "`linkend`" is here known as "`targ-txt`". The HyNames attribute is fixed in the DTD, so it will apply to all `txt-link` elements without needing to change their start-tags.

With the "HyNames" method, our markup tags would not change. All that has changed is that our document instance is now fully HyTime compliant.

Summary

This chapter has sought only to introduce you to HyTime as a functional extension of SGML. It is not a subset or superset, not a replacement, and not (as in the case of some widely used SGML applications) the product of some vertical industry or interest group. Nor is HyTime a revision to SGML meant to fix some deficiency. Rather it extends the facilities of SGML to enable the following:

1. Document reusability, as hypermedia, as intelligent retrieval, and within delivery methods yet undefined.

2. A flexible locating methodology, applying to all types of media, that requires less, not more, effort on the writer's part.

3. A formal method for identifying internal relationships and properties of items within the document.

4. Robust, standard support for media that is time-based and/or graphics-based.

5. A standard querying method to allow intelligent on-the-fly access to data in hypermedia documents.

Where to Go Next

This book has provided the necessary prerequisites to begin a further exploration of HyTime. Like SGML itself, HyTime offers you some powerful enabling tools for expanding the usefulness, portability, and life cycle of your documents. For that exploration, we urge you to read *Practical Hypermedia: An Introduction to HyTime* by W. Eliot Kimber (Englewood Cliffs, N.J.: PTR Prentice Hall, 1995).

In addition, Dr. Charles F. Goldfarb, the inventor of HyTime, has prepared a summary "Catalog of HyTime Architectural Forms and HyTime SGML Specification." You can get your own copy of the catalog by downloading it from the FTP site at the Institute for Informatics, University of Oslo. The full anonymous FTP address is as follows:

```
ftp.ifi.uio.no
```

You should find the document as `arch-form.catalog` under `/pub/sgml/HyTime`.

MORE ON THE
WORLD WIDE WEB

A.1   Uniform Resource Locators

The value of the HREF attribute in an HTML <A> "anchor" tag is one form or another of a uniform resource locator (URL). The URL represents one of the document locating standards within the HTML standard. It is your way of telling the current document (1) *how to access* the linked-to document (the access "scheme"), (2) the *name of the computer* where the linked-to document is to be found, (3) the *directory location* within the host computer, (4) the precise *file name* of the document on the remote computer (these last three specifiers comprise the reference document's "path"), and (5) the name of a specific anchor in that document. Let us dissect the following example to see how your HTML document will allow your document to access the remote document.

Here is an example of a URL for an HTML document:

```
http://our_server.com/book-lab/urls/url-page.html#Examples
```

In a general form the URL looks like this:

```
{scheme}://{host.domain}/{path}/{filename}#{location}
```

The first field, the access *scheme*, is the method of access and protocol (or "standard access method") that should be used to access the target document. There are six primary schemes you should be aware of:

1. `http`: HyperText Transfer Protocol.

2. `file`: file transfer protocol (ftp), this is also used to access a file on your local machine.

3. `ftp`: alternate method for specifying ftp.

4. `gopher`: gopher protocol, for accessing data stored on gopher servers.

5. `telnet`: to open a telnet session, for actual login to a remote system.

6. `wais`: to begin a wais search.

The Hypertext Transfer Protocol (http) is the most commonly used scheme within HTML documents. If we used the URL below inside an "anchor," we would be instructing our browser to use http as the method for locating the target ("referenced") document. Note that there are upwards of ten such protocols, some standard and some still undergoing experimentation, for accessing remote documents.

```
http://our-server.com/book-lab/urls/url-page.html#examples
```

Next we need to identify the location of the computer on which the target document resides. In the world of Web hypertext, a computer which is dedicated to transmitting a document whenever it is requested (as our document is about to do with its URL) is called a Web "host" or "server," and is identified by a "domain name" ({host.domain} in the template above). For practical purposes, we can consider the domain name to be the name of the computer, as seen by the Web. So in our example, "our-server.com" is the host domain name of the computer on which the document is to be found:

```
http://our_server.com/book-lab/urls/url-page.html#Examples
```

Note that when you use the "file" scheme to access a file on your local machine, there is no host domain name, so this field is left blank, resulting in three slashes after the scheme designation:

```
file:///C:/htmldocs/myresume.htm
```

Next, we need to let the addressing mechanism know just where within the computer the document is to be found, that is, the directory path to it ({path} in the template). This segment of the URL is a descriptor that is suggestive of the UNIX operating system, but it applies to any operating system that is running the server. Note however that, like UNIX and *unlike* DOS, all slashes are "forward slashes" (/) and not DOS-style "back slashes" (\).

```
http://our-server.com/book-lab/urls/url-page.html#Examples
```

So the server's pathname for the target file is "/book-lab/urls/".

We then provide the name of the document itself ({filename} in the template), "url-page.html" in this case

```
http://our-server.com/book-lab/urls/url-page.html#Examples
```

Finally, if the place we want to link to is identified with a named anchor, we can specify the name of the anchor ({location}).:

```
http://our-server.com/book-lab/urls/url-page.html#Examples
```

For our example there would be an anchor with a NAME attribute assigned the value "Examples", like this:

```
<A NAME="Examples">The Examples</A>
```

If we are not linking to a named anchor, we simply omit the "#{location}" portion of the URL.

It is worth observing some properties of the URL mechanism:

1. The term "locator" in "uniform resource locator" deals strictly with Internet access standards. As HTML and Web activity matures, and as we see the meaning of "information object"

expand, we will see other "flavors" of universal resource identifiers, of which the URL is one type.

2. The high popularity of the HTML URL has become almost a standard within the standard as a method for referencing a document electronically. That is, while with print media a researcher typically cites author, title, date of publication, and publisher, it is increasingly common to see writers reference some document by its HTML address.

3. The HTML address provides a direct access method within hypertext viewing methodology. We ordinarily think of the hypertext user's following the "canned" links from document to document, just as the authors imbedded them. This is why the software and hardware for viewing hypertext documents are collectively referred to as a "browser." But every browser available also offers the reader the option of moving directly to any document that bears a functional http address. True, it requires many characters' worth of perfect typing, but the access is as direct and immediate as Internet traffic will allow.

4. The "ugliness" of the URL remains almost totally hidden from the end user. Some browsers will display each linked-to document's URL in some unobtrusive screen location, and this may be of interest to a more serious reader. Otherwise, URLs simply do their job in an under-cover fashion, preserving all the tidiness and seamless screen presentation that the particular browser will allow.

5. URLs are standard by definition. There is an immense amount of global networking activity connected with every hypertext link. In the spirit of generalized markup, virtually all of this extremely complicated detail is hidden from the author, thanks to the URLs being standard. And as a major Internet benefit, the standard URL makes geography obsolete. That second field of the http address (host domain name) can reference *any* Web server on the planet, and how distant that may be is of little concern to you. The URL, as an Internet-based standard, simply handles it for you.

6. An HTML URL is a perfectly legitimate means of document addressing within any SGML application that supports it.

A good example document showing a variety of HTML links and URLs is the NCSA Mosaic Home Page. It is available at:

```
http://www.ncsa.uiuc.edu/SDG/Software/Mosaic/NCSAMosaicHome.html
```

A.2   Is HTML a Standard?

At the time of this book's publication, HTML will likely have evolved to support interactive fill-in forms, equations, tables, live database access, and many presentation effects. And the various browsers (client software) will have likewise evolved to keep pace. This rapidly evolving activity means that there are significant matters of which the writer and editor *must* be aware:

1.   Have HTML and HTML+ indeed become *de facto* international standards?

2.   If standards are in place for HTML+, what is the current version number, and where can the standards documents be obtained?

3.   Which versions of which browser software for which platforms support which version and level of HTML?

The somewhat free-flowing activity in HTML standards setting means that writing groups must be very careful not to exclude some significant audience by exploiting some exotic and attractive but non-standard HTML feature. The most likely scenario is that a small set of *de facto* HTML standards will fall out of the discussions and that it will be the popularity of presentation (browser) software for the various platforms that will be the deciding factor.

This situation contrasts sharply with most SGML application standards efforts, where the emphasis is on the document markup alone, independent of browsing or other processing. Instead, the objective of the standard is to preserve the document accurately, allowing its reuse for multiple purposes, on multiple platforms, over long periods of time.

A.3   Where to Go Next?

Not surprisingly the richest sources of information about HTML are on the Internet and are accessible through the World Wide Web. We assume that you know or can find out how to (1) use File Transfer Protocol (FTP) to access an "anonymous ftp site" (i.e., open to anyone) and (2) access a WWW document if you know its universal resource locator (URL). Note that the Web is in constant flux, and sometimes things move to new sites or simply disappear. Therefore these addresses are offered "as is," with no guarantee that they exist or contain anything useful.

There is a very good list of frequently asked questions (FAQs) about the World Wide Web itself at the following Web location:

```
http://sunsite.unc.edu/boutell/faq/www_faq.html
```

It is also available as a text file at the following ftp address:

```
rtfm.mit.edu/pub/usenet/news.answers/www/faq
```

This will provide you with an excellent overview of the simultaneously evolving areas of concern to Web authors and editors: URLs, browsers for all platforms, publication procedures, servers (software to allow you to become a live Web node), plus locators for various primers and tutorials.

For the very helpful "A Beginner's Guide to HTML," (National Center for Supercomputing Applications), go to the following Web location (URL) and browse through the document:

```
http://www.ncsa.uiuc.edu/General/Internet/WWW/HTMLPrimer.html
```

There is also a concise and well-written trilogy about the Web, Web servers, and HTML published by Nathan Torkington. It is available on the Web at the following URLs:

An introductory level primer on the WWW:

```
http://www.vuw.ac.nz/non-local/gnat/www-primer.html
```

HTML information targeted mostly to information providers:

```
http://www.vuw.ac.nz/non-local/gnat/www-html.html
```

Information about Web servers, also targeted to information providers:

```
http://www.vuw.ac.nz/non-local/gnat/www-servers.html
```

For the person who is seriously interested in what is happening on the Web and about the development of the Web, there are several usenet news groups dedicated to the topic:

```
comp.infosystems.authoring.html
comp.infosystems.www
comp.infosystems.www.users
comp.infosystems.www.providers
comp.infosystems.www.misc
alt.internet.services
comp.answers
alt.answers
news.answers
```

There is an HTML document on the disk that accompanies this title which has live links to the sites listed in this chapter as well as some others of interest. See the documentation on the disk for more information.

GLOSSARY OF *ISO 8879* TERMS USED IN THIS BOOK

Overview

This appendix is an excerpt from the ISO 8879 standard. We have only included the definitions of terms that are used in the book. If you want to read other definitions in the standard either purchase a copy of the full standard from your national standards body or get a copy of *The SGML Handbook*, by Charles F. Goldfarb (ISBN 0-19-853737-9) which incorporates the full text of the standard with helpful annotations.

Definitions

4.5 application: Text processing application.

4.9 attribute (of an element): A characteristic quality, other than type or content.

4.10 attribute definition: A member of an attribute definition list; it defines an attribute name, allowed values, and default value.

4.11 attribute definition list: A set of one or more attribute definitions defined by the *attribute definition list* parameter of an attribute definition list declaration.

4.12 attribute (definition) list declaration: A markup declaration that associates an attribute definition list with one or more element types.

4.28 CDATA: Character data.

4.33 character data: Zero or more characters that occur in a context in which no markup is recognized, other than the delimiters that end the *character data*. Such characters are classified as data characters because they were declared to be so.

4.35 character entity set: A public entity set consisting of general entities that are graphic characters.

NOTES

1. Character entities are used for characters that have no coded representation in the document character set, or that cannot be keyboarded conveniently, or to achieve device independence for characters whose bit combinations do not cause proper display on all output devices.

2. There are two kinds of character entity sets: definitional and display.

4.46 comment: A portion of a markup declaration that contains explanations or remarks intended to aid persons working with the document

4.51 conforming SGML document: An SGML document that complies with all provisions of this International Standard.

NOTE — The provisions allow for choices in the use of optional features and variant concrete syntaxes.

4.55 (content) model: Parameter of an element declaration that specifies the *model group* and *exceptions* that define the allowed *content* of the element.

4.72 data: The characters of a document that represent the inherent information content; characters that are not recognized as markup.

4.73 data character: An *SGML character* that is interpreted as data in the context in which it occurs, either because it was declared to be data, or because it was not recognizable as markup.

4.74 data content: The portion of an element's *content* that is data rather than markup or a subelement.

4.84 default value: A portion of an attribute definition that specifies the attribute value to be used if there is no *attribute specification* for it.

4.92 descriptive markup: Markup that describes the structure and other attributes of a document in a non-system-specific manner, independently of any processing that may be performed on it. In particular, SGML descriptive markup uses tags to express the element structure.

4.96 document: A collection of information that is processed as a unit. A document is classified as being of a particular document type.

NOTE — In this International Standard, the term almost invariably means (without loss of accuracy) an SGML document.

4.97 document architecture: Rules for the formulation of text processing applications.

NOTE — For example, a document architecture can define:

  a. attribute semantics for use in a variety of element definitions;

  b. element classes, based on which attributes the elements have;

  c. structural rules for defining document types in terms of element classes;

  d. link processes, and how they are affected by the values of attributes; and/or

  e. information to accompany a document during interchange (a "document profile").

4.99 document element: The element that is the outermost element of an instance of a document type; that is, the element whose *generic identifier* is the *document type name*.

4.100 document instance: Instance of a document type.

4.102 document type: A class of documents having similar characteristics; for example, journal, article, technical manual, or memo.

4.103 (document) type declaration: A markup declaration that formally specifies a portion of a document type definition.

NOTE — A document type declaration does not specify all of a document type definition because part of the definition, such as the semantics of elements and attributes, cannot be expressed in SGML. In addition, the application designer might choose not to use SGML in every possible instance — for example, by using a data content notation to delineate the structure of an element in preference to defining subelements.

4.105 document (type) definition: Rules, determined by an application, that apply SGML to the markup of documents of a particular type.

NOTE — Part of a document type definition can be specified by an SGML document type declaration. Other parts, such as the semantics of elements and attributes, or any application conventions, cannot be expressed formally in SGML. Comments can be used, however, to express them informally.

4.108 DTD: Document type definition.

4.110 element: A component of the hierarchical structure defined by a document type definition; it is identified in a document instance by descriptive markup, usually a start-tag and end-tag.

NOTE — An element is classified as being of a particular element type.

4.111 element declaration: A markup declaration that contains the formal specification of the part of an element type definition that deals with the content and markup minimization.

4.113 element structure: The organization of a document into hierarchies of elements, with each hierarchy conforming to a different document type definition.

4.114 element type: A class of elements having similar characteristics; for example, paragraph, chapter, abstract, footnote, or bibliography.

4.115 element (type) definition: Application-specific rules that apply SGML to the markup of elements of a particular type. An element type definition includes a formal specification, expressed in element and attribute definition list declarations, of the content, markup minimization, and attributes allowed for a specified element type.

NOTE — An element type definition is normally part of a document type definition.

4.119 end-tag: Descriptive markup that identifies the end of an element.

4.120 entity: A collection of characters that can be referenced as a unit.

NOTES

1. Objects such as book chapters written by different authors, pi characters, or photographs, are often best managed by maintaining them as individual entities.

2. The actual storage of entities is system-specific, and could take the form of files, members of a partitioned data set, components of a data structure, or entries in a symbol table.

4.121 entity declaration: A markup declaration that assigns an SGML name to an entity so that it can be referenced.

4.124 entity reference: A reference that is replaced by an entity.

NOTE — There are two kinds: named entity reference and short reference.

4.125 entity set: A set of entity declarations that are used together.

NOTE — An entity set can be public text.

4.135 external identifier: A parameter that identifies an external entity or data content notation.

NOTE — There are two kinds: system identifier and public identifier.

4.143 general entity: An entity that can be referenced from within the content of an element or an attribute value literal.

4.144 general entity reference: A named entity reference to a general entity.

4.145 generic identifier: A name that identifies the element type of an element.

4.146 GI: Generic identifier.

4.150 ID: Unique identifier.

4.151 ID reference list: An attribute value that is a list of ID reference values.

4.152 ID reference value: An attribute value that is a *name* specified as an *id value* of an element in the same document instance.

4.153 ID value: An attribute value that is a *name* that uniquely identifies the element; that is, it cannot be the same as any other *id value* in the same document instance.

4.160 instance (of a document type): The data and markup for a hierarchy of elements that conforms to a document type definition.

4.178 mark up: To add markup to a document.

4.179 marked section: A section of the document that has been identified for a special purpose, such as ignoring markup within it.

4.180 marked section declaration: A markup declaration that identifies a marked section and specifies how it is to be treated.

4.181 marked section end: The closing delimiter sequence of a marked section declaration.

4.182 marked section start: The opening delimiter sequence of a marked section declaration.

4.183 markup: Text that is added to the data of a document in order to convey information about it.

NOTE — There are four kinds of markup: descriptive markup(tags), references, markup declarations, and processing instructions.

4.187 (markup) minimization feature: A feature of SGML that allows markup to be minimized by shortening or omitting tags, or shortening entity references.

NOTE — Markup minimization features do not affect the document type definition, so a minimized document can be sent to a system that does not support these features by first restoring the omitted markup. There are five kinds: SHORTTAG, OMITTAG, SHORTREF, DATATAG, and RANK.

4.224 parameter: The portion of a markup declaration that is bounded by ps separators (whether required or optional). A parameter can contain other parameters.

4.225 parameter entity: An entity that can be referenced from a markup declaration parameter.

4.226 parameter entity reference: A named entity reference to a parameter entity.

4.228 parsed character data: Zero or more characters that occur in a context in which text is parsed and markup is recognized. They are classified as data characters because they were not recognized as markup during parsing.

4.229 PCDATA: Parsed character data.

4.239 public identifier: A minimum literal that identifies public text.

NOTES

1. The public identifiers in a document can optionally be interpretable as formal public identifiers.

2. The system is responsible for converting public identifiers to system identifiers.

4.258 reference concrete syntax: A concrete syntax, defined in this International Standard, that is used in all SGML declarations.

4.266 replacement text: The text of the entity that replaces an entity reference.

4.268 required attribute: An attribute for which there must always be an *attribute specification* for the attribute value.

4.275 SDATA entity: Specific character data entity.

4.278 SGML: Standard Generalized Markup Language

4.279 SGML application: Rules that apply SGML to a text processing application. An SGML application includes a formal specification of the markup constructs used in the application, expressed in SGML. It can also include a non-SGML definition of semantics, application conventions, and/or processing.

NOTES

1. The formal specification of an SGML application normally includes document type definitions, data content notations, and entity sets, and possibly a concrete syntax or capacity set. If processing is defined by the application, the formal specification could also include link process definitions.

2. The formal specification of an SGML application constitutes the common portions of the documents processed by the application. These common portions are frequently made available as public text.

3. The formal specification is usually accompanied by comments and/or documentation that explains the semantics, application conventions, and processing specifications of the application.

4. An SGML application exists independently of any implementation. However, if processing is defined by the application, the non-SGML definition could include application procedures, implemented in a programming or text processing language.

4.282 SGML document: A document that is represented as a sequence of characters, organized physically into an entity structure and logically into an element structure, essentially as described in this International Standard. An SGML document consists of data characters, which represent its information content, and markup characters, which represent the structure of the data and other information useful for processing it. In particular, the markup describes at least one document type definition, and an instance of a structure conforming to the definition.

4.285 SGML parser: A program (or portion of a program or a combination of programs) that recognizes markup in SGML documents.

NOTE — If an analogy were to be drawn to programming language processors, an SGML parser would be said to perform the functions of both a lexical analyzer and a parser with respect to SGML documents.

4.304 specific character data entity: An entity whose text is treated as *system data* when referenced. The text is dependent on a specific system, device, or application process.

NOTE — A specific character data entity would normally be redefined for different applications, systems, or output devices.

4.305 Standard Generalized Markup Language: A language for document representation that formalizes markup and frees it of system and processing dependencies.

4.306 start-tag: Descriptive markup that identifies the start of an element and specifies its generic identifier and attributes.

4.307 status keyword: A marked section declaration parameter that specifies whether the marked section is to be ignored and, if not, whether it is to be treated as character data, replaceable character data, or normally.

4.309 subelement: An element that occurs in the content of another element (the "containing element") in such a way that the subelement begins when the containing element is the current element.

4.313 system identifier: System data that specifies the file identifier, storage location, program invocation, data stream position, or other system-specific information that locates an external entity.

4.314 tag: Descriptive markup.

NOTE — There are two kinds: start-tag and end-tag.

4.316 text: Characters.

NOTE — The characters could have their normal character set meaning, or they could be interpreted in accordance with a data content notation as the representation of graphics, images, etc.

4.318 text processing application: A related set of processes performed on documents of related types.

NOTE — Some examples are:

a. Publication of technical manuals for a software developer: document types include installation, operation, and maintenance manuals; processes include creation, revision, formatting, and page layout for a variety of output devices.

b. Preparation of manuscripts by independent authors for members of an association of publishers: document types include book, journal, and article; creation is the only defined process, as each publisher has its own methods of formatting and printing.

c. Office correspondence: document types include memos, mail logs, and reports; processes include creation, revision, simple formatting, storage and retrieval, memo log update, and report generation.

4.324 unique identifier: A *name* that uniquely identifies an element.

4.329 validating SGML parser: A conforming SGML parser that can find and report a reportable markup error if (and only if) one exists.

SGML MARKUP OF CHAPTER 10

Overview

This appendix is to give an idea of what a real book looks like when marked up with SGML. We also include in this appendix the DTD that we created and used for the production of *ReadMe.1st*. Note that we have done some cleanup of the format (mostly the insertion of line breaks) so that it is easier to read and see the structure.

C.1   Markup of Chapter 10

```
<!DOCTYPE BOOK SYSTEM "tdt.dtd">
<CHAPTER><TITLE>Entity Management</TITLE>
<TERMSLIST><TITLE>SGML terms introduced or reinforced:</TITLE>
<PARA>entity, entity declaration, entity reference, entity set, general entity
reference, parameter entity reference, public identifier, replacement text,
specific character data entity.</PARA></TERMSLIST>
<OVERVIEW><TITLE>Overview</TITLE>
<PARA>Using parameter entities benefits the designer and human reader of a
document-type definition, as we saw in Chapter 7. And general entities simplify the
writer&rsquor;s task. But<INDEXTERM TERM="entity: purpose">entities accomplish far
more. Because an entity is declared <EMPHASIS>once</EMPHASIS> to be read
<EMPHASIS>many times</EMPHASIS>, we can use entities containing large sections of a
document to (1)  free the writer from concern over the specifics of computer
storage of the many parts of a large document, (2) ease the writer&rsquor;s task of
incorporating disparate types of media, and (3) enhance the reusability and
longevity of a document. We have distinguished between (1) the markup
representation of <EMPHASIS>element structure</EMPHASIS> (enabled by markup during
the authoring process) and (2) the <EMPHASIS>visual (or perceivable)
representation</EMPHASIS> of the document. We now propose a third layer: the
<EMPHASIS>storage representation</EMPHASIS>. This layer provides yet more relief to
the writer, since all of the system-specific detail can be isolated to entity
declarations separate from the body of the document.</PARA></OVERVIEW>
<SECTION><TITLE>Entities</TITLE>
```

<PARA>The SGML term <QUOTE>entity</QUOTE> is strikingly simple in its formal definition and highly pervasive in its actual usage. We studied two varieties of SGML entities in Chapter 7: <SGMLTERM>parameter entities</SGMLTERM> and <SGMLTERM>general entities</SGMLTERM>. There we hinted at benefits of entities and made some distinction between who benefits from each type. The designer or editor or reader of a DTD benefits from parameter entities, we said, while general entities benefit the author. We also distinguished between the objectives of each type of entity, that is, what sort of text each type of entity refers to and where each type of entity reference is used. Finally, we studied some examples of how we declare and use those two types of entities.</PARA>
<PARA>In this chapter we will expand on that why-who-what-where-how discussion in order to gain a larger view of entities in general. That will make it quite easy to introduce entity management. If you have been waiting for even more proof of the benefits and payoff of using SGML, then this discussion should help convince you that the SGML claims of document portability and reusability are indeed attainable. And entity management is, as we shall find, neither subtle nor revolutionary. It merely formalizes the way writers and writing groups have manipulated large documents all along.</PARA>
<SUBSECTION><TITLE>Formal Definition</TITLE>
<PARA>The <INDEXTERM TERM="entity: defined"> definition of <QUOTE>entity</QUOTE> is simple:
<ISOQUOTE> <PARA>entity: A collection of characters that can be referenced as a unit.</PARA><CITATION>ISO 8879: &secmrk;4.120</CITATION></ISOQUOTE>
While we do not intend for this chapter to be an exhaustive commentary on the ISO definition, we need to look closely at some important aspects of entities that the definition conveys.</PARA>
<PARA>There are two distinct activities implied by the formal definition. <QUOTE>Collection of characters</QUOTE> implies that someone points to or specifies or gathers or delineates some portion of text. For every type of entity we are discussing, SGML enables us to <QUOTE>collect</QUOTE> an entity by means of an <SGMLTERM><INDEXTERM TERM="entity declaration">entity declaration</SGMLTERM>. To declare an entity then means to collect some string of characters. The declaration is the formal <EMPHASIS>means</EMPHASIS> that SGML offers to make collection possible.</PARA>
<PARA>The <EMPHASIS><INDEXTERM TERM="entity: purpose">purpose</EMPHASIS> of declaring an entity is likewise explicit in the definition. The whole point is to enable us simply to <EMPHASIS>refer</EMPHASIS> to the collected text and not to be forced to repeat all of the same text string every time we use it.</PARA>
<PARA>The underlying principle of an <SGMLTERM><INDEXTERM TERM="entity declaration">entity declaration</SGMLTERM>—reference rather than repeated inclusion of text—is common to many activities in computer programming. The entity declaration enables us simply to point to (reference) the entity. The enabling mechanism for <QUOTE>pointing to</QUOTE> an entity is similar to pointing to (or addressing) data in computer storage in general. The entity bears a <EMPHASIS><INDEXTERM TERM="entity name: reference pointer">name</EMPHASIS>, and this name is the pointing apparatus for the entity. The ISO 8879 definition for <SGMLTERM>entity declaration</SGMLTERM> highlights the importance of the entity’s name:

<ISOQUOTE> <PARA><INDEXTERM TERM="entity declaration: defined">entity declaration:
A markup declaration that assigns an SGML name to an entity so that it can be
referenced.</PARA><CITATION>ISO 8879: &secmrk;4.121</CITATION></ISOQUOTE></PARA>
<PARA>In addition to <QUOTE>collection</QUOTE> and <QUOTE>reference,</QUOTE> there
is a third significant property of entities that the definition only implies but
that is the most powerful of all: declare <EMPHASIS>once</EMPHASIS> and reference
<EMPHASIS>many times</EMPHASIS>.</PARA>
<PARA>What we have said so far about entities applies to entities in general. The
difference between the various varieties of entity usage become clear when we ask
the various <QUOTE>wh—</QUOTE> questions: Why? who? what? and so
forth.</PARA></SUBSECTION>
<SUBSECTION><TITLE>Parameter Entities</TITLE>
<PARA><INDEXTERM TERM="<$startrange>parameter entity: discussion">What sort of text
does the declaration for a parameter entity collect? (A more formal way to phrase
the question is <QUOTE>What is its <INDEXTERM TERM="entity: replacement
text">replacement text?</QUOTE>) As we saw in Chapter 7, the text for a parameter
entity is a string of characters which itself is part of yet another declaration.
We declared a parameter entity <SGMLNAME>txm</SGMLNAME> which was our name for the
string <QUOTE>(p|l)+</QUOTE>.</PARA>
<PARA>We said in Chapter 7 that both of our reasons for using parameter entities
had to do with economy. First, by declaring the entity <SGMLNAME>txm</SGMLNAME> to
replace the fully spelled-out text string, we cut the length of each occurrence by
50 percent. This saving of three characters would not seem to justify the
complication of using a <INDEXTERM TERM="parameter entity declaration">parameter
entity declaration and references. But in Chapter 7 we also cited a five-line
string of parameter text which was replaced by a mere seven-character entity name.
So there is most definitely an economy possible with real-world DTDs. This is
an<INDEXTERM TERM="parameter entity: economy when creating DTD"> economy that
applies at the time of creating the document type definition.</PARA>
<PARA>The other <INDEXTERM TERM="parameter entity: economy of maintenance">economy
is one of maintenance. Even in our tiny WAE DTD we found three occurrences of
<QUOTE>(p|l)+</QUOTE>. If, for example, a DTD designer or an author should wish to
alter the content model of a very complex DTD (but one which used parameter
entities extensively), then it would be a simple matter to change only the
parameter entity declaration rather than having to search for and edit the same
string throughout the entire DTD. So for our WAE DTD we may wish to change
<QUOTE>(p|l)+</QUOTE> in the content model to <QUOTE>(p|l|blkq)+</QUOTE>. We would
only need to change it once in the declaration in order for the change to take
effect for the entire DTD. This economy therefore applies over the entire life
cycle of the document.</PARA>
<PARA>From our discussion it should be clear that parameter entities operate only
within markup declarations. Their <QUOTE>collections of characters</QUOTE> comprise
strings that belong only in declaration parameters. Since in typical documents,
most markup declarations occur in the DTD, it follows that the beneficiaries of
parameter entities are people who deal directly with the DTD. These include
designers of DTDs, but they may also include writers and managers who must simply
make slight modifications to a DTD.</PARA>

<PARA>But the greatest benefits of parameter entities come to the <EMPHASIS>human reader</EMPHASIS> of the DTD. This is most often the writer or editor who is seeking to understand the structure of a particular document type. A well-designed DTD that uses parameter entity declarations and references is far more readable than one that repeats long and complicated strings of parameter text.</PARA>
<PARA>The mechanics of declaring an entity (repeating our exhibit from Chapter 7) is as follows:<INDEXTERM TERM="parameter entity declaration: systax">
<DTDLISTING><SGMLDECLARATION>!ENTITY % <EMPHASIS>name</EMPHASIS> "<EMPHASIS>replacement text</EMPHASIS>"</SGMLDECLARATION></DTDLISTING>
When we reference a parameter entity in a content model we enclose its name within a <QUOTE><INDEXTERM TERM="parameter entity reference open (%)">%</QUOTE> (defined in ISO 8879 as <SGMLTERM>parameter entity reference open</SGMLTERM> or <SGMLTERM>PERO</SGMLTERM>) and a <QUOTE><INDEXTERM TERM="parameter entity reference close (;)">;</QUOTE> (<SGMLTERM>reference close</SGMLTERM>), as follows:
<DTDLISTING><SGMLDECLARATION>!ELEMENT sec   -- --   (shd?, (<STRONGEMPH>%txm;</STRONGEMPH> | ssec | txtref)+)</SGMLDECLARATION><INDEXTERM TERM="<$endrange>parameter entity: discussion"></DTDLISTING></PARA></SUBSECTION>
<SUBSECTION><TITLE>General Entities</TITLE>
<PARA><INDEXTERM TERM="<$startrange>general entity: discussion">The <QUOTE>collections of characters</QUOTE> referenced by general entities are of even more immediate concern to the writer, since these entities occur in the body of the document itself. As with all entities, the benefit is economy of some kind, and here again the benefit is at least twofold. First, a general entity could replace a character string that is long, difficult to type, and occurs frequently throughout the document. For instance, using the <SGMLTERM><INDEXTERM TERM="general entity reference">general entity reference</SGMLTERM> <QUOTE>cob</QUOTE> for the <SGMLTERM><INDEXTERM TERM="general entity replacement text">replacement text</SGMLTERM> <QUOTE>Chairman of the Board Linius Phelan Bennington III</QUOTE> clearly represents a <QUOTE>creation-time</QUOTE> benefit for the author, particularly if it is referenced 150 times in the document.</PARA>
<PARA>The additional creation-time benefit which we discussed in Chapter 7 is to enable the writer to incorporate foreign symbols that are not on the keyboard. Because an entity name merely <EMPHASIS>references</EMPHASIS> the character by some standard name, the author only needs to key in that name. So the <INDEXTERM TERM="general entity: text string example">Byelorussian <QUOTE>capital U</QUOTE> character, which is a non-Russian Cyrillic character, can be represented by the entity reference <QUOTE>Ubrcy,</QUOTE> which the writer enters as <QUOTE><SGMLTAG CLASS="GenEntity">Ubrcy</SGMLTAG></QUOTE> (without quotes). That character is defined as part of a standard character <EMPHASIS>entity set</EMPHASIS> known as ISOcyr2. We will discuss entity sets shortly.</PARA>
<PARA>Like parameter entities, general entities offer immense life-cycle (<INDEXTERM TERM="general entity: economy of maintenance">maintenance) benefits as well. Suppose, to everyone’s horror, that research of company dossiers revealed that the distinguished chairman is actually Bennington IV and not Bennington III. Just one change in the replacement text of the entity declaration would repair the entire document.</PARA>
<PARA>As for the mechanics of declaring a general entity, here is the declaration of the Byelorussian character we cited above:

<DTDLISTING><SGMLDECLARATION><INDEXTERM TERM="general entity declaration: syntax">!ENTITY ubrcy SDATA "[Ubrcy]"--=capital U, Byelorussian--</SGMLDECLARATION></DTDLISTING>
This declaration defines a character whose representation is likely to be dependent on system-specific output devices. So the ISO definition includes the SGML keyword <SGMLKEYWORD><INDEXTERM TERM="SDATA entity">SDATA</SGMLKEYWORD>, which informs the computer that this is a <SGMLTERM><INDEXTERM TERM="specific character data entity: defined">specific character data entity</SGMLTERM>. By definition, the text (the single character referenced here) is system-specific:
<ISOQUOTE> <PARA><STRONGEMPH>specific character data entity:</STRONGEMPH> An entity whose text is treated as <EMPHASIS>character data</EMPHASIS> when referenced. The text is dependent on a specific system, device, or application process.</PARA>
<PARA>NOTE -- A specific character data entity would normally be redefined for different applications, system, or output devices.</PARA><CITATION>ISO 8879: &secmrk;4.304</CITATION></ISOQUOTE>
In other words, the entity replacement text will be (probably) rendered differently on different types of systems<INDEXTERM TERM="<$endrange>general entity: discussion">.</PARA></SUBSECTION></SECTION>
<SECTION><TITLE>Benefits</TITLE>
<PARA><INDEXTERM TERM="general entity: summary">To summarize, we find entities to be beneficial in two respects. First, an entity has direct and immediate benefits to the portion of the document to which it applies. A <INDEXTERM TERM="parameter entity: summary">parameter entity makes for more concise and readable entity declarations and content models within a DTD. And a general entity declaration dramatically reduces keystrokes for the writer. Furthermore, a general entity enables the writer with only a standard keyboard to include characters from any written alphabet on earth. Entity declarations for many such characters have been collected into ISO standard character entity sets; we shall cite an example shortly.</PARA>
<PARA>The second general benefit of entities is that they enhance the maintenance task and hence the life cycle of the document. A parameter entity declaration allows a designer easily to modify a complex DTD at a single location without perturbing and perhaps <QUOTE>breaking</QUOTE> a complex definition. For the writer with a maintenance task in a large document, that task is immensely simplified if some string of characters (like a complicated list of current addresses that is repeated throughout a long document) is represented by a general entity.</PARA></SECTION>
<SECTION><TITLE>Entities in Pre-Electronic Writing and in SGML</TITLE>
<PARA>We turn now to<INDEXTERM TERM="entity management"> entity management, in which the <QUOTE>collection of characters</QUOTE> is within the body of the document and typically applies to larger portions of a document. While a single-character entity is theoretically treated identically to an entity of several million words, in practice there can be significant differences when dealing with entities whose texts are large chunks of a document, which will probably all be stored on a computer under different file names. For the remainder of this chapter we will be (1) examining what some of those differences are and then (2) determining how SGML helps us formalize the process of concurrent authorship of multiple portions of large documents.</PARA>

<PARA>A large documentation project will be fragmented, in the sense that several writers will be working simultaneously on different portions of the document. This is not bad… not even undesirable and certainly not uncommon. Instead of a writer’s doing an entire set of chapters, a single writer may be assigned to create sidebar, tabular, or other specialty material for the entire book. And within multiple-author projects, those authors may be geographically scattered across multiple continents.</PARA>
<PARA>The document itself, even a traditional publication, will be fragmented if it incorporates deliverables other than hard-copy print media. Some of this heterogeneous material is pure running character text, some is graphical, some is tabular, and some is not page-oriented text at all. Again, this is not at all peculiar to electronic documents. Even for something as common as a typical college textbook product (which includes the textbook and its ancillaries), the variety of deliverables for the final package is mind-boggling: running character text, graphics (line, greyscale, photo), tables, lists, indexes, glossaries, test item booklets, test generation software, spreadsheet software and templates (for an economics textbook), instructor’s manuals, overhead transparencies, accounting forms (for an accounting book), plus cover and promotional art. True, the editors would not consider this to be a single document, but with proper entity management and document markup techniques such a <QUOTE>package</QUOTE> can indeed be a <QUOTE>document.</QUOTE></PARA>
<PARA>Producing such a package is quite routine in major college textbook divisions, and it represents all of the problems that SGML can help to ease. The various editors, graphics specialists, software providers, and media producers somehow make it all come together. And this happens in spite of how separated all of the specialists (many of them third-party providers working in different countries) and components may be.</PARA>
<PARA>We urged in our early chapters that the author of an electronic publication be relieved from details of presentation. We are arguing here that the author should also be relieved from needing to know the actual file location of every storage unit (entity) of the entire document and its ancillaries. In slightly more formal terms, the writer and his or her document need system and device independence.</PARA></SECTION>
<SECTION><TITLE>Layered Activity</TITLE>
<PARA>All of the above has been true of documentation projects even without electronic tools. In a traditional publication environment, the central focus of all of the participating groups is on the final printed product (plus the non-print ancillaries). On the other hand, we have insisted for electronic publishing that as writers we disengage our focus on final presentation and concentrate rather on structure. We have therefore formalized a distinction between writing and editing on the one hand and production on the other. By disengaging these layers, we can theoretically guarantee that our product will potentially <QUOTE>play</QUOTE> on any device or medium, known or yet to be invented.</PARA>
<PARA>We have insisted on an <INDEXTERM TERM="author's responsibility: markup of representation of document's abstract, logical structure">authoring process whose output (marked-up text) is what we may call the markup representation of the document’s <EMPHASIS>abstract</EMPHASIS> (or<EMPHASIS><QUOTE>logical </QUOTE></EMPHASIS>) structure. How to do this is of course the focus of this book. On the other hand, we recognize a <EMPHASIS>perceivable</EMPHASIS> (<EMPHASIS>visual</EMPHASIS> or <EMPHASIS>audio</EMPHASIS>, normally)

<EMPHASIS>representation</EMPHASIS> (perhaps as data access and retrieval). But simply to formalize the activities of traditional publication into these two representations is not sufficient, because we still do not have an adequate mechanism for accomplishing what traditional publishers have done along. For a document of any magnitude we still must somehow pull together a large number of components in order to create the final unified document. We need therefore to formalize this activity of pulling it together.</PARA>
<PARA>The most critical problem in a highly decentralized document (many entities of many types in the hands of many authors in many places) is at all times to know what is where, so in addition to our <EMPHASIS>visual representation</EMPHASIS> layer, and our <EMPHASIS>markup representation</EMPHASIS> layer we need a <EMPHASIS><INDEXTERM TERM="storage representation: visual, markup and storage layers">storage representation</EMPHASIS> layer. This needs to be a totally separate layer because it is wrong for a <INDEXTERM TERM="marked-up document: free from location and text data">marked-up document (the representation of element structure) to incorporate system-specific data about locations of text and data. It is wrong for the same reason that that document should also not specify details of visual presentation, as we have insisted throughout this book. Any system-specific information is bound to change, so the document should contain nothing that is <INDEXTERM TERM="marked-up document: free from system-specific information">system dependent or device dependent.</PARA>
<PARA>Note that the layered representations do not necessarily represent sequential stages in a document’s production. On the one hand, a marked-up manuscript (representing the abstract or <QUOTE>logical</QUOTE> structure of the document) may indeed first be an SGML document and later be transformed to a non-SGML representation for rendition as hard copy. But in a retrieval system, all of the layers may coexist simultaneously.</PARA>
<SUBSECTION><TITLE>Markup Representation</TITLE>
<PARA>An <INDEXTERM TERM="conforming SGML document: abstract or logical structure information">SGML document, with its element structure properly marked and validated, represents the document’s abstract or logical information. We call this <QUOTE>abstract</QUOTE> because within this layer we do not account at all for the external realities of (1) how the document is to be rendered (the perceivable representation) or (2) where the various portions (entities) of the document may physically reside (the storage representation). The actual body of the document—the textual material that the writer creates—is of course anything but abstract. But we are talking now only about the SGML representation of structure of the document’s elements.</PARA></SUBSECTION>
<SUBSECTION><TITLE>Perceivable Representation</TITLE>
<PARA>In the earlier chapters of the book, we used various terms to describe the document’s existence beyond its abstract representation: rendition, presentation, appearance. And while we have urged the <INDEXTERM TERM="author's responsibility: conforming SGML document">writer to postpone concerns about appearance (page or screen layout, for example), we certainly do not ignore that final deliverable of the SGML document. In fact, because of SGML and the pervasiveness of the standard, there is not one but theoretically an infinite variety of renditions, presentation media, and appearances possible for a single SGML document.</PARA>

<PARA>And not all of the representations are necessarily visible. Postscript may be a means of representing the document for hard-copy typesetting or for specialized screen display. But the same document may be rendered as a database, to be visualized with a retrieval engine that matches the database. Or the SGML document may be rendered as Braille or as video or audio. Whether visible or not, these are all viable as perceivable representations.</PARA></SUBSECTION>
<SUBSECTION><TITLE>Storage Representation</TITLE>
<PARA>If we really want the abstract representation to remain abstract—even for large documents comprising hundreds of entities and residing on far-flung computers and storage devices used by dozens of co-authors—then the authors and editors need help. The document’s system dependence (what kind of computer?) and device dependence (what file structure?) must be handled elsewhere. So SGML enables us to manage these concerns through entity structure. We therefore confine all of the system and device dependencies (specifics of computers and file structures) to the <EMPHASIS><INDEXTERM TERM="storage representation: container for system and device information">storage representation</EMPHASIS>.</PARA>
<PARA>Just as for the entities we studied in Chapter 7, these larger document entities enjoy the benefits of <QUOTE>declare once reference many times.</QUOTE> We declare an entity once, including all of the specifics needed to display, retrieve, print, or otherwise play the document later on. A photograph of a newly released circuit board may reside now on a particular computer with the following file specification:
<MARKUP>/catalog/mod002/grafs/fig03.gif</MARKUP>
And we could include this specific file structure in the entity declaration as the location of the picture.</PARA>
<PARA>The newly released board presumably replaced an obsolete board whose photo may have had the following <QUOTE>address</QUOTE> in real storage (compare the two addresses carefully!):
<MARKUP>/catalog/mod001/grafs/fig03.gif</MARKUP></PARA>
<PARA>Fortunately for the writer, the entity’s
<EMPHASIS>name</EMPHASIS>—for both graphics—is <QUOTE>Fig-03,</QUOTE> and he or she only needs to <EMPHASIS>reference</EMPHASIS> the photo by that name. When the product was modified and the photo retaken and filed within a different directory structure on the computer, only the entity declaration needed to be changed. So we might <INDEXTERM TERM="entity declaration">declare that entity with a system-dependent storage location as follows:
<DTDLISTING><SGMLDECLARATION>!ENTITY Fig-03   SYSTEM
"/catalog/mod002/graf/fig03.gif" </SGMLDECLARATION></DTDLISTING>
Note that the <SGMLKEYWORD><INDEXTERM TERM="SYSTEM: replacement text not inserted into document">SYSTEM</SGMLKEYWORD> keyword indicates that the replacement text in the entity declaration is not to be inserted into the document itself but is the system storage location of the actual image. Exactly what the browser, viewer, or printer does with that image is system-dependent; it may be printed on a page, displayed on screen, or even simply referenced. This construct is known as a <QUOTE><INDEXTERM TERM="system identifier: external identifier">system identifier,</QUOTE> one of the two types of <QUOTE><INDEXTERM TERM="external identifier: identifying something outside the current entity">external identifier</QUOTE> we are going to discuss. They are called <QUOTE>external</QUOTE> because they are identifying something outside of the current entity.</PARA>

<PARA>We would store that entity declaration in some area separate from the document body, probably in a file containing the document’s <SGMLTERM><INDEXTERM TERM="entity set: list of entity definitions">entity set</SGMLTERM> (an entire list of entity definitions). Within the document content, the author would use the particular linking element type that is defined within the DTD to reference the graphic. It may be a special link for figures called <SGMLNAME>figref</SGMLNAME>:
<MARKUP>…. as you can see in Figure 3<STRONGEMPH><SGMLTAG CLASS="element">figref name="Fig-03"</SGMLTAG></STRONGEMPH>, the set screw is located just beneath the flange….</MARKUP>
That same marked-up text can remain untouched regardless of the modified photo and the revised location for its storage, because only the entity declaration would have changed.</PARA></SUBSECTION></SECTION>
<SECTION><TITLE>Lessons from Software Engineering</TITLE>
<PARA>Some 30 years ago software engineers recognized a similar commingling of information among portions of large programs. They referred to this unhealthy commingling as <QUOTE>modular glue.</QUOTE> This was bad programming practice because it made it difficult for a programmer to make changes within a single module when troublesome side effects were sure to follow elsewhere. So software engineering prescribed that modules should be isolated from one another as much as possible. <QUOTE>Hide something at every level</QUOTE> is one of the mandates of structured programming. Similarly, <INDEXTERM TERM="entity management: hide system-, device-, and file-specific details">entity management (the discipline we are introducing in this chapter) prescribes that we isolate (<QUOTE>hide</QUOTE>) or confine messy system-, device-, and file-specific details of an entity to its entity declaration. The result: A visible <QUOTE>virtual</QUOTE> storage structure, comprising entities on top of a concealed <QUOTE>actual</QUOTE> storage structure, comprised of system storage objects, such as files.</PARA></SECTION>
<SECTION><TITLE>Examples</TITLE>
<PARA>There is no single prescribed way to enable entity management in an SGML document. The point of this chapter is simply to survey the resources that SGML offers to add a <EMPHASIS><INDEXTERM TERM="storage representation: examples">storage representation</EMPHASIS>. Precisely how entity structures are defined is a matter of the designer’s choice. We close this chapter with two different examples of entity structuring. The first one demonstrates the ease with which SGML (including an adequate <EMPHASIS>entity manager</EMPHASIS>) enables a physically segmented document to exist as a logically unified one. In showing this we see how a document designer uses the <SGMLTERM><INDEXTERM TERM="entity declaration: examples">entity declaration</SGMLTERM> plus an <SGMLTERM><INDEXTERM TERM="entity set: examples">entity set</SGMLTERM> to hide system-specific details from the document instance, enabling all of the benefits that we have detailed in this chapter. Finally we see how the writer uses entity references rather than system-specific file names to refer to entities outside his or her current work space.</PARA>
<SUBSECTION><TITLE>A Document Type Definition in a Separate Entity</TITLE>
<PARA>One common use of entity management is for sharing and reusing the declarations of a document-type definition. One way of attaching the <INDEXTERM TERM="DTD: attaching to document instance">DTD to your document is by including the declarations between square brackets in the <INDEXTERM TERM="document type

declaration: examples">document type declaration—what is called the
<QUOTE><INDEXTERM TERM="internal declaration subset: in document type
declaration">internal declaration subset</QUOTE>—like this:
<DTDLISTING><SGMLDECLARATION>!DOCTYPE manual [
<SGMLDECLARATION>!ELEMENT manual . . .</SGMLDECLARATION>
<SGMLDECLARATION>!-- all the rest of the declarations here --</SGMLDECLARATION>
]</SGMLDECLARATION>
<SGMLDECLARATION>!-- your document goes here
--</SGMLDECLARATION></DTDLISTING></PARA>
<PARA>However, there is an alternative to repeating all the declarations in every
instance of a WAE document, as we illustrated but did not explain earlier. Instead
of declaring the <INDEXTERM TERM="DTD entity">DTD internally, you can put it in an
entity of its own—once—and reference it from the <INDEXTERM
TERM="DOCTYPE declaration: examples">DOCTYPE declaration of each WAE document
instance, like this:
<DTDLISTING><SGMLDECLARATION>!DOCTYPE manual SYSTEM
"C:\pub\dtds\wae.dtd"</SGMLDECLARATION></DTDLISTING>
As in the earlier example, the keyword <SGMLKEYWORD><INDEXTERM TERM="SYSTEM:
examples">SYSTEM</SGMLKEYWORD> introduces a system identifier that locates an
entity in a system storage location—in this case
<QUOTE>C:\pub\dtds\wae.dtd</QUOTE>. But because this is a
<SGMLKEYWORD>DOCTYPE</SGMLKEYWORD> declaration, rather than an entity declaration,
it references the entity immediately rather than declaring a name for it for later
reference.</PARA>
<PARA>For documents that are used in several different computer systems, system
identifiers typically need to be localized in each system, because real storage
structures can differ. In such cases, another type of external identifier, called a
<SGMLTERM><INDEXTERM TERM="public identifier: external identifier">public
identifier</SGMLTERM>, can be used:
<DTDLISTING><SGMLDECLARATION>!DOCTYPE manual PUBLIC "+//ISBN . . .//DTD Writers and
Editors DTD//EN"</SGMLDECLARATION></DTDLISTING>
Here, the public identifier uniquely identifies the DTD itself, rather than its
real storage location. SGML systems that support public identifiers maintain a
catalog that allows them to locate the local storage address for each public
identifier.</PARA></SUBSECTION>
<SUBSECTION><TITLE>A Logically Single Document Consisting of Several Physical
Entities</TITLE>
<PARA>Suppose a work group of five writers is to produce a maintenance manual. They
wish to divide a document <EMPHASIS>physically</EMPHASIS> so that each writer can
edit within his or her separate directory area of the computer. But the manual
itself of course is <EMPHASIS>logically</EMPHASIS> a single document. Here is the
marked-up document instance for an entire maintenance manual with the file name
<QUOTE>WDGTMMAN.SGM</QUOTE>:
<DTDLISTING><SGMLDECLARATION>!DOCTYPE manual SYSTEM "C:\pub\dtds\wae.dtd" [
<SGMLDECLARATION>!-- We "hide" the details of how the document is physically
divided by placing the entities into an entity set, which in turn resides in some
file of its own --</SGMLDECLARATION>
<SGMLDECLARATION>!ENTITY % MEnts SYSTEM "e:\sgmlab\MaintMan.ent" </SGMLDECLARATION>
%MEnts;
]</SGMLDECLARATION>

```
<SGMLTAG CLASS="element">manual last-rev="01/01/2000" last-au="Ron
Turner"</SGMLTAG>
<SGMLTAG CLASS="genentity">fm</SGMLTAG>
<SGMLTAG CLASS="genentity">ch01</SGMLTAG>
<SGMLTAG CLASS="genentity">ch02</SGMLTAG>
<SGMLTAG CLASS="genentity">ch03</SGMLTAG>
<SGMLTAG CLASS="genentity">bm</SGMLTAG>
<SGMLTAG CLASS="element">/manual</SGMLTAG></DTDLISTING>
```
Notice that the document type for the manual is our familiar <QUOTE>WAE,</QUOTE>
the declarations for which (the external <QUOTE>declaration subset</QUOTE>) are
stored at the system storage location <QUOTE>WAE.DTD.</QUOTE> Written into the
internal declaration subset (between the square brackets) there are declarations
that apply only to this instance of a WAE document: a comment declaration, entity
declaration, and an entity reference to still more declarations.</PARA>
<PARA>Note carefully that <QUOTE>MEnts</QUOTE> (the entity which we declare and
reference here) is actually a reference to a system-specific file name. The
external identifier parameter of the entity declaration is the only place in the
document that we specify that actual file location and name:
e:\sgmlab\maintman.ent. If we move or rename that file in the future, we only need
to alter the name in the declaration.</PARA>
<PARA>You should also note that there are no clues at this level (except for the
comment) that the purpose of the file is to contain the declaration for the
physically separate entities that comprise the document instance. That is only
clear within the entity set file itself <QUOTE>maintman.ent</QUOTE>, which contains
the following:
```
<DTDLISTING><SGMLDECLARATION>!-- Entity Set for Maintenance Manual
--</SGMLDECLARATION>
<SGMLDECLARATION>!ENTITY fm SYSTEM "e:\sgmlab\ron\front.doc" </SGMLDECLARATION>
<SGMLDECLARATION>!ENTITY ch01 SYSTEM "e:\sgmlab\tim\ch001.doc" </SGMLDECLARATION>
<SGMLDECLARATION>!ENTITY ch02 SYSTEM "e:\sgmlab\audrey\ch002.doc"
</SGMLDECLARATION>
<SGMLDECLARATION>!ENTITY ch03 SYSTEM "e:\sgmlab\cameron\ch003.doc"
</SGMLDECLARATION>
<SGMLDECLARATION>!ENTITY bm SYSTEM "e:\sgmlab\beth\back.doc"
</SGMLDECLARATION></DTDLISTING>
```
The quoted strings in the entity set file represent actual physical addresses of
each of the five entities that comprise the <SGMLTERM>document instance</SGMLTERM>
of the SGML document <QUOTE>wdgtmman.sgm</QUOTE>.</PARA>
<PARA>It is not required for us to imbed these system-specific declarations in a
separate entity set file (<QUOTE>maintman.ent</QUOTE> here). We could have declared
the five entities directly and in full within the internal declaration subset
itself:
```
<DTDLISTING><SGMLDECLARATION>!DOCTYPE manual SYSTEM "C:\pub\dtds\wae.dtd" [
<STRONGEMPH><SGMLDECLARATION>!ENTITY fm SYSTEM "e:\sgmlab\ron\front.doc"
</SGMLDECLARATION>
<SGMLDECLARATION>!ENTITY ch01 SYSTEM "e:\sgmlab\tim\ch001.doc" </SGMLDECLARATION>
<SGMLDECLARATION>!ENTITY ch02 SYSTEM "e:\sgmlab\audrey\ch002.doc"
</SGMLDECLARATION>
<SGMLDECLARATION>!ENTITY ch03 SYSTEM "e:\sgmlab\cameron\ch003.doc"
</SGMLDECLARATION>
```

```
<SGMLDECLARATION>!ENTITY bm SYSTEM "e:\sgmlab\beth\back.doc"
</SGMLDECLARATION></STRONGEMPH>
]</SGMLDECLARATION>
<SGMLTAG CLASS="element">manual last-rev="01/01/2000" last-au="Ron
Turner"</SGMLTAG>
<SGMLTAG CLASS="genentity">fm</SGMLTAG>
<SGMLTAG CLASS="genentity">ch01</SGMLTAG>
<SGMLTAG CLASS="genentity">ch02</SGMLTAG>
<SGMLTAG CLASS="genentity">ch03</SGMLTAG>
<SGMLTAG CLASS="genentity">bm</SGMLTAG>
<SGMLTAG CLASS="element">/manual</SGMLTAG></DTDLISTING>
```
But while this accomplishes the same purpose of identifying all the physically separated entities, it perhaps does so at the expense of cluttering the SGML document unnecessarily. As we have emphasized throughout the chapter, we are striving to separate the <EMPHASIS>storage representation</EMPHASIS> of the document from the other layers of the document’s existence. That is the reason for the extra apparatus of an entity set file.</PARA>
<PARA>Finally, here are the contents of the remaining entities (other than the DTD) that make up the maintenance manual document. The SGML parser uses the DTD and entity list to thread its way through the document. The parser (as well as whatever application will render or represent the document) treats the document as a single <EMPHASIS>logical</EMPHASIS> object, regardless of the number of entities in which it is stored:
```
<MARKUP><STRONGEMPH>e:\sgmlab\ron\front.doc:</STRONGEMPH>
<SGMLTAG CLASS="element">ti</SGMLTAG>The Greatest Maintenance Manual Ever<SGMLTAG
CLASS="element">/ti</SGMLTAG>
<SGMLTAG CLASS="element">au</SGMLTAG>Ron Turner<SGMLTAG
CLASS="element">/au</SGMLTAG>
<SGMLTAG CLASS="element">sec</SGMLTAG>
<SGMLTAG CLASS="element">p</SGMLTAG>This is the entire text for the front matter of
the manual<SGMLTAG CLASS="element">/p</SGMLTAG>
<SGMLTAG CLASS="element">/sec</SGMLTAG>
<STRONGEMPH>e:\sgmlab\tim\ch001.doc:</STRONGEMPH>
<SGMLTAG CLASS="element">sec</SGMLTAG><SGMLTAG
CLASS="element">shd</SGMLTAG>Section 1: Parts List<SGMLTAG
CLASS="element">/shd</SGMLTAG>
<SGMLTAG CLASS="element">p</SGMLTAG>Here is the list of parts for the
widget<SGMLTAG CLASS="element">/p</SGMLTAG>
<SGMLTAG CLASS="element">/sec</SGMLTAG>
<STRONGEMPH>e:\sgmlab\audrey\ch002.doc:</STRONGEMPH>
<SGMLTAG CLASS="element">sec</SGMLTAG><SGMLTAG
CLASS="element">shd</SGMLTAG>Section 2: Principles of Operation<SGMLTAG
CLASS="element">/shd</SGMLTAG>
<SGMLTAG CLASS="element">p</SGMLTAG>Here&rsquor;s the very ample discussion of how
the widget works.<SGMLTAG CLASS="element">/p</SGMLTAG>
<SGMLTAG CLASS="element">/sec</SGMLTAG>
<STRONGEMPH>e:\sgmlab\cameron\ch003.doc:</STRONGEMPH>
<SGMLTAG CLASS="element">sec</SGMLTAG><SGMLTAG
CLASS="element">shd</SGMLTAG>Section 3: User&rsquor;s Guide<SGMLTAG
CLASS="element">/shd</SGMLTAG>
```

```
<SGMLTAG CLASS="element">p</SGMLTAG>Here are the crystal-clear, no-fail
instructions for the user.<SGMLTAG CLASS="element">/p</SGMLTAG>
<SGMLTAG CLASS="element">/sec</SGMLTAG>
<STRONGEMPH>e:\sgmlab\beth\back.doc:</STRONGEMPH>
<SGMLTAG CLASS="element">sec</SGMLTAG><SGMLTAG
CLASS="element">shd</SGMLTAG>Appendix: Where we hide all the good stuff<SGMLTAG
CLASS="element">/shd</SGMLTAG>
<SGMLTAG CLASS="element">p</SGMLTAG>The back matter typically contains what the
user REALLY needs to know!<SGMLTAG CLASS="element">/p</SGMLTAG>
<SGMLTAG CLASS="element">/sec</SGMLTAG></MARKUP>
The complete list of the files that make up this document is:
<ORDEREDLIST>
<LISTITEM> <PARA><SGMLNAME>wae.dtd:</SGMLNAME> the DTD itself</PARA></LISTITEM>
<LISTITEM> <PARA><SGMLNAME>wdgtmman.sgm:</SGMLNAME> top level document instance
entity</PARA></LISTITEM>
<LISTITEM> <PARA><SGMLNAME>maintman.ent:</SGMLNAME> entity declarations for
external entities</PARA></LISTITEM>
<LISTITEM> <PARA><SGMLNAME>front.doc:</SGMLNAME> front matter entity text
file</PARA></LISTITEM>
<LISTITEM> <PARA><SGMLNAME>ch001.doc:</SGMLNAME> chapter one entity text
file</PARA></LISTITEM>
<LISTITEM> <PARA><SGMLNAME>ch002.doc:</SGMLNAME> chapter two entity text
file</PARA></LISTITEM>
<LISTITEM> <PARA><SGMLNAME>ch003.doc:</SGMLNAME> chapter three entity text
file</PARA></LISTITEM>
<LISTITEM> <PARA><SGMLNAME>back.doc:</SGMLNAME> back matter entity text
file</PARA></LISTITEM></ORDEREDLIST></PARA></SUBSECTION>
<SUBSECTION><TITLE>Details Isolated from the Body of the Text</TITLE>
<PARA>Segmenting the physical entities of the document is not the only reason for
maintaining a separate <INDEXTERM TERM="entity set: isolated file">entity set file.
This mechanism for separation allows us to <QUOTE>hide</QUOTE> declarations for
other entities as well. Suppose that the actual titles for the various sections of
our maintenance manual are yet to be determined. But the various authors need to
refer to those chapters <EMPHASIS>by name</EMPHASIS> from anywhere in the document.
And those references need to remain valid no matter how often or how drastically
the titles are changed.</PARA>
<PARA>To accomplish this we again use SGML&rsquor;s facility for
<EMPHASIS>indirection</EMPHASIS> through <SGMLTERM><INDEXTERM TERM="entity
reference: examples">entity references</SGMLTERM>. And again we use the mechanism
of an entity set. But now the items within the entity set in which we are interested
are character strings, the names of each chapter in the document. Here is a revised
version of our entity set (file <QUOTE>maintman.ent</QUOTE>):
<DTDLISTING><SGMLDECLARATION>!-- Entity Set for Maintenance Manual
--</SGMLDECLARATION>
<SGMLDECLARATION>!-- File locations for each chapter --</SGMLDECLARATION>
<SGMLDECLARATION>!ENTITY fm SYSTEM "e:\sgmlab\ron\front.doc" </SGMLDECLARATION>
<SGMLDECLARATION>!ENTITY ch01 SYSTEM "e:\sgmlab\tim\ch001.doc" </SGMLDECLARATION>
<SGMLDECLARATION>!ENTITY ch02 SYSTEM "e:\sgmlab\audrey\ch002.doc"
</SGMLDECLARATION>
```

```
<SGMLDECLARATION>!ENTITY ch03 SYSTEM "e:\sgmlab\cameron\ch003.doc"
</SGMLDECLARATION>
<SGMLDECLARATION>!ENTITY bm SYSTEM "e:\sgmlab\beth\back.doc" </SGMLDECLARATION>
<SGMLDECLARATION>!-- Chapter titles --</SGMLDECLARATION>
<STRONGEMPH><SGMLDECLARATION>!ENTITY cht01 "Section 1: Parts List"
</SGMLDECLARATION>
<SGMLDECLARATION>!ENTITY cht02 "Section 2: Principles of Operation"
</SGMLDECLARATION>
<SGMLDECLARATION>!ENTITY cht03 "Section 3: User&rsquor;s Guide"
</SGMLDECLARATION></STRONGEMPH></DTDLISTING></PARA>
<PARA>With the chapter titles now declared in the entity list as general entities,
the various authors do not need to be concerned about the precise wording of each
chapter title. Instead the text for the three chapters would now read as follows:
<MARKUP><STRONGEMPH>e:\sgmlab\tim\ch001.doc:</STRONGEMPH>
<SGMLTAG CLASS="element">sec</SGMLTAG><SGMLTAG
CLASS="element">shd</SGMLTAG><STRONGEMPH><SGMLTAG
CLASS="GenEntity">cht01</SGMLTAG></STRONGEMPH><SGMLTAG
CLASS="element">/shd</SGMLTAG>
<SGMLTAG CLASS="element">p</SGMLTAG>Here is the list of parts for the
widget<SGMLTAG CLASS="element">/p</SGMLTAG> <SGMLTAG
CLASS="element">/sec</SGMLTAG>
<STRONGEMPH>e:\sgmlab\audrey\ch002.doc:</STRONGEMPH>
<SGMLTAG CLASS="element">sec</SGMLTAG><SGMLTAG
CLASS="element">shd</SGMLTAG><STRONGEMPH><SGMLTAG
CLASS="GenEntity">cht02</SGMLTAG></STRONGEMPH><SGMLTAG
CLASS="element">/shd</SGMLTAG>
<SGMLTAG CLASS="element">p</SGMLTAG>Here&rsquor;s the very ample discussion of how
the widget works.<SGMLTAG CLASS="element">/p</SGMLTAG>
<SGMLTAG CLASS="element">/sec</SGMLTAG>
<STRONGEMPH>e:\sgmlab\cameron\ch003.doc:</STRONGEMPH>
<SGMLTAG CLASS="element">sec</SGMLTAG><SGMLTAG
CLASS="element">shd</SGMLTAG><STRONGEMPH><SGMLTAG
CLASS="GenEntity">cht03</SGMLTAG></STRONGEMPH><SGMLTAG
CLASS="element">/shd</SGMLTAG>
<SGMLTAG CLASS="element">p</SGMLTAG>Here are the crystal-clear, no-fail
instructions for the user.<SGMLTAG CLASS="element">/p</SGMLTAG> <SGMLTAG
CLASS="element">/sec</SGMLTAG></MARKUP>
So if the editor should decide finally to change <QUOTE>Section</QUOTE> to
<QUOTE>Chapter</QUOTE> in each of the titles, it would take only a single revision
to each of the three corresponding items in the entity set. The actual file with the
text of the chapter would remain untouched.</PARA>
<PARA>Cross-referencing the various chapters by their titles is also smoothed
considerably with an entity set. The author of Chapter 3 needs to refer to Chapter
2. A general entity reference accomplishes this very nicely:
<MARKUP><STRONGEMPH>e:\sgmlab\cameron\ch003.doc:</STRONGEMPH>
<SGMLTAG CLASS="element">sec</SGMLTAG><SGMLTAG
CLASS="element">shd</SGMLTAG><SGMLTAG CLASS="GenEntity">cht03</SGMLTAG><SGMLTAG
CLASS="element">/shd</SGMLTAG>
```

```
<SGMLTAG CLASS="element">p</SGMLTAG><STRONGEMPH>Now that we have an idea of how the
widget functions (see "<SGMLTAG CLASS="GenEntity">cht02</SGMLTAG>"),
h</STRONGEMPH>ere are the crystal-clear, no-fail instructions for the user.<SGMLTAG
CLASS="element">/p</SGMLTAG>
<SGMLTAG CLASS="element">/sec</SGMLTAG></MARKUP></PARA>
<PARA>With the replacement text fully expanded (<QUOTE>resolved</QUOTE>), the
marked-up paragraph would read as follows:
<MARKUP><SGMLTAG CLASS="element">sec</SGMLTAG><SGMLTAG
CLASS="element">shd</SGMLTAG><STRONGEMPH>Section 3: User&rsquor;s
Guide</STRONGEMPH><SGMLTAG CLASS="element">/shd</SGMLTAG>
<SGMLTAG CLASS="element">p</SGMLTAG>Now that we have an idea of how the widget
functions (see "<STRONGEMPH>Section 2: Principles of Operation</STRONGEMPH>"), here
are the crystal-clear, no-fail instructions for the user.<SGMLTAG CLASS="element">
/p</SGMLTAG>
<SGMLTAG CLASS="element">/sec</SGMLTAG></MARKUP></PARA></SUBSECTION></SECTION>
<SUMMARY><TITLE>Summary</TITLE>
<PARA>We have reviewed some essentials of entity structure in order to discover how
SGML and the various SGML systems might help us to manage the separate entities of
a major document. The character-only portions are typically parceled out among
several writers, and the various non-character entities (graphics) are also
separate. This is the way writing projects have always been. SGML&rsquor;s entity
structure allows us to manage these distributed entities in a standard and highly
efficient manner. Whether the entity is a file-sized portion for which a single
writer is responsible or whether it is a short character string of system-specific
data, SGML entity management saves work for the writer, eases the editor&rsquor;s
task, and enhances the life cycle of the document.</PARA></SUMMARY></CHAPTER>
```

C.2   DTD used

This DTD was developed specifically for the production of *README.1ST: SGML for Writers
and Editors*. It is not intended to be a complete or general purpose DTD, it is offered here only for
the purpose of making the sample chapter above more understandable.

```
<!ENTITY % isolat1 SYSTEM "isolat1.ent" >
<!ENTITY % isopub  SYSTEM "isopub.ent" >
<!ENTITY % isonum  SYSTEM "isonum.ent" >

%isolat1;
%isopub;
%isonum;

<!ENTITY secmrk    SDATA   "[secmrk]" --Section mark -->

<!ENTITY % inline.gp "Footnote | Quote | StrongEmph | Emphasis |
                      SGMLKeyword | SGMLTerm | SGMLName | SGMLTag |
                      IndexTerm" >
```

```
<!ENTITY % block.gp    "Para | Markup | BlockQuote | OrderedList |
                        ItemizedList | ISOQuote | DTDListing" >
<!ENTITY % dtd.gp      "%inline.gp | SGMLDeclaration" >

<!ELEMENT Book              - -     (Foreword?, Preface?, Chapter+, Appendix*) >

<!ELEMENT (Preface
          | Foreword)       - -     (Title, (%block.gp; | Section)+) >
<!ELEMENT Chapter           - -     (Title, TermsList?, Overview, Section+, Summary*) >
<!ELEMENT Appendix          - -     (Title, (%block.gp; | Section)+) >

<!ELEMENT Section           - -     (Title, (SubSection | %block.gp;))+) >
<!ELEMENT SubSection        - -     (Title, (%block.gp;)+) >
<!ELEMENT TermsList         - -     (Title, Para+) >
<!ELEMENT (Overview
          | Summary)        - -     (Title, (%block.gp;)+) >

<!ELEMENT Title             - -     ((#PCDATA | %inline.gp;)+) -(Footnote)>

<!ELEMENT Para              - -     ((#PCDATA | InlineMarkup | (%block.gp;))+)
                                                        +(%inline.gp;) >

<!ELEMENT (Markup
          | InlineMarkup)   - -     ((#PCDATA | (%inline.gp;))+) >
<!ELEMENT BlockQuote        - -     ((#PCDATA | Para |(%inline.gp;))+, Citation?) >
<!ELEMENT ISOQuote          - -     ((#PCDATA | Para |(%inline.gp;))+, Citation) >
<!ELEMENT Citation          - -     (#PCDATA) +(%inline.gp) >

<!ELEMENT (OrderedList
          | ItemizedList)   - -     (ListItem+) >
<!ELEMENT ListItem          - -     ((%block.gp;)+) >

<!ELEMENT DTDListing        - -     ((#PCDATA | SGMLDeclaration)+) +(%dtd.gp;) >
<!ATTLIST DTDListing
          Numbering   (ON | OFF)                        OFF >
<!ELEMENT SGMLDeclaration   - -     (#PCDATA) >

<!ELEMENT Quote             - -     (#PCDATA) +(%inline.gp) >
<!ELEMENT Footnote          - -     (Para+) -(Footnote)>
<!ELEMENT Emphasis          - -     ((#PCDATA | %inline.gp;)+) -(Emphasis)>
<!ELEMENT StrongEmph        - -     ((#PCDATA | %inline.gp;)+) -(StrongEmph)>
<!ELEMENT (SGMLKeyword
          | SGMLTerm
          | SGMLName)       - -     (#PCDATA) >

<!ELEMENT SGMLTag           - -     (#PCDATA) >
<!ATTLIST SGMLTag
          Class       (Attribute | Element
                       | GenEntity | ParamEntity)   #IMPLIED >

<!ELEMENT IndexTerm         - O     EMPTY >
```

```
<!ATTLIST IndexTerm
          Term          CDATA                    #REQUIRED >
```

INDEX

A

anchor

    defined 117

    initiating 120

ANSI Z39.18-1987 52–55

application

    defined in ISO glossary 203

application: text processing application

architectural form declaration

    compared with element type
        declaration 193

architectural forms

    as a documentation techniques 192

    HyTime's formal specifications 192

    markup declarations that define HyTime
        standard 189

    templates, not defined element types 191

ATTLIST

    attached to element type 108

    identifies attribute definition list
        declaration 108

attlist

    used in HyTime 193

attribute

    characteristics 104

    communicates information about an
        element 104

    defined 104

    defined in ISO glossary 203

    examples 105–107

    power used by HyTime 191

    purpose 103

    required or implied value 108

    using for system-specific presentation 105

    value or type of value 108

attribute definition

    defined in ISO glossary 203

attribute definition list 110, 119

    defined in ISO glossary 203

    example 108, 111

attribute definition list declaration 108

    defined in ISO glossary 203

    HyTime 192

    syntax 108–110

attribute form

    used in HyTime 193

attribute link 108

attribute value

    syntax 107

U

unique identifier

  defined in ISO glossary 208

V

validating SGML parser

  defined in ISO glossary 208

  mode of operation 60

value-added links 119

W

WAE DTD

  attribute 107

  attribute modified form 110

  declaration of an element type 108

  formalization 74

  hypertext linking 120, 121

  intuitive approach 63

  structure definition 86

  structure definition revision 74

  table-based form into SGML notation 74

WAE: writers and editors

word processed document 62

word processors 60

World Wide Web (WWW) 169–173

  browsers 171, 174

  characteristics 172

  defined 170

  documents 170

  locating/transporting infrastructure 174

  network infrastructure 170, 171

  reasons for rapid growth 171

  standards 174

  viewers 171

ABOUT THE DISKETTE

The diskette that accompanies this book contains a variety of files and freely available software, which the authors consider useful in your study of SGML. The SGMLab viewer allows you to validate and view documents written to conform with the WAE DTD (developed in the book). With SGMLab you will simultaneously view your SGML structural markup of a document and a formatted on-screen representation of that document. In addition the disk contains a copy of the public domain validator SGMLS. This will allow you to validate any SGML document using any DTD. Several sample documents, taken from the examples in the book, illustrate various important SGML concepts. Finally, for more information, we include a World Wide Web page with links to sites containing SGML- or HTML-related information. See the file DSK-CONT.TXT for a complete listing of the contents of the diskette.

Installation

To install the SGMLab files insert the diskette into your disk drive. From a DOS prompt type:
`A:\INSTALL`
(if your floppy drive is not drive A: substitute the appropriate drive letter)
Follow the on-screen instruction for selecting a directory in which to install SGMLab.

License Agreement and Limited Warranty

READ THE FOLLOWING TERMS AND CONDITIONS CAREFULLY BEFORE OPENING THIS DISK PACKAGE. THIS LEGAL DOCUMENT IS AN AGREEMENT BETWEEN YOU AND PRENTICE-HALL, INC. (THE "COMPANY"). BY OPENING THIS SEALED DISK PACKAGE, YOU ARE AGREEING TO BE BOUND BY THESE TERMS AND CONDITIONS. IF YOU DO NOT AGREE WITH THESE TERMS AND CONDITIONS, DO NOT OPEN THE DISK PACKAGE. PROMPTLY RETURN THE UNOPENED DISK PACKAGE AND ALL

ACCOMPANYING ITEMS TO THE PLACE YOU OBTAINED THEM FOR A FULL REFUND OF ANY SUMS YOU HAVE PAID.

    1. **OWNERSHIP OF SOFTWARE:** You own only the magnetic or physical media (the enclosed disks) on which the SOFTWARE is recorded or fixed, but the Company retains all the rights, title, and ownership to the SOFTWARE recorded on the original disk copy(ies) and all subsequent copies of the SOFTWARE, regardless of the form or media on which the original or other copies may exist. This license is not a sale of the original SOFTWARE or any copy to you.

    2. **MISCELLANEOUS:** This Agreement shall be construed in accordance with the laws of the United States of America and the State of New York and shall benefit the Company, its affiliates, and assignees.

    3. **LIMITED WARRANTY AND DISCLAIMER OF WARRANTY:** The Company warrants that the SOFTWARE, when properly used in accordance with the Documentation, will operate in substantial conformity with the description of the SOFTWARE set forth in the Documentation. The Company does not warrant that the SOFTWARE will meet your requirements or that the operation of the SOFTWARE will be uninterrupted or error-free. The Company warrants that the media on which the SOFTWARE is delivered shall be free from defects in materials and workmanship under normal use for a period of thirty (30) days from the date of your purchase. Your only remedy and the Company's only obligation under these limited warranties is, at the Company's option, return of the warranted item for a refund of any amounts paid by you or replacement of the item. Any replacement of SOFTWARE or media under the warranties shall not extend the original warranty period. The limited warranty set forth above shall not apply to any SOFTWARE which the Company determines in good faith has been subject to misuse, neglect, improper installation, repair, alteration, or damage by you. EXCEPT FOR THE EXPRESSED WARRANTIES SET FORTH ABOVE, THE COMPANY DISCLAIMS ALL WARRANTIES, EXPRESS OR IMPLIED, INCLUDING WITHOUT LIMITATION, THE IMPLIED WARRANTIES OF MERCHANTABILITY AND FITNESS FOR A PARTICULAR PURPOSE. EXCEPT FOR THE EXPRESS WARRANTY SET FORTH ABOVE, THE COMPANY DOES NOT WARRANT, GUARANTEE, OR MAKE ANY REPRESENTATION REGARDING THE USE OR THE RESULTS OF THE USE OF THE SOFTWARE IN TERMS OF ITS CORRECTNESS, ACCURACY, RELIABILITY, CURRENTNESS, OR OTHERWISE.

    IN NO EVENT, SHALL THE COMPANY OR ITS EMPLOYEES, AGENTS, SUPPLIERS, OR CONTRACTORS BE LIABLE FOR ANY INCIDENTAL, INDIRECT, SPECIAL, OR CONSEQUENTIAL DAMAGES ARISING OUT OF OR IN CONNECTION WITH THE LICENSE GRANTED UNDER THIS AGREEMENT, OR FOR LOSS OF USE, LOSS OF DATA, LOSS OF INCOME OR PROFIT, OR OTHER LOSSES, SUSTAINED AS A RESULT OF INJURY TO ANY PERSON, OR LOSS OF OR DAMAGE TO PROPERTY, OR CLAIMS OF THIRD PARTIES, EVEN IF THE COMPANY OR AN AUTHORIZED REPRESENTATIVE OF THE COMPANY HAS BEEN ADVISED OF THE POSSIBILITY OF SUCH DAMAGES. IN NO EVENT SHALL LIABILITY OF THE COMPANY FOR DAMAGES WITH RESPECT TO THE SOFT-

WARE EXCEED THE AMOUNTS ACTUALLY PAID BY YOU, IF ANY, FOR THE SOFT-WARE.

SOME JURISDICTIONS DO NOT ALLOW THE LIMITATION OF IMPLIED WARRANTIES OR LIABILITY FOR INCIDENTAL, INDIRECT, SPECIAL, OR CONSEQUENTIAL DAMAGES, SO THE ABOVE LIMITATIONS MAY NOT ALWAYS APPLY. THE WARRANTIES IN THIS AGREEMENT GIVE YOU SPECIFIC LEGAL RIGHTS AND YOU MAY ALSO HAVE OTHER RIGHTS WHICH VARY IN ACCORDANCE WITH LOCAL LAW.

ACKNOWLEDGMENT

YOU ACKNOWLEDGE THAT YOU HAVE READ THIS AGREEMENT, UNDERSTAND IT, AND AGREE TO BE BOUND BY ITS TERMS AND CONDITIONS. YOU ALSO AGREE THAT THIS AGREEMENT IS THE COMPLETE AND EXCLUSIVE STATEMENT OF THE AGREEMENT BETWEEN YOU AND THE COMPANY AND SUPERSEDES ALL PROPOSALS OR PRIOR AGREEMENTS, ORAL, OR WRITTEN, AND ANY OTHER COMMUNICATIONS BETWEEN YOU AND THE COMPANY OR ANY REPRESENTATIVE OF THE COMPANY RELATING TO THE SUBJECT MATTER OF THIS AGREEMENT.

Should you have any questions concerning this Agreement or if you wish to contact the Company for any reason, please contact in writing at the address below.

Robin Short
Prentice Hall PTR
One Lake Street
Upper Saddle River, New Jersey 07458

SGMLab

Software Copyright 1995 by Soph-Ware Associates Spokane, WA.
swa@comtch.iea.com

SGMLab is the property of Soph-Ware Associates and may not be distributed except to accompany the book README.1ST: SGML for Writers and Editors

SGMLS

LICENSE AND DISCLAIMER OF WARRANTIES

Standard Generalized Markup Language Users' Group (SGMLUG), SGML Parser Materials
1. License

SGMLUG hereby grants to any user: (1) an irrevocable royalty-free, worldwide, non-exclusive license to use, execute, reproduce, display, perform and distribute copies of, and to prepare derivative works based upon these materials; and (2) the right to authorize others to do any of the foregoing.

2. Disclaimer of Warranties

(a) The SGML Parser Materials are provided "as is" to any USER. USER assumes responsibility for determining the suitability of the SGML Parser Materials for its use and for results obtained. SGMLUG makes no warranty that any errors have been eliminated from the SGML Parser Materials or that they can be eliminated by USER. SGMLUG shall not provide any support maintenance or other aid to USER or its licensees with respect to SGML Parser Materials. SGMLUG shall not be responsible for losses of any kind resulting from use of the SGML Parser Materials including (without limitation) any liability for business expense, machine downtime, or damages caused to USER or third parties by any deficiency, defect, error, or malfunction.

(b) SGMLUG DISCLAIMS ALL WARRANTIES, EXPRESSED OR IMPLIED, ARISING OUT OF OR RELATING TO THE SGML PARSER MATERIALS OR ANY USE THEREOF, INCLUDING (WITHOUT LIMITATION) ANY WARRANTY WHATSOEVER AS TO THE FITNESS FOR A PARTICULAR USE OR THE MERCHANTABILITY OF THE SGML PARSER MATERIALS.

(c) In no event shall SGMLUG be liable to USER or third parties licensed by USER for any indirect, special, incidental, or consequential damages (including lost profits). (d) SGMLUG has no knowledge of any conditions that would impair its right to license the SGML Parser Materials. Notwithstanding the foregoing, SGMLUG does not make any warranties or representations that the SGML Parser Materials are free of claims by third parties of patent, copyright infringement or the like, nor does SGMLUG assume any liability in respect of any such infringement of rights of third parties due to USER's operation under this license.

DocBook DTD

DocBook DTD Revision: 2.1

Copyright 1992, 1993 HaL Computer Systems International, Ltd., and O'Reilly & Associates, Inc.

Permission to use, copy, modify and distribute the DocBook DTD and its accompanying documentation for any purpose and without fee is hereby granted, provided that this copyright notice appears in all copies. If you modify the DocBook DTD, rename your modified version. HaL Computer Systems International, Ltd., and O'Reilly & Associates, Inc., make no representation about the suitability of the DTD for any purpose. It is provided "as is" without expressed or implied warranty.

The DocBook DTD is maintained by HaL Computer Systems International, Ltd., and O'Reilly & Associates, Inc. Please direct all questions, bug reports, or suggestions for changes to: davenport@ora.com or by postal mail to either: Terry Allen, O'Reilly & Associates, Inc., 103A Morris Street, Sebastopol, California, 95472; or Conleth O'Connell, HaL Computer Systems, 3006-A Longhorn Blvd., Austin, Texas, 78758.

Please note that an SGML declaration is provided for this DTD.

Public Identifier: "-//HaL and O'Reilly//DTD DocBook//EN"

HTML Level 2 DTD

Document Type Definition for the HyperText Markup Language (HTML DTD)
$Id: html.dtd,v 1.28 1995/06/16 18:54:22 connolly Exp $
Authors: Daniel W. Connolly <connolly@hal.com>, Tim Berners-Lee

The World Wide Web Consortium (W3C) works to develop common standards for the evolution of the World Wide Web. Information about W3C is available online at:

http://www.w3.org/hypertext/WWW/Consortium/

The comp.infosystems.authoring.html newsgroup is chartered for discussion about HTML and authoring with HTML.

The HTML working group of the IETF is chartered both to describe and to develop the HyperText Markup Language (HTML). For more information see:

http://www.ietf.cnri.reston.va.us/html.charters/html-charter.html

Tim Berners-Lee chairs this group.

See Also: html.decl, html-0.dtd, html-1.dtd
    http://www.hal.com/%7Econnolly/html-spec/index.html
    http://www.w3.org/hypertext/WWW/MarkUp/